# Genre and White Supremacy in the Postemancipation United States

OXFORD STUDIES IN AMERICAN LITERARY HISTORY

Gordon Hutner, Series Editor

---

# Genre and White Supremacy in the Postemancipation United States

Travis M. Foster

OXFORD
UNIVERSITY PRESS

# OXFORD
## UNIVERSITY PRESS

Great Clarendon Street, Oxford, OX2 6DP,
United Kingdom

Oxford University Press is a department of the University of Oxford.
It furthers the University's objective of excellence in research, scholarship,
and education by publishing worldwide. Oxford is a registered trade mark of
Oxford University Press in the UK and in certain other countries

First Edition published in 2019

Impression: 1

Published in the United States of America by Oxford University Press
198 Madison Avenue, New York, NY 10016, United States of America

British Library Cataloguing in Publication Data

Data available

Library of Congress Control Number: 2019941418

ISBN 978-0-19-883809-8

DOI: 10.1093/oso/9780198838098.001.0001

Printed and bound by
CPI Group (UK) Ltd, Croydon, CR0 4YY

# { CONTENTS }

# { LIST OF ILLUSTRATION }

# Introduction

## GENRES OF THE NEW RACIAL ORDINARY

Writing in 1891, Reverend Albery Allson Whitman, known during his lifetime as "Poet Laureate of the Negro Race," delivered a blunt assessment: emancipation had failed.[1] Delineating the contributing factors, he describes a newly vibrant white nationalism organized through "the common heritage of the Blue and the Gray," scenes of "[m]utual admiration" between former white enemies, "bonds of Anglo-Saxon brotherhood," and an invigorated racial capitalism in which industrialists "of the Atlantic seaboard will do nothing to unsettle the labor on the plantations." First observing that "[s]trife between the white people is at an end," Whitman then wryly concludes: "Profitable industry is a great peace-maker."

Titled "A Bugle Note," Whitman's argument takes on the urgency of a cavalry charge: "The Colored people of the South are *just now* being tried as by fire."[2] But the white nationalism he describes—its scenes of everyday affection between whites cohering into the racialized sense of a common people positioned over and above nonwhite others—cannot exactly be seen as the crisis his title and "just now" implies. Or, at least, the processes he delineates don't unfold with the sudden tempo, unpredictability, or spectacular eventfulness we associate with emergency. Instead, Whitman alerts his readers to what had already become a commonplace feature of their everyday existence: antiblackness instilled within the unfolding of ordinary life; a counterrevolution to Reconstruction arrayed in the calm and orderly peace of conflict resolution.

By the early 1890s, Whitman's story of resubjugation was already familiar among his fellow black intellectuals, who decades previously had already begun describing emancipation's faltering promise and the resurgence in white supremacy.[3] Yet in his emphasis on the ordinary, Whitman's essay adds a significant element to the story. He suggests that when we look for either the historical agents of black resubjugation or the constituents of white supremacy's postemancipation reorganization, we would do well to examine more than the monumental gestures of reunion and reconciliation, the trans-sectional circulation of white money and capital, or even the disciplinary techniques newly imposed for enforcing and reproducing hierarchy across the color line.[4] We should direct our attentions as well, he suggests, toward habitual practices and the commonsense of implicit, taken-for-granted

*Genre and White Supremacy in the Postemancipation United States*. Travis M. Foster, Oxford University Press (2019).
© Travis M. Foster.
DOI: 10.1093/oso/9780198838098.001.0001

knowledge. Entering into his essay's most prophetic mode, Whitman writes: "The proud descendants of Lee's ragged veterans are mingling with the splendid hosts of Grant and Sheridan, and fraternizing in hope, they are to join hands in all perils, and open the gate of the Twentieth Century with a music that will respond to the music of the spheres."[5] The sentence captures a sentiment sweeping Northern and Southern whites into a mutual, forward-looking embrace, anticipating not only the national futurity and hopeful modernity of the twentieth century but also the certitude of divine approbation: whiteness in its rightful place as the nation's past, present, and God-given destiny. Notably, Whitman grounds this racial momentum in two gerunds describing run-of-the-mill social practices, *mingling* and *fraternizing*. Placing emphasis on the ongoing normalization of white affinity and the consequent social reproduction of black subjugation, the verbs orient our attention to everyday rhythms and repetitions. Such a shift in scale reveals a history of antiblackness that otherwise occludes its own historicity, falling outside our historiographical and analytical purviews. Hence we might say that Whitman's urgent summons, his bugle call, amounts more than anything to a methodological plea. What tools can we bring to bear for analyzing, assessing, historicizing, and diagnosing a mode of subjugation that obscures its own function as such? What are we to do with a system of domination and exploitation so ordinary it has become utterly asymptomatic?

*Genre and White Supremacy in the Postemancipation United States* takes up Whitman's summons through an analysis of four genres that arose into widespread popularity during the years following emancipation and emancipation's rapid demise.[6] By historicizing and theorizing genre's role in unfolding the era's new racial ordinary, this book tracks the interplay between aesthetic conventions and social norms, identifying this dynamic relationship as a key influence in how Americans understood their affiliations, their citizenship, and their race. The result is both a historical argument about postemancipation white supremacy and a methodological argument insisting on genre's paramount significance within projects, like Whitman's, aspiring to turn the ordinary world into an urgent object of study. The first three chapters highlight how white popular genres—campus novels, the *Ladies' Home Journal*, and Civil War elegies—secured fraternal and sororal identifications with white supremacy and expanded the elasticity of white belonging to include new European immigrant populations, white feminism, and even expressions of dissent against white nationalism's large-scale interpellations. The final chapter turns from whites' mutually affirming interactions with white genres to black collectivities made possible through participation in what was arguably the era's most popular mode of African American popular expression, the gospel sermon. By highlighting the performative and aesthetic conventions of a popular black genre, this final chapter uncovers an alternative relationship between genre and white supremacy: one in which generic conventions worked to collectivize and propagate black affirmations of freedom rather than to naturalize and implement a racist status quo.

During the concluding decades of the nineteenth century, generic literature reached an unprecedented level of social and cultural influence, circulating and recirculating conventions within Americans' everyday lives. Steam press innovations during the 1850s and a rise in commercial paper mills beginning during the late 1860s made print cheaper, more accessible, and more prevalent. Improved transportation networks, the introduction of second-class postage rates for newspapers and magazines, and the explosion of book subscription services meant that popular literature showed up regularly at Americans' front doors.[7] Through these technologies, the aesthetic conventions of popular genres entered into and influenced people's day-to-day experiences and guided how they located themselves within larger social and political organizations.[8]

More specifically, popular genres influenced a new ordinariness in the experience, social reproduction, and significance of race. They maintained racial belonging as the overarching criterion for white social organization in the wake of emancipation; naturalized for white readers the hierarchy through which white supremacy reproduced itself; and, for African Americans, provided a method for affirming, energizing, and organizing radical collectivities. Genre worked so well—even for such diametrically opposing projects—because it operated as a technology, a machine, unfolding through the self-greasing mechanism of expectation and satisfaction. It entered social life by suffusing the desire for convention into encounters with texts and performances, creating expectations for recurrence and then satisfying through the circulation of ever-new instantiations.

And so it is that an engine of desire becomes an engine of history. When popular genres rise up, satisfying and demanding attention, they reflect the shared assumptions and loyalties of their audiences, operating to make certain futures seem possible, likely, appealing. Put differently, out of the multiple, layered interactions between the individuals and the conventions of genre, new social and ideological conventions first emerge and then become taken-for-granted features of daily experience. Analysis of postbellum popular genres thus facilitates a historicism uniquely invested in Albery Allson Whitman's history of the ordinary, providing access to the obscured stakes and elided thickness of everyday life through an archive and a method that highlight the textured ongoingness of antiblackness and its discontents.[9]

Yet as a methodological scale and framework, genre also productively complicates this picture in two significant ways. First, while genres certainly do survive through the reproduction of conventions over time, they also survive through the novelty of new instantiations, each one presenting what has already become familiar with its own small twist. Within this play of repetition and difference even highly stable patterns become vulnerable to erosion and change. Hence this book's first three chapters, all focusing on popular white genres, document a movement toward racial belonging and a countermovement in which the reproduction of such belonging demands supplementation by something more than mere likeness, more than mere being-in-common. On the one hand, newly significant literary and cultural genres lent potent momentum to the white supremacist project of sectional reconciliation, easing white Northerners into a feeling of kinship, solidarity, and fraternity with their Southern counterparts and eclipsing even tenuous commitments to racial justice or multiracial democracy. On the other hand, analysis of these same popular white genres captures the sometimes-fragile quality of racial affinity for whites in the postbellum North and helps us to see how, on its own, the racial kinship of whiteness remained an insufficient basis for collective identification. Hence the aesthetic conventions that we find in popular white genres reveal crucial features in the constitution and social reproduction of white supremacy: namely, that while whiteness operated as a tremendous force for bridging sectional, ethnic, economic, and political differences in the postbellum United States, it did so primarily through incorporation, accommodation, and even celebration of white particularity.[10] In short, genre reveals whiteness's seemingly limitless capacity to reproduce its supremacy through adaptation and elasticity.

Second, genre provides an aesthetic vehicle for collectivizing social and political potential aslant, underneath, and against dominant whiteness. More specifically, the pleasures and satisfactions of black popular genres underwrite fugitive experimentation and contra-fraternal collectivity.[11] Genre analysis therefore revises an overly narrow sense of the political that tends to dominate in literary studies—one that situates opposition in the exceptional, lone, and spectacular work of individual texts heroically bucking convention while ignoring or even deriding the unoriginal, collective, and pooled work of generic texts and the capacities for conventionality to nurture shared life.[12] In this sense, my fourth chapter's analysis of black gospel sermons serves as a counterweight to its first three chapters, insisting that the politics of genre—and, indeed, the genre of politics—cannot be determined in advance. Close examination of sermons' tenacious and multilayered conventionality reveals a widespread and collective black religio-aesthetics that resists the very terms available for political dissent.[13] The sermon's proffered alternatives root racial community within an improvisational performance enabled precisely through the shared conventions of genre. Gospel sermons thereby provided an infrastructure for experiments with blackness and freedom apart from either an interracial liberal project of diversified inclusion or racial fraternity's a priori being-in-common.

## Postemancipation, Sectional Reconciliation, and the Racial Ordinary

Historians, far more than literary critics, have taken up questions of emancipation's aftermath in the postbellum United States, compiling a robust historiography unique for being as invested in tracking stasis over time as it is in historical change. Collectively, these histories survey a process initiated when the gradually unfolding events known as emancipation produced new crises in the underwriting logic of white supremacy: "No longer could racial meanings be anchored in the exclusivity of both slavery (black) and full citizenship (white, as well as male)," writes historian Hannah Rosen. "Nor was it inevitable that distinctions based on European versus (any) African descent would continue to structure the postemancipation polity—its public life, family patterns, personal identity, and constructs of community and nation."[14] After surveying the varieties and extents of emancipation's disruptions, histories of postemancipation turn to the institutional, juridical, paralegal, and cultural tools whites used to restore and re-naturalize white supremacy as the engine of US sociopolitical life. Most notably, they have documented the Ku Klux Klan's and the White Leagues' successes in stripping black citizenship rights, lynching's reign of terror, the rise of mass incarceration and enslaved inmate labor, the reconfigured regulations of black labor and housing, and the emergent networks of jurisprudence that would come to be known as the "Black Codes," all pursued under the mocking aegis of an illusory freedom.[15] To date, then, histories of US postemancipation have primarily located resubjugation where it occurs explicitly and, most often, spectacularly—as racism carried out through actions, speech, physical brutality, imprisonment, and legislative action. What they've largely neglected, however, has been the frequently unremarked, ambient way that antiblackness came to underwrite everyday white life.

In contrast to the emphasis on explicit, interracial resubjugation in the South, this book's first three chapters focus on antiblackness as an implicit, constitutive feature within *intra*racial scenes, primarily in the white North.[16] I argue that white antiblack racism should not be understood merely as content, defined by a particular kind of thought or activity, but also as rhythm, repetition, seriality, and festivity. Its social reproduction and affirmation occurs more frequently through daily patterns of, say, white fraternizing and mingling than it does through more direct enactments of brutality and subjection. Critic Arif Dirlik makes a similar point when he describes the "habitualness" of racism that took hold in the wake of emancipation: "Slavery may have produced racism, but it was arguably the end of slavery that would render racism into a virulent principle of social distancing and repression, able to achieve through ideology what could no longer be guaranteed through legal oppression and exploitation."[17] Significantly, though, we must not limit the habitual practices of racism to scenes of interracial exploitation. Hence philosopher Charles W. Mills's essential revision of political theory's "social contract" into a racial contract: "it is not a contract between everybody ('we the people'), but between just the people who count, the people who really are people ('we the white people')."[18] This racial contract frames all intrawhite interactions within raced space. It operates by "distinguishing on the level of everyday interaction...person–person from person–subperson social intercourse" while affirming consent to the contract's terms, privileges, and regulations. These intraracial white interactions comprise antiblackness's most generative praxis, constituting as they do the vast bulk of its pedagogy, reinforcement, and regularization.

By focusing primarily on racist regulatory apparatuses that arose following slavery or on scenes of explicit resubjugation of the formerly enslaved, we miss out on the ways that white supremacy's restoration transpired in everyday, common-place, routine interactions that are not in any explicitly discursive way *about race*. In other words, we miss out on those interactions that may otherwise remain unavailable to racial analysis, shielded as they are by whiteness's incessant self-fashioning as the agent rather than the object of racial logic. While it has now been over twenty-five years since Toni Morrison's insistence, in *Playing in the Dark*, that literary historians and critics attend to the systems and legacies of enslavement "[e]ven, and especially, when American texts are not 'about' Africanist presences or characters or narrative or idiom," American literary histories still too frequently, albeit implicitly, attribute racelessness to the texts, spaces, and scenes of white literature.[19] Such a failure causes too many literary histories implicitly to mis-represent antiblackness as a confined phenomenon, germane to scenes featuring interracial character interactions or white writers' representations of nonwhite characters, rather than as an atmospheric condition of US life that shapes social experience both across the color line and also far apart from the color line's scenes of abuse and subjugation.[20]

In the postbellum United States, as Albery Whitman has already reminded us, white consent to the racial contract—to belonging together as one white people over and against nonwhite others—required bridging sectional divisions of the Civil War and at least approximating shared memory over how that war transpired and what it meant, leaving the South "beaten but unconquered."[21] For the past two decades, historians like Nina Silber, David Blight, and Edward J. Blum have elaborated, in significant ways, on the postbellum history of trans-sectional white belonging, tracing how white Protestant institutions, Memorial Day rituals, popular literature such as plantation stories and reunion romances, and soldiers' reminis-cences all inclined white Northerners toward sectional reconciliation. As they describe it, the process succeeded through parallel procedures: reestablishment of antiblackness as a defining, unifying, and shared attribute of the white North and South; and affirmation of the Confederate cause as morally just or, at the very least, honorably fought.[22]

Literary critics have likewise documented the seemingly unavoidable impulse toward sectional reconciliation over and against emancipationist possibility. Elizabeth Duquette describes this transition in white Northern literature as a shift from sympathy to loyalty. Such a transition reconfigured allegiance to race and nation in ways, Duquette argues, that led Northern white writers toward "narra-tive structures that reduce contingency and diminish the potential difference between both [white] persons and moments in time."[23] For critics working on Walt Whitman's and Herman Melville's Civil War poetry, by far the largest body of Americanist literary scholarship to address white sectional reconciliation, such a turn to loyalty meant diminishing antagonisms between the white North and the white South and minimizing the overly disruptive theme of black emancipation.

Ed Folsom, for instance, details how Walt Whitman edited out "the prospect of America as a biracial democracy" when revising his wartime writing for postbellum publications like the 1875 *Memoranda During the War* and the 1882 *Specimen Days*.[24] Likewise, multiple critics cite Melville's 1866 "Supplement" to *Battle-Pieces*, which claims that "kindliness" toward African Americans should "not be allowed to exclude kindliness to communities who stand nearer to us in nature."[25] Yes, slavery may have been wrong and, yes, emancipation may be cause for celebration, yet, for the vast majority of white Northern writers, sectional reconciliation and white national loyalty took clear precedence over even inchoate imaginings of what emancipation might look like or entail.[26]

In recent years, historians have challenged the extent and speed of sectional reconciliation, asserting that the process was both more prolonged and more precarious than initially argued. They have documented, for instance, extensive commitments among many white Union veterans and their women relations to honoring black heroism during the war, leading this subpopulation of Northern whites to hold more firmly to emancipationist principles than their counterparts.[27] So, for example, Brian Matthew Jordan notes several instances in which white Grand Army of the Republic members angrily assailed the racism of D. W. Griffith's wildly popular *The Birth of a Nation* upon its 1915 release.[28] Moreover, historians have noted that the Republican Party, which remained the nation's dominant political force through the early twentieth century, regularly continued its legislative attempts to check antiblackness in the South up until 1891, a full fourteen years after the Compromise of 1877 and the ostensible end of Reconstruction.[29] While neither line of argument intends to overturn the central thesis that sectional reconciliation ultimately succeeded at the expense of emancipation for the formerly enslaved, each suggests that the reconciliationist outcome was far from inevitable. They therefore provide a strong correction to recent cultural tendencies toward alternate histories premised on Confederate victory, inviting us instead to imagine the very real possibility that an emancipationist vision—even a compromised one—had prevailed. How would the US now be different had the white South not, as Cecilia Elizabeth O'Leary puts it, "won in the cultural arena what it lost on the battlefield"?[30] More to the point for this project, these arguments suggest that we still have much to understand about what happened in the white North during the decades following the Civil War, that period Timothy Sweet refers to as "the unsettled moment when the memory of the war was not yet overwritten by topoi that would later come to dominate, such as the Lost Cause, the romance of reunion, and the reconciliation of veterans."[31] What caused the white North, by the mid-1890s, to forswear any commitment to the imagination and implementation of anything approaching a vision for emancipation? If, as Colleen C. O'Brien argues, "what ushered the United States into the modern era—and marked the demise of American romanticism's quest for freedom—was the relative abandonment of antiracist work by white reformers," then we still need more ways to understand what made the racial contract of antiblackness more appealing, acceptable, and agreeable than pursuing the antiracist ideals of emancipation.[32]

This emergent postbellum reality is what I describe as the new racial ordinary. Like Pierre Bourdieu's *habitus*, the term *ordinary*—along with the grouping of terms critics use in ways roughly synonymous, like everyday, mundane, commonplace, unoriginal, and quotidian—flags how a reconciliationist vision ultimately saturated the white North so thoroughly that it became unthinking, taken for granted, and frequently implicit: "internalized as a second nature and so forgotten as history."[33] As a complement to analyses of the biopolitical transformation of individuals into racialized and hierarchically distributed populations, measured and managed within unequal distributions of capacity, the racial ordinary functions to shape behavior, interpersonal interactions, and the interpretation of experience while simultaneously providing the ubiquitous, ongoing, and constitutive elements of racial belonging.[34] Unlike analyses and histories of biopolitics, however, which tend to place their greatest emphasis on the structuring interactions between aggregates (populations and science, racialization and organic matter, health and the optimization of life), the racial ordinary tracks how the small-scale interactions, reactions, thoughts, and feelings making up everyday experience align with—and, in some instances, complicate—the aggregate patterns such everyday life reproduces and naturalizes. The new racial ordinary, as this book describes it, lurks in practices and dispositions that constituted whites' "common-sense world," and it therefore structured intraracial practices for getting along and being together as well as actions and thoughts across the color line.[35]

Yet such an observation risks making the process seem cleaner and more self-evident than I intend. "Attending to the ordinary," writes Heather Love, "means understanding and accepting the mixed nature of reality."[36] We might take this a step further to say that it means understanding and accepting the contradictory, paradoxical, and profoundly unreasonable nature of reality itself. Indeed, ordinariness remains implicit in no small part by taking contradictions and turning them into basic understandings about how things work. The racial ordinary for whites means living out what Mills refers to as the many forms of "white misunderstanding, misrepresentation, evasion, and self-deception...prescribed by the terms of the Racial Contract," and, moreover, expressing that ignorance as a form of commonly held knowledge, certitude, privilege, and self-possession.[37] Nor, as I've already suggested, can we rest on any easy assumption that ordinariness is intrinsically reactionary. Indeed, it's within the ordinary more so than within the individual (in the multitude of ways we might understand such a term) that alternative ways of knowing and experiencing the world can take hold as shared resistance to white supremacy. While the first three chapters of this book focus on ordinariness within an incipient Northern white racist status quo, then, its final chapter takes a crucial turn to how, for many African Americans, the conventions of ordinary, shared experience manifested as potent vehicles for affirming a mode of freedom that resisted both the content of antiblackness (its racial hierarchy) and the form of antiblackness (its privileged fraternity).

In considering the history of white supremacy as an outgrowth of ordinary life, I build on extensive recent work within critical race studies concerned with implicit epistemic frameworks for reproducing racial hierarchy. Focusing on what Mills terms "the more primeval sense of underlying patterns and matrices of belief," these scholars work to show how ordinariness assimilates history into the lived background of white experience, reconstituting legacies of enslavement and settler colonialism into the unnoticed, seemingly transhistorical footholds around which white life continues to be organized.[38] Philosopher George Yancy describes the process of white racialization as a "lived density" in which the repetition of performed behaviors produces "the reality of white identity as spatial distance and ontological difference from blacks," giving to racial hierarchy "the appearance of being something natural and inevitable."[39] For Yancy, antiblackness becomes internalized through the socializing force of ordinary experience: "white children are oriented, at the level of everyday practices, within the world, where their bodily orientations are unreflected expressions of the background *lived* orientations of whiteness, white ways of being, white modes of racial and racist practice."[40] Similarly, scholarship within Native studies highlights how settler colonialism created the material conditions for the normalization of white supremacy. Aileen Moreton-Robinson describes this process as the production of "white possessive logics," which circulate "as part of commonsense knowledge, decision making, and socially produced conventions" and underpin white "rationalization" with "an excessive desire to invest in reproducing and reaffirming the nation-state's ownership, control, and domination."[41] In other words, as Mark Rifkin writes in *Settler Common Sense*, "the juridical dimensions and dynamics of settlement impress upon and are lived and reconstituted as the material animating ordinary nonnative experience."[42] In all of this work, sustained attention to the everyday ongoingness of white supremacy brings the thickness and dynamism of ordinary life—its repetitions, its dependence upon familiarity, its practices of habit and routine—into critical focus, turning those most mundane and, therefore, most overlooked aspects of experience into urgent objects for our sustained attention.

Such work on the racial ordinary has and will continue to have much to say about the history and social reproduction of whiteness, yet its emphases depart from those of the so-called "whiteness studies" that publishers institutionalized as an autonomous field during the 1990s. Texts like Noel Ignatiev's *How the Irish Became White* and Theodore Allen's *The Invention of the White Race* focus primarily on the social construction of whiteness—how certain groups, such as the Irish or European Jews, came to see themselves and be seen by others as white, thereby securing a place atop the racial hierarchy.[43] Work in critical race studies instead tends to conceptualize whiteness as a key mechanism in structures of domination and privilege, particularly those anchored by the legacies of enslavement and dispossession: more "a strategy than an ethnic nomenclature," to borrow from a discussion of whiteness in Mat Johnson's 2011 novel *Pym*.[44] So, for example, within the framing of this latter scholarship, it is of course still accurate to say that European immigrants were assimilated into whiteness, but we get closer to the underlying nature of the process when we observe, as does Morrison in *Playing in the Dark*, that European immigrants came to understand "their 'Americcanness' as an opposition to the resident black population."[45] For work on antiblackness, such a distinction is vital because it highlights racism as a constitutive feature of white experience, underscoring what Mills refers to as "the crucial reality that the *normal* workings of the social system continue to disadvantage blacks in large measure *independently* of racist feeling."[46] Within the postbellum United States, these normal workings suffused antiblackness into a wide array of white scenes, from the football match between sophomores and freshmen that opens so many campus novels to the networked sorority experienced and treasured by readers of the *Ladies' Home Journal*.

## White Suffering, Black Suffering, and the Long Civil War

The term *postbellum* I've just used to index this project's historical moment relies on a typical periodization of the US Civil War, positing it as a singular event on a timeline, 1861–5, that divides the nineteenth century—and, indeed, all of US history—into two distinct eras. This version of the war prevails in history and literary studies, shaping established curriculum, monograph subtitles, anthologies, and job ads for the hiring of faculty.[47] In a moment I'll turn to the insufficiencies of such a historicization and the ways, in particular, that it prioritizes the eventfulness of white suffering over the uneventfulness of black suffering. First, though, let me stress why we need to augment our notion of the Civil War as an event rather than dispense with it.

To no small extent, this conventional periodization captures something crucial about the war's immensity, its extraordinary devastation, and its momentous impact. It underscores, for instance, the significance of the shift in white supremacy, which, prior to the war, had organized itself around an inextricable link between blackness and chattel. And it therefore emphasizes emancipation and Reconstruction, even in their historically and ethically limited varieties, as tremendous and rare moments of promise in American history when different futures were imagined and made possible before being all too rapidly set aside. Hardly a liberal theorist of progress, W. E. B. Du Bois nevertheless celebrates emancipation as a radical and singular event: Joy rose in the South "like perfume—like a prayer," he writes, giving birth to a "new song" that "swelled and blossomed like incense, improvised and born anew out of an age long past, and weaving into its texture the old and new melodies in word and in thought." Using scent, sound, and spirit metaphors, Du Bois emphasizes the widespread and readily dispersed character of emancipation's unprecedented newness, which permeated consciousness and unconsciousness alike, giving birth to an incipient reality that "grew and swelled and lived."[48]

This vision of the war and emancipation comports with that put forward by many of its historical actors in the North. Consider the opening stanza of abolitionist John Greenleaf Whittier's 1861 "Ein feste Burg ist unser Gott," the Union rallying hymn Lincoln cited as an influence on his Emancipation Proclamation.[49] In this verse, Whittier represents the war as divine purification produced through restorative violence:

> We wait beneath the furnace blast
> The pangs of transformation;
> Not painlessly doth God recast
> And mould anew the nation.
> Hot burns the fire
> Where wrongs expire,
> Nor spares the hand
> That from the land
> Uproot the ancient evil.[50]

An Old Testament conflagration, the Civil War promised to destroy and purify the nation, breaking massively and all but completely with the past. Whittier imagines the "pangs of transformation" to be capable of instituting patterns in American life neither foreclosed nor predetermined by what had come before. This vision underlay Radical Republicans' foremost aspirations for the project of Reconstruction. Providing African Americans with military protection from white antiblack violence in the South, punishing racist aggression swiftly and harshly, and eliminating Confederate nationalism would, they anticipated, continue and then finish the work of the Civil War, utterly remaking the nation through the fulfillment of an emancipationist vision.

At the same time, however, so long as we ground scholarship—and structure the field as a whole—on this version of the Civil War, conceiving it as an event with a distinct four-year periodization, we miss out on a more expansive way the war has been understood, particularly in black and radical white antiracist thought: as an unending struggle between antiblackness and black freedom. Take Isabella MacFarlane's Civil War elegy "The Two Southern Mothers," published in the fall of 1863 by both *Continental Monthly*, one of the most prominent white publications within the Northern home front, and Martin Delany's *The Anglo-African*, perhaps the 1860s' most significant vehicle for circulating black intellectual and radical thought. The poem's first half describes the battle death of a Confederate soldier, crushed under the weight of his own horse, asking its readers to sympathize with the grief of that soldier's mother, and, through such feeling, to connect with her in a shared scene of loss, a noble and unifying collectivity of suffering. The poem additionally acknowledges honor on either side—"Northern valor, Southern pride"—anticipating the white reconciliationist agenda that later elegies, like

Francis Miles Finch's wildly popular "The Blue and the Gray," will take up with fervor. Most importantly for our purposes, it transforms Civil War death into an event, a cacophonous, gruesome, and monumental "scene of slaughter" that stands apart from the unfolding of diurnal time, providing an image and a frame for those lives lost that makes possible attention and memorialization.

But midway through, the elegy quickly shifts its focus, giving voice to a black woman who has been enslaved by the white mother, a woman who likewise grieves her children:

> As she mourned her slaughtered brave,
> Came and spake her aged slave—
> Came and spake with solemn brow:
> "Misses, we is even, now.
>
> "I had ten, and you had one;
> Now we're even—all are gone;
> Not one left to bury either—
> Slave and mistress mourn together.
>
> "*Every one of mine you sold—*
> Now your own lies stark and cold:
> To the just Avenger bow—
> Missis! I forgive you *now*."
>
> Thus she spoke, that sable mother;
> Shuddering, quailed and crouched the other.
> Yea! although it tarry long,
> *Payment shall be made for wrong!*[51]

When it refocuses its primary object of loss from the white Confederate soldier, spectacularly killed upon the battlefield, to the enslaved woman's children, routinely sold for profit, the poem reconfigures from within both the genre of the Civil War elegy and the Civil War itself. Knitting its two parts together with unbroken iambic meter, rhyming couplets, and the doubling of second-person address (initially from speaker to reader, then from enslaved mother to Confederate mother), "The Two Southern Mothers" embeds the everyday violence of antiblackness within its catalog of Civil War losses and makes black suffering a visible and significant object within the war's elegiac attention. The elegy thus argues against any neat periodization that would mark the war's beginning and end according to violence wrought upon white bodies alone and brings into the foreground a much longer timeline of antiblack subjection. Yet its aim is not merely to antedate the Civil War to the initiation of Atlantic world enslavement; it also looks to the present and future of antiblackness as a long-term, durable, and structuring commonplace in US history. By twice offsetting the word *now* (first as a standalone clause at the beginning of the enslaved mother's speech and second with italics at that speech's end) and by underscoring in its final couplet the deferred tarrying of racial justice, the elegy proleptically incorporates future abuses of black lives, anticipating those new techniques for re-enslavement—what Saidiya Hartman memorably terms "the forms of discipline unleashed by the abandonment of the whip"—that will emerge in the wake of emancipation.[52]

Historical periods, as Caroline Levine reminds us, act as "bounded wholes," "forms for organizing heterogeneous materials." They "afford constraints and opportunities, bringing bodies, meanings, and objects into political order."[53] Literary scholars are only beginning to think critically about what conventional periodization of the Civil War brings into focus and what it leaves out of sight. In his recent book *Nineteenth-Century American Literature and the Long Civil War*, for instance, Cody Marrs fruitfully traces the "transbellum" careers of Whitman, Douglass, Melville, and Dickinson to reconceptualize the war as a "nonsynchronous upheaval," "an event that outsteps the discrete, four-year span with which it is often associated."[54] Yet Marrs remains more focused on the questions conventional Civil War periodization raises for authorship, the conceptualization of literary careers, and the institutionalization of canonical literary history, rather than on the questions it raises for racialized history and the critical study of antiblackness.

To better understand the alternative periodization of MacFarlane's elegy, we should turn instead to a black intellectual tradition that conceptualizes Civil War periodization apart from the organizational structure of bounded forms. In the chapter of *Black Reconstruction* devoted to the nadir's forms of re-enslavement, for example, W. E. B. Du Bois describes "how civil war in the South began again— indeed, had never ceased."[55] Likewise in his masterpiece *Just Above my Head*, James Baldwin decries the notion of the Civil War as "an event skewered and immobilized by time," calling instead for us to witness how antiblackness was hardly "stopped at Shiloh, still less at Harper's Ferry."[56] Similarly, Christina Sharpe describes the inadequacy of a term like *postbellum* for capturing the reality of the formerly enslaved and their descendants, "still on the plantation, still surrounded by those who claimed ownership over them and who fought, and fight still, to extend that state of capture and subjection in as many legal and extralegal ways as possible, into the present."[57] All of these instances resist the temporality of an eventfulness that steps out of time and calls attention to itself, preferring instead to conceptualize the Civil War as a rolling and forceful ongoingness in both the ordinariness of antiblackness and the struggle against it. "Who fought, and fight still": this too is the Civil War, which began long before 1865 and continues into the present day.

In these pages, I attempt to heed the nineteenth century split by the war and the postbellum era's mirrored reiterations of its antebellum counterpart; the historical significance of white sectional reunion and the fractures that reconciliation and white nationalism opened within white consciousness and social worlds; white exploitation of black life and the unfailing pursuit of new forms of freedom that characterized so many dimensions of black intellectual, artistic, and religious creation. I describe the late nineteenth century's combination of profound uncertainty and sense of itself on the cusp of something new, and I track how the end of slavery did indeed restructure American life, even if only in ways that endeavored to maintain the antebellum racial order. Simultaneously, I trace the no-less-profound regression, loss, and subjection experienced at the hands of a white supremacy that was reconfigured and, in many instances, invigorated rather than weakened.

I do so primarily in two ways. First, the palimpsestic form of this book's historical argument enables it to dig through layers in ordinary life rather than trace a cause-and-effect historical narrative. Because all of the book's chapters overlap chronologically, the effect of the whole is to trace the coexistence of contradictory, complex impulses within time. History here is more inclined to turn inward than to arch toward progress. Second, I call readers' attention to the scale and conventions of genre. To track literature through genre's repeated conventions is, as Northrop Frye puts it, to refuse liberalism's emphasis on the autonomous, self-possessed individual and to overcome our wrongheaded tendencies to think of any such "individual as ideally prior to society."[58] It is to understand the social and the literary as deeply enmeshed within relationships that cannot be isolated through linear cause-and-effect historical arguments but instead must be understood as polyrhythmic and recurrently, often unpredictably, interactive networks of world making. Genre analysis enables literary histories that loosen the edges of periods and events, rendering them temporally diffuse and heterogeneous.

## Genre and Ordinary Life

The last ten years have witnessed something of a reawakening in genre analysis and, in particular, the development of new methods for conceiving of genre beyond the classifying functions of taxonomy, underscoring it instead as an interchange between aesthetic objects and social life. Casting aside any sense of what Virginia Jackson calls an "an old-fashioned, belletristic frame," recent critics are revealing genres as dynamic processes of interaction, "communally held forms of recognition" that first "hail us" and then invite us to "enter that scene of address."[59] This process occurs in part through the very form that genre assumes: a regularized recurrence, a rhythm. Put differently, genre comes into being through the regularized repetition of its iterations, each of which amounts to a temporal beat that echoes the past and creates anticipation for the future.[60] A meeting ground for memory and expectancy, genre makes and fulfills promises. Hence, in *The Female Complaint*, Lauren Berlant describes genre as an absorbent institution that incorporates small differences and variations, all the while delivering on its assurance "that the persons transacting with it will experience the pleasure of encountering what they expected."[61] These repeated aesthetic patterns anchor us within the present moment, providing the comfort of familiarity and stability. If, as Jeremy

Rosen argues, "[g]enres make visible…the role of literary forms in articulating broader social and ideological formations," then genre analysis provides the best method available to literary critics for tracking conventions as they enter into daily life.

Readers familiar with theorizings of the everyday—from Judith Butler's gender performativity to Bourdieu's habitus to Henri Lefebvre's dialectics of control and helplessness—will already notice a recognizable pattern of repetition, expectation, and fulfillment linking genre and the ordinary.[62] "As day follows trivial day," writes Lefebvre in exploring how ordinary life comes into being, "the eye learns how to see, the ear learns how to hear, the body learns how to keep its rhythms."[63] Genres and ordinary life gain meaning and significance within a similar shape and pattern, both organized through the regular sequence of expectations producing expectations. They each come into existence through reiterated citations recurring with regularity over time, transpiring into categories that become recognizable, familiar, second nature, and, indeed, generic. Yet the relationship between genre and everyday life goes much deeper than their mere sharing of formal properties. Genres produce and give substance to the ordinary. They are "the things we have in common."[64]

Of course, the "we" in Stanley Cavell's phrase here is never stable. It shifts between groups, across geographies, and over time, all the while acting as a dividing marker between "us" and "them." Nor is it possible to take for granted the sequence Cavell implies, that the "we" coheres into a recognizable mode of belonging and, only then, produces the common things of ordinary life. To study, describe, and analyze genre is to trace ordinariness entering into the world provisionally and contingently, solidifying into overlapping groupings of "we," and then—perhaps gradually, perhaps with surprising speed—transforming into something newly desirable and newly ordinary.

That is to say, genres come and go. Aesthetic, formal, and thematic characteristics become newly familiar generic groupings when they fulfill a function for their particular present and their particular audience, fading once that function loses its urgency.[65] There are, as Bruce Robbins describes it, "social tasks that cause a genre to be seized on at a given historical moment and invested with special energy and representativeness."[66] So, for instance, campus novels, the topic of my first chapter, provided white postbellum Americans with a scaled down idealization of the national community as a conciliatory, jovial commingling of peers, turning intraracial, internecine agonism into skirmishes quickly overcome through banter and merriment. Or, to take a more recent example, we might think of our own era's penchant for novels and films narrating survival in the wake of apocalypse—narratives that channel our anxieties related to the precarious global economy and the inevitability of ecological crisis by inviting us collectively to identify with the survivors of catastrophe. These popular modes of expression come together in the repeating conventions of genre when we need them to ameliorate tensions and ease social and psychic pressures. Genre exists in no small part to smooth over antagonisms and conflicts, to re-attach us to social belonging, and to help us feel a sense of connection to the conventions that enable shared experience. It mediates the "we" and maps our belonging within it.

How literary historians access and interpret this process presents a set of methodological and archival questions that can make genre criticism strangely reminiscent of the editorial prefaces to scholarly editions. This is because what belongs to or participates in any given genre always amounts to a vexed question, just as so frequently is the case with decisions about what belongs and doesn't belong in the authoritative edition of, say, Melville's "Hawthorne and his Mosses." Genres, as Wai Chee Dimock writes, amount to "fields of knowledge": "none is a closed book, none an exhaustive blueprint."[67] This open-endedness comes into play when attempting to ascertain any given genre's lifespan, and it often comes into play again when interpreting any given text's relationship to generic grouping. Yet only by positing the straw horse of absolute generic purity, as Jacques Derrida does in "The Law of Genre," can we conclude that such open-endedness means that "genre declasses what it allows to be classed," thereby rendering it all but meaningless as a critical concept.[68] What such open-endedness does mean, however, is that ascertaining and then analyzing a genre's defining conventions cannot be strictly empirical or quantitative—cannot, that is, be addressed more through data sets than the professional reading practices typical of graduate literary training.[69] Dimock, in her argument against quantitative reading practices, refers to genre criticism as a "fluid continuum" between the large-scale conventions binding groups of texts and the small-scale manifestations of those conventions within single texts. When the "micro evidence is sufficiently detailed and precise," she argues, we can bring close reading methods to those patterns and conventions that bind texts into "extended kinship."[70]

In the process of researching white campus novels, Civil War elegies, the *Ladies' Home Journal*, and gospel sermons, my initial aim has been to identify each genre's defining conventions, or what Jeremy Rosen refers to as the "relatively stable center" that binds them and makes them recognizably related to their generic peers.[71] To do so, I've read as close to the entirety of the genre as possible, a process of necessarily incomplete archive assembly and study that each chapter describes explicitly. The analysis I compile here, however, depends on close readings of texts and moments drawn from a selection of this archive. In choosing which examples to describe and analyze, I looked for moments that stand out either for their exemplariness (their close adherence to the defining conventions of their genre) or their metaliterary self-awareness (their expression of how their genre's defining conventions interact with each other and the outside world). This method provides one way to work through the problem of scale we face whenever attempting to negotiate the flux between the conventions binding texts into genres and the uniqueness of individual iterations within those genres. It enables analysis of the significance and complexity of conventions while also facilitating understanding of the relationship between those conventions and the departures from them.

This process will always be partial. Just as there can be no exhaustive reading of an individual text, so too is it impossible to provide an exhaustive reading of any given genre. What I've attempted instead is to open new possibilities for understanding the interaction between popular genre and race, proposing how we might better appreciate the interrelationship of conventions within genre and the links between generic aesthetics and social life.

## Popular Intraracial Genres

Campus novels, white women's magazines, Civil War elegies, and gospel sermons became popular during the nineteenth century's latter decades in no small part for their ability to help individuals feel connected to a racial community, to provide patterns for relating to others within that community, and, in some instances, to negotiate feelings of unease and misrecognition in the interchange between individual identity and racial belonging. I term them *intraracial genres* because they focus almost exclusively on the patterns, textures, and feelings of social life between whites or between blacks and, in so doing, conceptualize the binding agents of racial membership and its forms of belonging. By *intraracial*, therefore, I do not refer to genres with an exclusively homogeneous cast of characters. Indeed, white intraracial genres in particular often include minor characters of color and racist humor about people of color in the service of affirming racial belonging through the naturalization of white supremacist racial hierarchy.

The genres collected here are but a few of the many modes of popular literature and culture operating within and against the postbellum color line. Minstrel performances and songs circulating after the Civil War, for instance, shifted their focus in response to new demands the war placed on white supremacy. Antebellum minstrelsy, as Eric Lott has argued, organized white fascination with black men and black culture, negotiating between the allure of a subject position deemed transgressive and the threat such an allure posed to racial and sexual autonomy.[72] Yet postbellum minstrelsy, responding simultaneously to the aftermath of sectional discord between whites and to the late-century rise in European immigration, could not take white affinities as self-evident and therefore tended to focus primarily on securing white racial belonging through the white entertainments and white pleasures of antiblackness. The genre came to emphasize the black figure as grotesque and barbaric. It enabled, as Bill Brown notes, native-born and immigrant whites to secure themselves within America by "identifying against the nation's internalized, perpetual other," while simultaneously earning the wages of whiteness afforded through the spectacle of racist mockery.[73] Hence the affinities between postbellum minstrelsy and a Civil War genre that emerged only after formal emancipation: the novels of white supremacist melodrama, including, among many others, Thomas Nelson Page's *Red Rock* (1898), Thomas Dixon's *The Leopard's Spots* (1902) and *The Clansman* (1905), and J. W. Daniels's *A Maid of the*

*Foot-Hills* (1905). These novels—most familiar to us through the film adaption of *The Clansman, Birth of a Nation*—bemoan Reconstruction's challenge to white supremacy as a national threat advanced by an avaricious white minority against the white majority, implicitly outlining the condition for national reunion as a welding of white power and citizenship.[74] In a similar vein, sectional reunion romances worked toward producing white Northern sympathy toward former white Confederates. In fictions like Julia Magruder's *Across the Chasm* (1885), Constance Fenimore Woolson's "Old Gardiston" (1876), S. T. Robinson's *The Shadow of the War* (1884), Charles King's *A War Time Wooing* (1888), and Joel Chandler Harris's *A Little Union Scout* (1904), white Northerners and Southerners transfer the marriage plot into the sectional reunion plot, figuring white national mutuality as the progeny of heterosexual desire.[75] Along with the genres collected in the first three chapters of this study, these genres became, for postbellum white Americans, the "things we have in common."

This brief survey points to a distinguishing factor in the genres I've assembled and studied. Three of the four featured in this book do not prominently feature slavery, the Civil War, or Reconstruction. Unlike minstrel performances, with their Lost Cause reminiscences of antebellum plantation life or their caricatures of Reconstruction-era black politicians; white supremacist melodramas, with their explicit analysis of the racial politics of Reconstruction and the antebellum South; or sectional reunion romances, with their none-too-subtle prescriptions for national unity, campus novels, regionalist sketches, and gospel sermons treat the war as at best peripheral to their central investments. Moreover, where minstrelsy, supremacist melodrama, and reconciliation romance feature regular scenes of cross-racial interaction, such scenes remain rare in the genres featured here.

This project instead highlights worlds and relationships a far remove from white supremacist exploitation across the color line. That, in crucial ways, is their very point: such supposed distance—from the Civil War, from the debates surrounding Reconstruction, from explicit scenes of racist assault—has distinct advantages for this book's aim to track a new racial ordinary. The archive here helps us to trace affective attachments within white and black America, respectively, and to better understand daily practices that propelled and resisted the emergent color line, its social logics, its patterns, and its contradictions. The genres I analyze allow us to historicize and conceptualize the ordinary in all of these textures, uncovering the social reproduction of white supremacy and resistance to white supremacy as outgrowths of everyday experience.

My first three chapters trace the role played by white campus novels, the *Ladies' Home Journal*, and Civil War elegies in soliciting white consent to white supremacy. Yet while their focus overlaps, there's also an organizational logic to their sequence. Each successive chapter tracks increasingly less certain, contradictory, ambivalent, and even frustrated instances of consenting affirmation. My point is not that failure amounts to a destination, as though the rigidity of white nationalist social practices gradually undoes itself. Rather, the book's sequence underscores the thick texture of ordinary life, in which norms and conventions exist in networks of successes, failures, compensations, and adjustments. If the dominant narrative of these first three chapters pertains to the mutually beneficial relationship between popular generic aesthetics and white racial fraternity, a clear secondary narrative pertains to the capacious elasticity of whiteness, which incorporates European immigrants as well as seemingly disruptive strains such as intra-white gender conflict and feelings of misrecognition between the white individual and the racial fraternity.

The first chapter documents and clarifies the nature of this fraternal structure. It does so by studying the surprisingly popular genre of campus novels, which became prominent from the late 1860s through the early twentieth century. Combining picaresque with Bildungsroman, campus novels document the merry frolicking, naughty pranking, and classroom avoiding behavior of white college students. Through these good times the novels register a joyousness experienced through commonality organized, first, by membership within the same collegial institution, and then, metonymically, by racialized membership within the same nation. Campus sociality thus became a white national fantasy with influence that far exceeded the small percentage of whites going on to higher education, offering a set of practices, such as banter and good-humored joshing, for affirming similarity, flattening difference, and managing conflict. Moreover, campus novels developed a ready-to-hand solution for the vapidity that so frequently plagues social organizational forms that distribute their affections too widely. By saturating their scenes with nostalgia, campus novels gave depth and a sense of weightiness to relationships frequently divorced of intimacy or meaning. In this way, their affective energies connect them to the culture industry of white nationalist nostalgia characterizing Civil War memory and Lost Cause mythology that, by the 1890s, was spreading through the white North as rapidly as it was through the white South.

My second chapter turns from white fraternity to white sorority, focusing on how the *Ladies' Home Journal* fashioned white women's culture as a mediating force for an imagined sisterhood and intimate public that provided the comforting sense of familiarity across distance, while also responding to a perceived crisis in the conditions of white women's intimate friendship. I argue that both scales of white social practice, the mass belonging promised by sorority and the closeness facilitated through friendship, attached white women's social forms to antiblackness. On the one hand, the *Journal* infused its imagined sisterhood with a deep sense of racial supremacy through frequent use of racist humor, blackface minstrelsy, and social segregation, providing white women a compensation that at least partially made up for the harms and alienations produced by heteropatriarchy and gender inequality. On the other hand, by revitalizing intraracial, intimate friendship as a necessary departure from antiseptic social life, the *Ladies' Home Journal* engaged an Aristotelian politics of friendship in which the precondition for befriending (whiteness) naturalizes itself as the precondition for larger-scale modes of belonging. In this sense, intimate friendship acted to reinforce and invigorate the large-scale, racialized social forms of white sorority, white fraternity, and white nationalism.

Chapter 3 looks at white fraternity's ability to incorporate and put to use the discontent it simultaneously produced by analyzing those Civil War elegies circulating widely throughout the North from 1861 through the 1890s. Like white campus novels, many of these poems enthusiastically celebrate the ability for racial bonds to overcome intraracial differences and heal sectional division. Elegies like Finch's "The Blue and the Gray" take loss as an occasion to forge national community out of shared mourning while also, by frequently depicting Southern benevolence toward Northern dead, disciplining their white Northern readers' lingering sectionalism and pushing them toward a more reconciliationist frame of mind. Yet where campus novels supplement their fraternal social organization with nostalgia and the *Ladies' Home Journal* supplements its with intimate friendship, nontrivial subsets of Civil War elegies tend to supplement theirs with dissent. Antiwar elegies, for instance, describe a set of feelings—such as exhaustion, despair, and even boredom—that seem inassimilable within nationalist celebration. Likewise, melancholic elegies, by refusing and even mocking the admonition to cease mourning and move on, depict the sentiment frequently found in their nationalist counterparts as fraudulent, obtuse, and even grotesque. While we might expect antiwar elegies and melancholic elegies to comprise distinct alternatives to more explicitly nationalist verse, their publication history instead indicates surprisingly easy alignment. Indeed, nationalist and dissenting elegiac modes sometimes appear side by side in patriotic anthologies or even within the very same poem. Instead of historicizing dissenting elegies apart from the racial community of white nationalism, I argue we should consider them as key particulars in nationalism's appeal. Doing so reveals the tremendously incorporative drive through which white nationalism could include intra-white dissent and misrecognition without disrupting the fundamental shape of white belonging.

My first three chapters focus on the fraternal organization of white racial community in the North, highlighting its organizational emphasis on being-in-common and its remarkably elastic capacity to incorporate internal difference. My fourth chapter shifts from white to black attachments, from fraternal to more provisional modes of belonging, and from a regional process within the white North to a trans-regional network of black Protestantism. In doing so, it also shifts from examining genre as an accomplice and agent of the status quo to examining genre as a mechanism for organizing alternatives to the status quo. The chapter analyzes the conventions and frequently contentious reception history of the gospel sermon, a performative and collaborative oral poetics that arguably became the most popular African American literature of the postbellum era.

Turning religious enthusiasm into a durable genre and rendering it a recurrent feature of black Protestant worship, the gospel sermon facilitated ecstatic experiences that reoriented congregants' relationships to their selves, to the divine, and to each other, enabling a provisional fellowship oriented around shared encounter with the uncanniness of the Holy Ghost. The presence of the unknown and divine suffused this fellowship with what its participants frequently compared to electricity, madness, and contagion, binding agents that render its community un-chosen yet also contingent, local, and experiential. Doing so constituted an essential aspect of the gospel sermon's fundamental alignment toward improvisation, experimentation, and openness to otherwise unimaginable futures. Against a backdrop of white supremacist notions harnessing black freedom to self-possessed individuality and rational consent to the status quo, gospel sermons enabled practices of freedom unburdened by liberalism's notions of institutional organizing, community, or personhood.

In the ongoingness of the new racial ordinary, generic and social conventions circulated promiscuously, attaching white postbellum subjects to race and linking their everyday lived existence to the reproduction of racial hierarchy, while also providing African Americans with collectivizing possibilities for new forms of living, resisting, and being together. Race, within this framework, comprises an interactive set of affinities and practices: a social framework governing how people enter into relation with one another, how they behave within those relationships, and how those relationships accrue into aggregate scales of belonging. It emerges out of the machinations in which the interactions between cultural consumers and their generic texts mirror and shape the relationships between men and other men, women and other women, mourners and their beloved dead, subjects and the nation, congregants and other congregants, worshipers and the Holy Ghost—a system for reinforcement and reproduction that locates both the ongoingness of white supremacy and the seeds for its undoing at the level of our most commonplace and everyday interactions.

# Campus Novels, Camaraderie, and White Nationalist Merriment

Elizabeth Stuart Phelps's 1893 *Donald Marcy* begins, as do many postbellum campus novels, with the annual freshmen–sophomore football match. Unlike her genre cohorts, however, Phelps uses the sporting event—and, indeed, her narrative as a whole—to reenact slavery's violence, the Civil War, Emancipation, Reconstruction, and, above all, white sectional reconciliation. During the match, Southerner Lee Calhoun, "white with rage," strikes down George Washington Clay, "[a] colored student," who "played quite fair, and dealt no foul blows."[1] Calhoun provides a simple and, for him, sufficient explanation: "He is a nigger, and I knocked him down."[2] The Northern white students react swiftly and punitively. Trouncey O'Grian, a prizefighter's son, knocks Calhoun "flat upon the ground" and instructs him in the ways of Northern justice: "'This is a free college and a free country.'"[3] Reconstruction proceeds apace: "Calhoun was subjected to almost every indignity that Harle"—Harvard + Yale = Harle—"Sophomores, in those long-past days, ever inflicted upon an unpopular Freshman."[4] Perhaps unsurprisingly, Calhoun's resentful threat to "shoot every man of you down as I would so many niggers" fails to win him any reprieve;[5] nor does a letter from the elder Calhoun to Harle's President ("My son complains to me that he is required to sit by the side of a negro student").[6] Calhoun's actions, we're told, constitute racism, sure. But even more feloniously they constitute "snobbishness"—"the last fault which a college full of sturdy young democrats will overlook"—and we're led to believe that he will endure continued punishment until he can thoroughly reform his ways.[7]

As a sophomore, Calhoun does indeed reform his snobbish ways, losing "most of the swagger with which he had ornamented Freshman year," even as he refuses to reform his racist ways.[8] Nevertheless, the hazing ceases and he begins to relate more easily to his white Northern compatriots. Then, in the novel's junior-year climax, a dramatic near drowning gives the Southern Calhoun the opportunity to team up with his former adversary, O'Grian, saving the life of the popular and eponymous Donald Marcy. Within the novel's historical allegory, this is the Compromise of 1877, the moment that secures peaceful reconciliation between the white North and the white South without demanding racism's reformation:

*Genre and White Supremacy in the Postemancipation United States.* Travis M. Foster, Oxford University Press (2019).
© Travis M. Foster.
DOI: 10.1093/oso/9780198838098.001.0001

The three principals in that memorable event looked at each other with something of the curious tenderness of reconciled sections after civil war.... It is the delightful thing about college friendships, that they easily override grudges and trifles, and gather together all sorts of sympathies and loyalties, from all kinds of natures; each bound to many by that young glow and fervor of feeling which adoration for his Alma Mater, and nothing else in life, can give a man.[9]

Phelps uses the scene to represent a metamorphosis in white feeling that naturalized and affirmed black resubjugation, or, at the least, that no longer took antiblackness as a justifiable source for internecine rancor. She foregrounds the tremendous appeals of intraracial affinities—"tenderness," "glow," and "fervor of feeling"—which overwrite lingering commitment to antiracist or Radical Republican principles (including, if we recall the novel's 1893 publication date, attempts to reinstate Reconstruction, such as the 1891 "Lodge Force Bill," which would have restored Federal supervision of Southern elections).[10] Phelps records a newly reconciled world in which opposition to resubjugation finds itself removed from political discourse, turned into so many "grudges and trifles," overridden by "college friendships," and neutered by the more potent force of "sympathies and loyalties."

Phelps's representation of "college friendships" distills an entire generation of popular novels: campus fictions, focusing all but exclusively on homosocial scenes of undergraduate merriment, published between the Civil War and World War I. Centering on the camaraderie of fraternal sociality, the genre models friendship as a democratic ideal for dispensing with conflict, featuring plot lines that progress inexorably toward resolution in an intense affirmation of unity. As a new student in William Tucker Washburn's *Fair Harvard: A Story of American College Life* (1869) puts it, campus novels pit "class feeling" against the "clique."[11] By locating their impetus for national belonging ("class feeling" writ large) in the extracurricular activities of college kids, these popular texts help us to see the historical momentum toward white reconciliation in places we're not accustomed to look—the joyous cavorting of drunken Harvard students, say—rather than those more frequently studied vehicles of cross-regional weddings and interregional progeny.[12] This shift in historical attention from heterosexuality to homosociality requires that we also augment our ideas about how and where white sectional reconciliation occurred or even what it looked like. If national reunion proceeded through "sympathies and loyalties" that made it a desirable and presumed outcome, rather than merely through the historical revision of conflict-producing differences, then reconciliation manifested in settings and situations that failed to bring the previously warring parties face to face or even to address the fact of conflict in the first place. It emerged through an implicit ethos underwriting white social patterns. The "delightful thing about college friendships" is that they provided this ethos with a popularizing ideal.

So although *Donald Marcy* is alone in crafting a historical allegory between Calhouns and O'Grians, its counterparts remain no less in tune with campus friendships' reconciliationist significance. To be sure, almost all the novels under consideration here do feature at least one Southerner, and they rarely miss an opportunity to reference the mutual nobility of the blue and the gray. Lest he be misunderstood, for instance, the narrator of Owen Wister's *Philosophy 4: A Story of Harvard University* (1903) hastily clarifies that his compliment, "true son of our soil," applies equally to sons "Northern or Southern."[13] Likewise, those campus novels that take their student-heroes to the Civil War—Frederick Loring's *Two College Friends* (1871), Mark Sibley Severance's *Hammersmith: His Harvard Days* (1879), and John Seymour Woods's *Yale Yarns: Sketches of Life at Yale University* (1895)—do so in order to demonstrate the overwhelming power of collegial feeling to undo sectional animosity even in the midst of strife.

Yet I will propose that the genre's representation, popularization, and idealization of camaraderie promulgated reconciliationist sentiment more so than its depictions of any particular amity between the white North and South. Indeed, as we'll see, camaraderie deployed an extraordinary ability to alleviate multiple social tensions within the status quo—including those produced by European immigration, feminism, and the anarchism and populism of the 1890s—a quality that allowed campus novels, over four decades of prominence, to widen and adjust their ameliorative scope to multiple sources of potential disruption. Even so, white sectional reconciliation remained the genre's foremost concern into the early twentieth century.[14]

To make this argument, I survey almost thirty novels, from Washburn's 1869 *Fair Harvard* to Owen Johnson's 1912 *Stover at Yale*, all of which focus primarily on extracurricular, undergraduate merriment. I've compiled this archive primarily using John E. Kramer's meticulous *The American College Novel: An Annotated Bibliography* (2004), which built on the list of novels first identified in John O. Lyons's monograph, *The College Novel in America* (1962), through an extensive survey of nineteenth-century book reviews.[15] What I refer to as "campus novels," rather than "college novels," comprises a subset of this larger group that emerged in the 1860s, became increasingly popular into the 1890s, and then faded from prominence in the first decade of the twentieth century. Defined by their almost-exclusive focus on the homosocial experiences of undergraduate peers, campus novels starkly contrast the twentieth-century academic novels full of depressed and predominantly male professors that recent critics have tended to study.[16] Indeed, we might even see this latter subset as a negative image of the former: they share a setting but, in all other respects, reverse their emphases. In *Faculty Towers: The Academic Novel and its Discontents*, for instance, Elaine Showalter describes academic novels as narratives that "experiment and play with the genre of fiction itself, comment on contemporary issues, satirize professorial stereotypes and educational trends, and convey the pain of intellectuals called upon to measure themselves against each other and against their internalized expectations of brilliance."[17] Showalter's description, when almost entirely reversed, perfectly sums up the work of the campus novel: putting aside political or social concerns in favor of more immediate enjoyments; forsaking all forms of intellectualism, competitive or otherwise; and focusing on externalized social patterns more than internal experience.

Where academic novels trace their genealogy to nineteenth-century precursors such as Anthony Trollope's *Barchester Towers* (1857), campus novels trace their conventions to immensely popular schoolboy works such as Cuthbert Bede's Mr Verdant prankster narratives (published serially in the US during the 1850s) and Thomas Hughes's *Tom Brown at Oxford* (1861), a novel so popular in the US that booksellers kept advertising it until at least 1932.[18] Campus novels track their hero from her or his freshman to senior year, recording the trials and subsequent maturation that ensue, ultimately ending with graduation, followed occasionally by marriage to the sister or brother of a friend. Or, as Lyons's *The College Novel in America* dismisses them: "These works are uniformly episodic accounts of pranks, athletic events, and tavern bouts, ending with the young men getting the right girls."[19] The novels thus amount to breezy Bildungsromans, in the sense that they trace a young person's emergence from the family into the social world and, as Franco Moretti puts it, negotiate "the conflict between the ideal of *self-determination* and the equally imperious demands *of socialization.*"[20] Yet, collectively, they work to render socialization anything but imperious— as, instead, the very apex of fun, a vehicle into the more aspirational ideal of fraternal belonging. Throughout, the momentum of narrative arc and moral development thus cedes ground to the picaresque verve of the chapter as the novels relocate their energy to episodes—pranks and good times—that comprise for their student-characters and readers the university's foremost pleasures, value, and significance.

In their eager production and reproduction of these pleasures, postbellum writers and readers pushed the form, as Jeffrey J. Williams has recently argued, "into the mainstream of American fiction" and presented a remarkably consistent vision of college life across regional difference.[21] Distinctions do emerge: L. L. Jones's *Oberlin and Eastern School Life* (1889), for instance, paints a stark contrast between Ivy League tomfoolery and the hard-working seriousness of the rugged Oberlin undergraduate; Anson Uriel Hancock's *John Auburntop, Novelist: His Development in the Atmosphere of a Fresh-Water College* (1891) demonstrates the same with 275 pages featuring little other than University of Nebraska students discoursing portentously on Hawthorne, Emerson, Ambrose Bierce, and the like; and Princeton novels such as the anonymously published *His Majesty, Myself* (1880) and James Barnes's *A Princetonian: A Story of Undergraduate Life at the College of New Jersey* (1886) all tend to be somewhat less rollicking then their Harvard and Yale counterparts. Nevertheless, the genre remains largely consistent across time and place, as though in implicit support of Washburn's subtitle declaring his Harvard novel "a story of American college life." We thus find the social life and narrative structure that characterizes Ivy League novels replicated in those set at mid-western and western public institutions, such as Joy Lichtenstein's Berkeley novel *For the Blue and Gold* (1901), and George Fitch's *At Good Old Siwash* (1911), set at a fictionalized Knox College in Illinois. Nor was the "brotherhood" of camaraderie exclusively male. We also find camaraderie's fraternal patterns replicated in novels set on women's campuses, such as Helen Dawes Brown's *Two College Girls* (1886) and Caroline Fuller's *Across the Campus* (1899), set respectively at fictionalized versions of Vassar and Smith, and enacted by white women students featured in novels set within coed institutions.

The campus's potential to merge disparate people into a solid whole drew the attention of writers outside the immediate genre of campus fiction, who cited campus life particularly when addressing the problem of white national reconciliation. The most famous Civil War antagonist, for instance, Stephen Crane's Henry Fleming (*The Red Badge of Courage*, 1895), imagines battle as a college football game, a metaphor that registers not only, per Bill Brown, the era's "conflation of war and sport,"[22] but also football's collegiate resonance with its accompanying "mysterious fraternity," which the novel celebrates as an overarching "brotherhood more potent even than the cause for which they were fighting."[23] James's *The Bostonians* (1886) likewise mends hostile feelings between its Northern feminist heroine and its emblem of unreconstructed Southern manhood by taking the couple on a stroll through "the great university of Massachusetts," which "exhaled for the young Mississippian a tradition, an antiquity," such that even Memorial Hall, honoring Harvard's Union dead, cathects the scene with a "sentiment of beauty" that arches "over friends as well as enemies."[24] Elegies for college students killed during the Civil War, such as Herman Melville's "On the Slain Collegians" (1866), similarly rest on the seemingly natural or innate affinities of young Union and Confederate soldiers mutually motivated by honor more than politics. Melville's poem, for instance, pauses to address and then chastise his Northern readers who may have been harboring lingering resentment: "What could they else—North or South? | Each went forth with blessings given | By priests and mothers in the name of Heaven | And honor in both was chief."[25] Likewise, many of the era's explicitly white supremacist texts—including Thomas Nelson Page's *Red Rock* (1898), Thomas Dixon's *The Leopard's Spots* (1902), and the Dixon-inspired film, *The Birth of a Nation* (1915)—turn to college friendships or similarly modeled prep-school friendships as vehicles for fraternal bonds that affirm white affiliation. Taken as a whole, all of these texts exhibit an implicit awareness of the campus's remarkable, outsized, and likely exceptional ability to generate allegiance toward a white national citizenship that transcends politics and sectional difference while presenting itself as the natural outgrowth of good-natured fun. As the most sustained and popular representation of white postbellum student culture, the campus novel genre provided postbellum whites with a self-consciously nationalizing instruction in the feelings and practices of citizenship.

## Camaraderie's Textbooks

And, yet, as an early reference in F. Scott Fitzgerald's *This Side of Paradise* (1920) makes clear, it's odd to associate campus novels with instruction of any sort, let alone something so ostensibly austere as civic pedagogy. Running through a list of literary texts that influenced his hero, Fitzgerald cites Johnson's *Stover at Yale* as "somewhat of a text-book."[26] The sardonic quality of Fitzgerald's term, "text-book," which he underscores with the winking "somewhat," points out a central irony of the entire genre: these are books that detest books in general and "text-books" most of all; they're novels set within institutions of higher learning that position themselves entirely in opposition to instruction. The genre deals with formal education either by ignoring it entirely or assuming an actively hostile stance toward the faculty who so rudely impose it. In valuing "college life" over book learning and social experience over rote memorization, campus novels suggest the civic qualities of a college degree come about through relaxed sociality rather than the acquisition of any formal knowledge. As such, the genre aims to produce a very particular reading experience that, in turn, aims to reproduce the merry loafing of "college life." To borrow from Michael Warner's description of uncritical reading, campus novels value "unsystematic and disorganized" practices such as "identification, self-forgetfulness, reverie, sentimentality, enthusiasm, literalism, aversion, [and] distraction" over any "cultivated and habitual disposition" to read *for* something.[27] They insist on being read as "generic" and not "literary," for it is only by doing so that readers will glean anything at all.

Owen Wister's slender *Philosophy 4* devotes itself entirely to this idea. The novel features two young men, Bertie Rogers and Billy Schuyler, preparing for the eponymous course's final. They do so first with the aid of a tutor so serious he "never yet had become young" and then, more successfully, with a day of play—the partial catalog of which includes skinny dipping, driving about town, locating a famously out-of-the-way tavern, feasting, and drinking themselves far beyond tipsy—before finally returning home in the early morning hours and, as readers have all along known they would, easily outperforming their grind of a tutor.[28] Acing the exam is not the only confirmation of their decision to bypass study for leisure. Throughout their outing, spectators look upon the two with great pleasure: "Pleasantness so radiated from the boys' faces ... that a driver on a passing car leaned to look after them with a smile and a butcher hailed them with loud brotherhood";[29] and, later, when the two head back to Cambridge in the early morning hours, they're sighted "by the street-car conductors and the milkmen, and these sympathetic hearts smiled at the sight of the marching boys, and loved them without knowing any more of them than this."[30] The boys thereby become the focal point for an idealization of American democracy, through whom a Whitmanian cast of intra-white diversity finds hope for the future. Bringing together the glowing representation of idleness and loafing and the multiple appeals of radiant college boys—productive, as they are, of pleasure, brotherhood, sympathy, and love—Wister's novel reflects on the entire genre, suggesting that the nation's future success depends far more on following the lead of campus novel characters than it does from undertaking a course of formal instruction.

Most readers of the time agreed wholeheartedly with Wister's high esteem for the edifying value of student life, even as they viewed campus novels as significant opportunities to experience it. Muckraker Lincoln Steffens, for instance, reported that campus fiction prepared his entire cohort of peers for 1880s University of California customs: "The stories and the life are pretty much the same for any college."[31] Yet campus fiction was not merely a prep school. It also constituted a key activity in the merry life such fiction aims to represent. Reading campus novels was itself an extracurricular pleasure, and campus newspapers frequently mention the novels in ways that assume readers' familiarity. Hence after Washburn's *Fair Harvard* received a handful of scornful reviews for its scandalous portrayals (per a letter from William James to little brother Henry, complaining about its popularity: "[n]othing but drinking & 'going to Parker's' which are spoken of as if they were the highest flights human freedom cd. soar to"[32]) sales rapidly increased and "the work became required extracurricular reading for the Harvard undergraduates of the period."[33] Moreover, the same novel represents its own hero as a reader of school-boy stories, indicating that, along with various issues of *Harvard Magazine* and *Atlantic Monthly*, his coffee table featured "Mr. Cuthbert Bede's celebrated history of Verdant Green."[34] It comes as no surprise, then, that the supposedly nonfictional memoir most often cited by historians documenting nineteenth-century student antics, Lyman Bagg's *Four Years at Yale* (1871), itself reads like a campus novel.[35]

If undergraduates and pre-undergraduates learned in part how to become college students and interact within college social networks precisely by becoming familiar with a novelistic genre, then a feedback loop finds itself completed when contemporaneous reviewers praise the novels' verisimilitude. One reviewer lauds Severance's *Hammersmith* for its "faithful description of college life."[36] The *Atlantic Monthly* similarly praises Brown's *Two College Girls* because "[o]ne may by means of it get a glimpse into the interior of a girl's college,"[37] and the *New York Times* refers to Charles Macomb Flandrau's *Harvard Episodes* (1897) as, simply, "an accurate picture of college life."[38] We can understand this attachment to the novels' striking accuracy as an effect of what, for readers, constituted their appealing conventionality. Fitzgerald, it turns out, was exactly right. Campus novels entered into their readers' lives as "text-books" of standard behavior and confirmations of common practice, providing an easygoing education that presented itself as the unschooled product of intuition and instinct. Nor was such pleasurable instruction limited to college students, future, past, or present. As the Chicago newspaper *Daily Inter Ocean* notes of John Seymour Wood's *Yale Yarns*, "bright sketches of college life at Yale will be enjoyed as much by those who are not Yale men or college men as by the men of whom they are told."[39]

Indeed, campus novels' pedagogical influence acquired political zeal on a national scale precisely as higher education and the practices of student life began to assert themselves as epicenters of American futurity, models for new configurations of democratic community and networks for installing a more robust national identity. Admittedly, this claim rests on an improbable disparity between the handful of Americans who actually attended college (from 1 per cent in 1865 to roughly 4–5 per cent by the century's turn) and the influence of higher education over late-nineteenth-century US life. Recent historians, however, argue compellingly that higher education became a vital extension of postbellum governmentality, both through specific state enterprises (including the 1862 and 1890 Morrill Land-Grant College Acts, the newly established Bureau of Education, and the public university extension movement) and through nonstate national academic networks (including lecture circuits, the growing academic press, popular textbooks, and widespread newspaper interest in university life)—all of which led Americans to experience the curricular university as part and parcel of expanding federal power.[40]

At the same time, if academic culture nationalized the university as "a many-sided academic public sphere," campus culture provided an underwriting social network. Although historians of higher education largely neglect the extracurricular, a good deal of evidence suggests that postbellum whites likely valued activities out of the classroom as much or even more than those inside of it.[41] In 1870, for instance, Yale's president Noah Porter echoed campus novels when he argued that for the "many who persistently neglect the college studies, the college life is anything rather than a total loss."[42] Alumni, too, began targeting their financial support to extracurricular activities as when Yale graduates sponsored an 1877 student minstrel show, adamantly opposed by faculty, at the Union League Theater in New York.[43] Even an occasional professor, precisely the group most frequently set in opposition to college life, joined in a celebration of all things extracurricular. In 1892, philosopher and Harvard professor George Santayana praised college students for living "in a sort of primitive brotherhood, with a ready enthusiasm for every good or bad project, and a contagious good-humor."[44] Nor was it merely the elite or the people directly associated with university life who praised student cultures. Helen Lefkowitz Horowitz, one of the few historians to examine extracurricular life, extensively documents instances when public support for fraternities and athletics and even local authorities' collaboration in elaborate student pranks stymied professors' efforts to exert any taming force outside of the classroom.[45] Ultimately, Horowitz concludes, "[c]ollege life—which had begun in the interstices of the early-nineteenth-century college—emerged by the end of the century as the handsomely endowed center of campus."[46]

This transition tracks the university's shift from a religious institution with the primary mission of educating clergy to a secular institution with the primary mission of educating and reproducing a professional class.[47] As businessmen and politicians replaced ministers on university governing boards, the university increasingly fell under the control of the dominant financiers, industrial capitalists, and philanthropists who only decades previously had seen higher education as entirely irrelevant. In 1891 Andrew Carnegie, to name just one prominent example, mocked a university degree as "adapted for life upon another planet," but he was simultaneously relishing his position on the Cornell University Board of Trustees and just ten years later worked to found the Carnegie Institute of Technology. In this sense, the university transitioned from a religious to a secular institution in order to maintain its cultural and national influence, assuming service to industry just as industrial leaders began to characterize the dominant class, and thereby functioning to reproduce in its students the values of American business interests.

In what remains one of the more prescient analyses of US higher education, *The Higher Learning in America: A Memorandum on the Conduct of Universities by Business Men* (1918), Thorstein Veblen delineates these values as "a spirit of quietism, caution, compromise, collusion, and chicane."[48] Veblen links this transition directly to the new importance of campus social life. He complains that university administrations increasingly subsidized camaraderie's "politely blameless dissipation" in order to attract the increasingly important and numerous members of the middle and genteel classes as well as to bolster the university's reputation among the nation's elite. For, he argues, the extracurricular in fact produced in the young person proficiency for "tactful equivocation and a guarded habit of mind, such as makes for worldly wisdom and success in business."[49] No surprise, then, when the closing paragraph of Wister's *Philosophy 4* celebrates that its two heroes have become professional successes as, respectively, the treasurer for a Wall Street bank and an upper-level manager for the New York and Chicago Airline, while their grind of a tutor has taken up that most worthless of occupations, literary criticism and book reviewing.[50] To recall President Porter, for the future businessmen of America what mattered most was not anything in the classroom but the social skills learned and associations entered outside of it.[51]

Veblen's almost entirely class-driven analysis can only take us so far. It can periodize the solidification of institutional change within the US university system to "the Civil War and Reconstruction," but it cannot explore these events' systemic ties.[52] It can note the remarkable collaboration between the middle and genteel classes and between regionally diverse students within the activities of college life, but it cannot broach an explanation for this newfound alliance. And it can hint at the university's role in the service of increasing nationalism and "vainglorious patriotism," but it cannot sustain the analytical attention such an observation demands.[53] Missing is an analysis of the university's role in reproducing white supremacy and facilitating white reconciliation. Administrators like Porter, professors like Santayana, and, of course, the genre of the campus novel all came to value the segregated, extracurricular sociality of the university at precisely the moment when, as historian Michael David Cohen writes, "a significant though small number of African Americans" integrated the university's curricular space.[54]

The remainder of this chapter brings these segregated extracurricular scenes into Veblen's analysis, observing that the university extended white power and supremacy by bestowing upon young white men and women the social capital that would maintain their economic dominance, thereby helping to sustain in a post-slavery world the value of white identity as a propertied investment. It also, and more significantly, instructed white students—and, via campus novels, white readers—in the dominant social protocols through which white supremacy constructs whiteness as exceptional and exerts itself above and against nonwhite people: through the assumption of universality; through exclusive claim on the right to appropriate, territorialize, and define difference; and through the maintenance of a monopoly on social and geographic mobility.[55] The university and its culture of college life functioned to consolidate a mobile and readily abstracted white racial affiliation that would, at least fantastically, cut across divisions of class and region while at the same time allowing for the particularity of identification as student. White supremacy, as we'll see, could have its class and its fraternity, its elitism and its democracy, its particularity and its universality.

## The Nation of Peers

I turn now to campus novels' content and, specifically, to the novels' two foremost properties. The first, fraternity, manifests in their pages as an everyday, local practice of homosociality as well as, on a larger scale, momentum toward forms of belonging organized around sameness. The second, nostalgia, provides the genre with a pleasantly melancholic affect that lends emotional momentousness to fraternal belonging.

Fraternity constitutes a central concern in Olive San Louie Anderson's anonymously published and autobiographical *An American Girl and her Four Years in a Boys' College* (1878), which tracks the first coeducational class at a fictionalized University of Michigan. Perhaps strangely, given its focus on girls and women, the novel provides one of the genre's most telling representations of college students' enthusiasm for fraternity, cataloging the violence of its inaugural moments, the involuntary means through which it takes hold, and the democratic joy it finds in citing its ability to accommodate difference, even, at least partially, gender difference. So doing, Anderson introduces her readers—and us—to campus novels' particular mode of fraternity, which orients its characters, through the practices and rituals of college life, toward fused union and holds itself out as a model for national citizenship.[56] Simultaneously, by focusing on a woman character within a boyish environment, Anderson outlines fraternity's ability to produce feelings of belonging across difference, while also highlighting the levy imposed upon women seeking inclusion.

In an early chapter, Anderson's heroine, Will Elliott, writes a letter to her sister, detailing her first chapel and explaining that she almost immediately came to feel

"large as life," a "member of the freshman class," despite her rather abject relationship, as a woman, to the student body. I quote at length:

> It was terrific, and I did not know as there would be a vestige of me left to send to
> you. You see, we have prayers every morning in the law lecture-room, as our hall
> is not done yet; it is an immense room, and the freshmen sit on one side and the
> sophs on the other, so that the two combustibles are separated by the grave upper-
> classmen. We girls (there are nine of us) went fifteen minutes before time, and,
> when we entered the door, we heard the most uproarious din, and, on coming up
> the stairs, found the fresh and sophs joined in mortal combat, while, above all,
> rose the chorus, "Saw freshman's leg off—*short!*" We were terribly frightened,
> thinking that some one would surely be killed; but at last we were all in the room
> and no lives lost....
>
> We, poor little wretches, did not know where to sit, of course, and not one boy
> was polite enough or dared to face the crowd and show us a seat; so we kind of
> edged around into not much of anywhere, but found to our cost that it was in
> direct line of the missiles between the hostile classes, which missiles consisted of
> hymn-books, sticks, anything movable; a great apple-core struck me right in the
> eye, which caused me to see a whole solar system of stars; but I bore it bravely,
> feeling something of that rapture that the old martyrs must have felt—for, was
> I not suffering in the cause of co-education?
>
> I thought that I was used to boys; but I must say that I never met boy in his
> most malignant form until I came to college. In looking at my own class, every
> variety can be seen—long boys, short boys, fat boys, lean boys, boys pious and
> boys impious, gathered from one hundred and fifty families all over the land,
> from Maine to Mexico, a most heterogeneous collection, fused into one solid
> mass by the common bond "our class."... The girls are not expected to have much
> class-spirit yet, but are supposed to sit meekly by and say "Thank you" for the
> crumbs that fall from the boys' table; but, in spite of that, I feel my bosom swell
> with pride when I look at these one hundred and fifty heads, and think that I, too,
> as much as the best of them, am a member of the freshman class of the University
> of Ortonville.[57]

The passage amounts to a "text-book" on textbooks. It decodes a familiar momentum in campus novels toward a mode of belonging so "terrific" that Will is unsure
"there would still be a vestige of me left." At first glance, violence seems to be the
central motivating agent behind such belonging, hinging class feeling on common
injuries—an apple core to the eye—along with common enmities. Yet an appealing
lightness and goodwill cuts through the terror even here, in this nascent scene of
class feeling, for Will represents the events in a mock heroic tone. Her military
language makes a grand spectacle of the freshman–sophomore rivalry; her good-
natured jibing of "boy in his most malignant form" betrays a teasing approval of the
unfolding events; and her expression of martyrdom "in the cause of co-education"
allows for the playful expression of feminist argument from a location within
fraternal boisterousness. One effect of this humor, given the sophomores' threat to
amputate freshmen legs, is to tame the memory of Civil War violence by relocating

it from the battlefield to the campus. For Will, the humor more palpably signals that the scene has been one of pleasure rather than injury, such that "in spite" of an intense devaluation of women, who get merely "the crumbs that fall from the boys' table," she feels her "bosom swell with pride" for her membership in this "one solid mass." Like her masculine nickname, Will's humorous tone further signals the ultimate success of her assimilation by reproducing the raillery characterizing campus novels and undergraduate dialogue, and it thus comes as no surprise that, by her senior year, Will "had won a place of high standing in her class."[58]

The passage celebrates campus life as a pleasant coercion, all in the service of unity. In this, it is far from alone. Time and again, campus novels turn merry episodes into populist fables. Their student characters see even the most sophomoric pranks as engines of equality and even the most heinous hazing as anti-elitist adjudication. Even as they compete for limited resources, such as admission into a secret society, these students laud the extracurricular American campus as neo-Athenian. Recall, for instance, that *Donald Marcy*'s Calhoun is primarily guilty of "snobbery," not racism, and that correcting the former rather than the latter brings him back into his peers' good graces. Indeed, the same novel also charts its northern hero undergoing a parallel transition; upon imbibing the democratic virtuousness of college life, the wealthy Donald Marcy decorates his room "less gorgeous[ly]" in his Sophomore year, for as a freshman "he had learned...the healthy pleasure of adapting one's self to the circumstances of one's comrades."[59] Likewise, at Yale, observes the narrator of *Yale Yarns*, "[t]he rich man's son...has to overcome a certain democratic prejudice,"[60] a point echoed in *Two College Girls*, when a new student meets the daughter of Wisconsin's governor and is then hastily reminded: "fathers don't amount to a row of pins here, let me tell you. Neither do clothes."[61] The pattern emerges clearly: campus novels cite difference as a celebration of sameness—a way of highlighting their settings' remarkable ability to fuse Will Elliott's "most heterogeneous collection" into a coherent and self-identical unity.

Most obviously, this power comes from the appealing quality the campus lends to fraternal belonging. The "pleasure of adapting one's self to the circumstances of one's comrades" need hardly take an ascetic form when said circumstances include, as *Fair Harvard* catalogs them, "convivial ale, the social oyster, jolly songs, and conversation."[62] Hence the narrator of *Hammersmith* asks: "what meager description can do justice to the abounding gaiety, the full, throbbing life, the buoyant festivities?"[63] What, indeed? Yet if a full, throbbing life suggests the affirmative bribe forming one end of fraternity's disciplinary mechanics, then the enforced universality of collegial experience signals what, to be something of a spoilsport, I'll call the positively hegemonic nature of its will to good times. Campus novels announce themselves as the archenemy of enmity (except that between freshmen and sophomores). They work against divisions prophylactically, tightening the spheres of acceptable deviation and transforming real differences into those faux differences that produce banter rather than disagreement, accord rather than discord, and reconciliation rather than resentment. The "certain democratic prejudice" in these novels suppresses differences to favor the "one solid mass" and renders consent to the status quo a predetermined criterion for its uniquely conciliatory mode of democratic organization—a potent mechanism through which Will ends up happily acquiescing to patriarchal impositions.

Over the duration of their prominence, campus novels directed this mechanism to multiple sources of disruptions, acting as a barometer for the degree to which postbellum whites assessed threats to national unity. Novels published before 1900, for instance, remain particularly anxious to accommodate European immigrants. *Fair Harvard* describes a capacious model for national whiteness and celebrates the campus's ability to expand it even farther: "Under the influence of freedom, and the discipline of our schools, the children of the foreigner will grow worthy of their adopted home; in time we shall mould these different nationalities into one."[64] By the turn of the century, however, *Philosophy 4* seems less concerned with assimilating Oscar Marioni, its studious, immigrant character, than with ostracizing him for his academic rigor.

The novel's hints that Oscar may have socialist inclinations reveal what may be its more pressing concern with radicalism—a threat *Stover at Yale* takes up extensively. In that novel, radicalism takes two forms: a handful of articulate though vague dissenters who at once champion individualism and defend socialism; and, more significantly, a successful challenge to the tradition wherein sophomore clubs were to the sole point of entry for campus-wide leadership positions. While other campus novels take for granted the easy cohesion of class feeling, here factionalism emerges as disgruntled students increasingly challenge Yale's internal elitism. For Dink Stover, the novel's hero, this turn of events is devastating:

> Where had it all gone—that fine zest for life, that eagerness to know other lives and other conditions, that readiness for whole-souled comradeship with which he had come to Yale? Where was the pride he had felt in the democracy of the class, when he had swung amid the torches and the cheers past the magic battlements of the college, one in the class, with the feeling in the ranks of a consecrated army gathered from the plains and the mountains, the cities and villages of the nation, consecrated to one another, to four years of mutual understanding that would form an imperishable bond wherever on the face of the globe they should later scatter?[65]

The novel ultimately restores "whole-souled comradeship" and assimilates radicalism when Stover, in line to be captain of the football team and secure coveted admission to Skull and Bones, dramatically relinquishes his own elite position and befriends the dissenters. As he works to bring about a "new harmonizing development," the novel uses friendship between the popular Stover and the potentially disruptive campus forces to absorb the threat of socialism, channeling its radical challenge to class hierarchy into the restoration of campus novels' benign anti-elitism, thereby restoring the campus to "a community of interest and friendly understanding."[66]

I've been using *fraternity* and *camaraderie* as shorthand for this fraternal campus community, but I might just as aptly use *whiteness*. For the novels rely on a capacious model of nationalizing whiteness that readily accommodates wide-ranging difference. They thereby challenge a central thesis of 1990s "whiteness studies," which holds that immigration from Europe during the latter decades of the nineteenth century led to what Matthew Frye Jacobson terms a "paradigm of plural white races."[67] Campus novels instead represent whiteness as a paradigm of elasticity, nodding toward white particularity precisely in order to emphasize whiteness's generous liberalism and, in turn, to elide—or, at least, minimize—their social scenes' reliance on black exclusion.[68]

The inclusion of women within coed campus settings and women's campus novels' strict adherence to their genre's conventions provide a case in point. Campus novels featuring women students explicitly and implicitly make arguments on behalf of women's higher education, which, given the coextension between the campus and camaraderie, also meant making arguments on behalf of women's inclusion into fraternal social arrangements. Yet while brotherhood social arrangements may include women, such inclusion will never be easy or seamless; "the sister," as Jacques Derrida puts it, "will never provide a docile example for the concept of fraternity."[69] To ease the inclusion of both white women's homosocial networks on all-women's campuses and white heterosociality on coed campuses, novels featuring female characters adapt two different strategies. First, as we've seen with Will Eliott and *An American Girl and her Four Years in a Boys' College*, some coed novels allow their female characters to be, as it were, one of the boys, sanctioning, participating in, and excelling at the social practices of campus life.[70]

Second and more commonly, both coed novels and those set on women's campuses incorporate racial exclusion more visibly than their all-male counterparts. Their white feminist arguments on behalf of women's higher education therefore link female opportunity to white privilege and nonwhite exclusion, as though the "brotherhood" of whiteness might triumph over fraternity's otherwise constitutive exclusion of women. Fuller's *Across the Campus*, set at a fictional Smith College, for instance, begins when a new college girl hires a "grin[ning]" "negro boy" ("Enter, African, and hang my pictures") despite her roommate's entreaty not to "bring any miscellaneous kind of creature up here,"[71] an opening scene that rests white women's inclusion on African Americans' doubled exclusion from the national domestic ("African") and the human ("creature"). Similarly, in *For the Blue and Gold*, set at the coeducational University of California, white women are enthusiastically included within camaraderie's social conventions, while people of color are just as pointedly excluded. "The whole college [is here]," we're told of an early-season football game, "including co-eds and digs." A page later, however, the narrator qualifies his description with an apparent exception to the "whole college": the "Japs" remain in the library studying.[72] Far from marginal incidents or asides in the novels' narratives, these instances instead mark a recurring pattern that underscores white women's inclusion as the outgrowth of nonwhite characters' exclusion, revealing how such racial exclusion served as compensation for white women's necessarily uncertain belonging within fraternal social worlds. This perhaps also explains why, as W. E. B. Du Bois notes in his 1900 study of black students in US colleges and universities, black men gained entrance into universities more easily than black women gained access to Northern women's colleges. "Among the women's colleges," writes Du Bois, "the color prejudice is much stronger and more unyielding."[73] He cites the Secretary of Vassar College, who reports that there "is no rule of the college that would forbid our admitting a colored girl, but the conditions of life here are such that we should hesitate for the sake of the candidate to admit her and in fact should strongly advise her for her own sake not to come."[74] The inclusion of white women may have perturbed campus fraternity's "solid mass," yet it also provided occasion to reinforce through gender diversity the social justifications of racial hierarchy and white nationalism.

Largely, however, the novels leave race implicit, a fact that both elides racial exclusion and signals their preoccupation with the race that announces itself through its refusal to do so. It is, then, a good-natured joke between friends that best illustrates how campus fraternity remained inextricable from both the furtherance of white supremacy, antiblackness, and the social realization of white nationalism. After spending an entire period in front of the classroom, unable to solve a math problem, a student in Washburn's *Fair Harvard* tells his fellows: "It would try the soul of an abolitionist to stand a weary hour, staring at the black face of a long board as I did."[75] The joke most readily assumes a white audience that would rather not look upon black faces at all. Yet we cannot simply chalk its success up to the individual prejudices of speaker and audience. It relies on banality, at once enacting and affirming racism as a structure of white social solidarity. Discipline follows from the joke as a kind of preemptive strike against any auditor who may be harboring antiracist or Radical Republican thought, shaping the very conditions that make the joke possible in the first place. It succeeds because it economically brings together the various expressions that camaraderie permits: an antischolarly sentiment that affirms sociality, an antipolitical sentiment that affirms jocularity, and a pejorative commentary on black appearance that has the benefit of affirming whiteness as a prerequisite to class feeling. Camaraderie, in this sense, facilitates an economy of signs that continually renews white social belonging.

## Compensatory Nostalgia

In *Absalom, Absalom!* (1936), William Faulkner's narrator jabs at the fraternal feeling in campus novels by contrasting the famously "happy marriage" between Quentin and Shreve with the "ritual as meaningless as that of college boys in secret rooms at night."[76] Pitting the marital exclusivity of intimate friendship against the democratic openness of camaraderie, Faulkner's point is more quantitative than qualitative, for how can friendship remain friendship when it's spread across 20, 50, or even hundreds of fellow students? As a character in *Two College Girls* puts it: "'you do have to take most people superficially here.... You just touch so many people, without any close contact with them. It is like a book overcrowded with characters,—the life here is.'"[77] The observation points to a central conundrum: as a genre built in part around the ideal of "class feeling," campus novels have to manage the discrepancy between a large-scale distribution of student affections and the potentially "meaningless" nature of friendship spread too thin.

Their obvious solution—nostalgia—is, it turns out, ready to hand. For nostalgia lurks as a built-in function of the campus's neoclassical architecture and Greek-life customs, lending an aura of timelessness to everyday experience. Thus the opening pages of *Fair Harvard* turn a stroll between two brand-new acquaintances into a transcendent and collectivizing encounter with the ghosts of Harvard past and Harvard future: "The sight of the classical grounds, rich with memories of the past and hopes of the future, touched the minds of the young fellows with a pleasant melancholy."[78] The memories that affect each student so palpably in no way derive from either's immediate experience or previous intimacies. It is only because of their impersonal relationship to the memories, their pleasant longing for the newly possessed yet never experienced past, that the "classical grounds" effectively provides the two with a doubled sense of belonging—primarily to the collective student body, past, present, and future, and secondarily to one another. Likewise, in *For the Blue and Gold*, the narrator asks: "Who does not experience this uplifting, enlarging emotion when he stands, taking in the beauty and dwelling on the significance of the dear old campus and its sights? It comes to the new sophomore, just returned from his first long vacation; and to the staid alumnus, too, the old longing, unappeased, returns when, after each absence, he views the old, familiar scenes."[79] The passage hails a binding attachment, uniting the returning sophomore and the "staid alumnus" to the "dear old campus," while also, through the shared experience of such longing, to each other and, by extension, to all their fellow students.

In case the campus grounds prove insufficient, several campus novels additionally feature student deaths. As the *Hammersmith* narrator puts it, this death instills in students a "greater longing" and "deeper purpose," as "an unexplained tenderness of grace, seemed to fill all the old familiar scenes."[80] The previously marginal nature of the newly beloved dead provides a necessary component for "greater longing," because it enables the absent student to be efficiently abstracted into universally shared sentiment. The dead student quickly becomes everyone's dearest friend so that everyone might collectively mourn her or his passing. This death additionally anticipates the inevitably finite nature of college life, with its relentlessly approaching class days and graduation: "The seniors grew closer together," notes the narrator of Fuller's *Two College Girls*, reflecting on this finiteness; "new friendships were formed, old friendships were strengthened. That it was 'for the last time' tinged every pleasure with a gentle sadness."[81] Taken together, this mixture of pleasure and sadness, meaning and mourning, enables a nostalgia that is timeless both in the sense that it transpires in no time at all and in the sense that it invites students into the enlarging pleasures of belonging to something temporally sweeping and ineffably grand. If, as Elisa Tamarkin argues, in one of the only critical analyses of antebellum campus fiction, "the elaborate world of ritual allows for students to live out their commitments to their friends…in terms that also emphasize their reverence for the principle of belonging to an institution," then nostalgia gives such reverence a widely lateral momentum, such that the students simultaneously learn to revere their connections to one another precisely for their shared institutional belonging.[82]

Such nostalgia thus solves a problem introduced by the flatness and, per Faulkner, potential meaninglessness of fraternity by inserting a divide between lived experience and the affective response students have to that experience. It intensifies, injects with significance, and ennobles even the most banal of banalities. College students thus maintain and nurture an a priori nostalgia for campus life even as it transpires, allowing the "greater longing" and "pleasant melancholy" to compensate for the absence of sustained intimacy. Far from the backward looking and petrifying force critics sometimes take it to be, this nostalgia makes life meaningful for students and cathects their social beings with a momentum through which certain futures achieve inevitability. Such a "restorative nostalgia," as Svetlana Boym names it, prioritizes futures characterized by group feeling, because it offers a "comforting collective script for individual longing" that promises to rebuild lost community and cohesion.[83]

Nostalgia's "collective script" returns us to sectional reconciliation and transsectional whiteness, which I've been arguing comprised the most urgent demands on campus novels' facility for conflict resolution and group feeling. For through nostalgia, campus novels tap into the governing affect of the reconciliationist industry: the cultural machinery surrounding plantation mythology; the memory and commemoration of the Civil War (which, as David Blight notes, continues to serve as a "mother lode of nostalgia"[84]); and Dunning School national fantasies, from The Birth of a Nation through Gone with the Wind (1936)—all of which create smooth, easily accessible pasts that gloss over the analytic category of race in the service of reinvigorated fraternal nationalism. As Tara McPherson compellingly argues in her analysis of Ken Burns's famous documentary, nostalgia remains the preeminent vehicle and hermeneutic lens for representing the Civil War to a sentimental white American public.[85] Such nostalgia facilitates reconciliationist sentiment, and nostalgia for fraternity's manifestation through celebration of post-Civil War reconciliation (as with images of previously warring veterans now shaking hands and exchanging stories) in turn works with self-regenerating efficiency to drive yet further reconciliationist nationalism. Campus novels enter this self-reproducing economy of feeling by representing campus experience as the microcosmic model for a newly unified national life and the ideal adhesive for white racial unity.

## These Friends, These Brothers: Overwritten by Genre

I've been tracing fraternity and nostalgia as recognizable and defining conventions across campus novels, using a method of genre criticism that underscores the sociopolitics of generic patterns, although one, too, that can sometimes occlude the fluid interrelationships within any given genre. I turn now to a single novel that, by virtue of its marginal location within the genre, highlights precisely these movements of relation. So doing, I aim to trace not merely campus novels' coherence as a genre—that is, the genre's ability to include even seemingly exceptional texts within its conventions and features—but also their contradictions and exceptions, revealing how the porousness of generic conventions abets the relationship between genre and history.[86]

More love story than buddy tale and more Civil War novel than Harvard picaresque, Fredrick Loring's *Two College Friends* (1871) would seem to have very little to do with what I've been describing. The narrative exerts no energy on the high jinks of college life; its heroes pass very little time on any actual campus; and, perhaps most profoundly, the novel focuses on the romantic affections between two young men, Ned and Tom, rather than the dispersed and fraternal bonds of class feeling. Ned buys an Etruscan locket, has Tom's initials carved into it, and expresses bafflement when a young woman, with identical initials, assumes he intends the locket for her—" 'She!' I answered; 'it isn't any girl; it's my chum, Tom, you know.' "[87] After the two leave Harvard to fight for the Union in the Civil War, he expresses pointed hostility towards heterosexual family life, writing to himself, "When this war is over, I suppose Tom will marry and forget me. I never will go near his wife—I shall hate her."[88] When Ned ultimately dies a hero's death, he is buried with a picture of Tom dressed as a "dear little peasant girl."[89] Given this seemingly queer narrative and literary history's tendency to prioritize singularity over ordinariness, we shouldn't be surprised that *Two College Friends* is also the only novel under consideration here to receive considerable scholarly attention. Recent critics and editors have recuperated it as a key piece within an ambivalent grouping of texts that struggle to represent affectionate, erotic relationships between men.[90] Far from constituting a training ground in normative sociality, they argue, the novel archives queer behaviors, relationships, and possibilities "beneath the dominant narrative."[91]

The circumstances of Ned's death and the novel's conclusion, however, suggest just the opposite: that precisely because of its representation of homosexuality, *Two College Friends* works to energize and even enhance the conventions of the campus novel genre. After Confederate soldiers capture Ned and Tom behind enemy lines, Stonewall Jackson himself allows the couple to rest overnight, honor bound to remain in place until they can be transported to a Confederate prison. Instead, Ned relies on the help of a Southern soldier, smitten by Tom's beauty, to smuggle his perilously ill friend back to Union territory. The next morning, his honor at stake, Ned leaves an injured and unconscious Tom with his final farewells

("And calmly, yet with a dreadful pang at his heart, he stooped, and once more kissed the flushed face of his friend"[92]) and then returns to the rebel camp to meet certain execution.

Already, the plot suggests a reconciliationist outcome, underscoring as it does a system of honor that exceeds the war's particular politics. In a final letter to his and Tom's favorite professor, however, Ned shifts from a familiar narrative about the mutual nobility of the fight, North and South, to campus novels' more particular focus on the fraternal feelings of college life:

> But if you ever want to think of me, and to feel that I am near, walk through the yard at Harvard, in the lovely evenings of the spring weather. It was at such a season, and at such a time, that I last saw the dear old place; and, if I ever can be anywhere on earth again, it is there. Ah, if I could only see Harvard once again! God bless it forever and forever! I wonder how many visions of its elm-trees have swept before dying eyes here in Virginia battlefields![93]

The passage shifts scale through three spatio-temporal registers in which Ned pre-figures his death within the timelessness of Harvard nostalgia and, ultimately, as the scale of his attention increases, imagines himself to constitute a ghostly agent for fraternity on a national scale. He begins as a specific person, remembering a specific spring and a specific location on the Harvard campus. The pending execution then allows him to transform *that* season and *that* time into "such a season, at such a time," a shift that anticipates the timelessness Ned attributes to Harvard when he asks that "God bless it forever and forever." Finally, the particular act of site-specific melancholia disperses into a nostalgia that expands into national identification when Ned again shifts registers, this time to the Civil War heroism of all Harvard alumnae, whose Northern or Southern allegiances eviscerate through their common deaths in "Virginia battle-fields."

In case we miss the point, the penultimate sentence begins with a compact phrase: "these friends, these brothers."[94] The first subject names the novel's epony-mous pair, while the second names the fraternal ties their romance energizes. Working together, the pairing subordinates the exceptional to the fraternal as the latter position of "brothers" works to clarify "friends," neutering the term of its previously intimate associations. Indeed, earlier in the paragraph, a nursing meta-phor has already begun directing the narrative away from romance and towards what we might call a campus-inspired national fraternity: "This wonderful coun-try, that is still in its infancy, that is nursing men of every nation to form a new nation ... justifies not merely enthusiasm, but any loss of human life which may aid in its preservation."[95] The text here directs the tragic energies of its conclusion into what it calls the "enthusiasm" of national belonging, a shared brotherhood binding "men of every nation" into the strange infant motherhood of "[t]his wonderful country." Simultaneously, it turns to the campus—the *alma mater* or nourishing mother—into an organizing matrix for this newly binding sentiment. Yet as the text frames it, this campus also names the site of past male romance and the site of

Ned's future ghostly return. So, even though romance ultimately finds itself set aside in favor of fraternity, the sentiment behind "brothers" cannot entirely erase the energies of intimacy that have, to this point, been the novel's primary concern. White homosexual passion lingers on as a ghostly resource, supplementing the homosocial bonds of "brothers" and national "enthusiasm," its energies targeted toward cohering fraternal sentiment by cathecting it with the memories and promises of intimate attachment.

## Conclusion: Du Bois's Strange Melody

I end where I began: a story that makes explicit the significance of postbellum campus life and campus novels for the history of American race relations. Where Elizabeth Stuart Phelps's *Donald Marcy* uses a moment of interracial violence during a football game in order to celebrate the "delightful" powers of college friendships to unite whites across sectional difference, W. E. B. Du Bois's short story "Of the Coming of John" (1903) uses a much more severe and historically common act of white antiblack violence to reveal the underlying white supremacy on which those friendships depend. Du Bois was intimately familiar with white campus camaraderie. When describing his own experiences at Harvard, he underscores racial segregation as the defining feature of campus life and compares it to that in the South. "Had I gone from Great Barrington high school directly to Harvard," he reports, "I would have sought companionship with my white fellows and been disappointed and embittered by a discovery of social limitations to which I had not been used." But, Du Bois continues, he's spared that experience, for, having come "by way of Fisk and the South," he has already accepted the "color caste" defining Harvard's social scenes.[96] On a few occasions he did attempt "to enter student organizations," but was always refused: "My voice, for instance, was better than the average. The glee club listened to it but I was not chosen a member. It posed the later recurring problem of a 'nigger' on the team."[97] In this context, we can see "Of the Coming of John" as Du Bois's attempt to link the casual antiblackness of Harvard's glee club and campus life to the more spectacularly and murderously violent antiblackness of the Jim Crow South. Specifically, the story uses two instances of antiblack violence—at attempted rape and a lynching—to clarify and make visible the mutually reliant relationship between white intraracial social patterns, such as camaraderie, and the devastating consequences of white supremacy.

In the story, two small-town Southern boys, both named John, head off to college: one to the Wells Institute and one to Princeton, that Northern institution of higher education preferred by the white South; one to the kind of black uplift educational setting Booker T. Washington describes in *Up from Slavery* (1901), a rigorous institution that rewards hard study (what the white characters in campus novels would deride as "grinding" or "digging"), and one to an idle atmosphere that comprises the typically jovial campus novel setting. Upon graduating, the former bristles against a world refuses to recognize his labors and hard-won achievements and then punishes him precisely for his success, while the latter returns home "tall, gay and headstrong," "spoiled and self-indulgent," entitled to the world.[98] The story ends tragically, and perhaps inevitably, when the town's whites lynch the black John, who has just saved his sister from rape by striking the white John dead.

Throughout, Du Bois cites campus novels and the reputation enjoyed by white college life, depicting his Princeton graduate as a quintessential campus novel character, a "young idler" bored by the offerings of small-town life, who sees the sister's "trim little body" as a means to return to the pleasures of Princeton leisure.[99] In so doing, Du Bois positions his story, with its neatly symmetrical pairing of two jarringly different experiences, as a prophetic counternarrative that rises through "dark shadows," very much like "the strange melody" in the story's conclusion, drifting up from the sea to fill his doomed hero's ears.[100] By indexing white campus idiom ("trim little body"), which in his autobiographical writings he cites mockingly, and by underscoring the neat fit between Princeton's extracurricular mores and the rape of black women, Du Bois roots the camaraderie of white campus life in a sociopolitical history that chose white affiliation over Reconstruction and brought about resubjugation of the formerly enslaved.[101] If campus novels were indeed "text-books" for the easy transmission of conventions and social norms, then, Du Bois suggests, a brutal education was in fact at stake—an education in tactfully and tacitly negotiating the "recurring problem of a 'nigger' on the team." And, thus, in "Of the Coming of John," a remarkably compact airing of the story white reconciliation has never wanted to tell about itself, Du Bois responds to an entire genre of popular fiction, placing it into new relationships and highlighting its white supremacist registers of history and meaning.

# The Ladies' Home Journal, Sororal Publics, and the Wages of White Womanhood

Unlike the designation chosen by its predecessor, *Godey's Lady's Book and Magazine*, the *Ladies' Home Journal* opted for a plural possessive. It proclaimed itself an object shared among the many, and it encouraged readers to imagine themselves part of a larger collectivity, a population defined by shared identity and characteristic. Over the course of its first decade, the magazine presented itself as an anthology of content, and, even more forcefully, a coherent and corporate genre with a recognizable identity, turning the tempo of monthly subscription into a cycle of expectation and fulfillment that both satisfied and produced an audience.[1] As a business plan, this agenda succeeded in spades. The magazine inaugurated late nineteenth-century mass culture, became the world's first periodical to surpass a million in paid subscribers, and turned itself into the model for a new group of white women's magazines that would come to include *Good Housekeeping* (1885), *Vogue* (1892), *McCall's* (1894), and *Redbook* (1903), among many others.[2] The *Journal* thus played a pivotal role in producing the intimate public sphere Lauren Berlant has labeled "women's culture," providing "a porous, affective scene of identification among strangers" that promised its subscribers "a better experience of social belonging."[3] It turned itself into a mediating agent binding white women into sororal community. Like campus novels—one of which, Ralph Henry Barbour's *The Land of Joy* (1903), it serialized—the *Ladies' Home Journal* taught its readers to fashion and recognize themselves as a collective body with shared hardships, experiences, concerns, and desires, and it cathected that group subject position with feelings of warmth, mutual familiarity, and social purpose.

Through analysis of the *Journal's* generic conventions and prevailing concerns, this chapter argues that the intimate or sororal public of women's culture operated as a vital layer within the postbellum era's new racial ordinary.[4] Unlike the camaraderie and fraternity of campus novels—which, as we saw, included white women in part through the effacement of gender difference—the sorority of the *Ladies' Home Journal* depended upon affirmatively recognizing and validating its members' identities as white women. In so doing, the *Journal* participated in an evolving conversation about what constituted ideal or proper womanhood around the turn of the century, and it offered itself as compensation for the gendered burdens

*Genre and White Supremacy in the Postemancipation United States*. Travis M. Foster, Oxford University Press (2019).
© Travis M. Foster.
DOI: 10.1093/oso/9780198838098.001.0001

characterizing its readers' lives: the isolation and loneliness that accompanies raising children, the dispiriting effects of ceaseless household labor, the psychological damage wrought by heteropatriarchy's debasement of women. At the same time, the *Journal* infused its conversations about white womanhood and its compensations for readers' burdened lives with an antiblackness that was frequently more explicit than that found in those campus novels set on all-male campuses, including regular anecdotes about "darkies," jokes about black porters and preachers, and the reprinting of minstrel plays and songs for readers to recreate with family in their homes. Like the more explicit racism found in those campus novels set at women's colleges, such antiblackness vouched for white women's position within white national belonging. Yet the *Journal's* antiblackness also offered something more, what we might term a premium for its white women readers. It lent white women's sorority a powerful sense of supremacy and rightfulness that at least partially assuaged intraracial gendered tensions and defused the pressures of surviving the gendered subjection of white patriarchy.

Yet sorority required another layer of connection; for the *Ladies' Home Journal*, the large-scale belonging of white women's culture and white nationalism was insufficient and unsatisfying if left without supplementation by the more intimate social form of friendship. If sorority comprised their primary or sole avenue for interpersonal affinity, then, the *Journal* worried, it would leave women deprived of more authentic and lived forms of interpersonal connection. Hence the magazine frequently alerted its readers to a crisis in the underwriting conditions of women's friendship and provided tools for forging and sustaining intimacy with other women. In a strictly segregated social world and within the pages of a segregated magazine, such a turn to intimate friendship strengthened the *Journal's* participation in postbellum antiblackness and white nationalism. In this context, a discourse and idealization of intimate friendship between white women transpired and became meaningful only through a white sororal—which is to say, racist, nationalist, and supremacist—politics of friendship in which intimacy between white women naturalized whiteness as the foremost precondition for American citizenship.

My foremost purpose in this chapter, then, is to describe how white women's culture and white women's friendships collaborated as constituents within the ordinariness of postbellum antiblackness. Yet it's impossible to address the racial politics of friendship in the *Ladies' Home Journal* without also addressing the racial politics of literature. There are two reasons for this. First, the *Journal* crafted deep associations between literary reading and befriending, instructing its readers that close and careful attention to literature provided the best possible apprenticeship in the skills necessary to bridge lasting connections across interpersonal difference. Second, unlike the *Atlantic Monthly* and similar magazines, the *Journal* systematically segregated its pages, publishing no African American writers or fiction. In the final section of this chapter, I argue that this segregation occurred because, for the *Journal*, books were "so much like friends," while for the *Atlantic*-group magazines, as Michael A. Elliott and Nancy Glazener have shown, they were objects of study: the *Journal* turned to books as extensions of their readers' intimate and social lives, the *Atlantic*-group magazines as extensions of their readers' worldly knowledge.[5] This publication history suggests a normative reading formation wherein white readers could study African American literary texts from an appropriate critical or ethnographic distance but couldn't, as it were, enter into their pages and befriend them.

## *Journal* Sisters

White women readers of the *Ladies' Home Journal* came to imagine and value their relationship to one another as a far-reaching sisterhood. Take the artist Lida Clarkson. During the 1880s, Clarkson wrote a regular *Journal* column, "Brush Studies," on painting and pictorial art. In an 1886 open letter to the editor, however, she details the *Journal's* foremost value for her and, she imagines, her fellow readers, in the process providing a succinct record for what it felt like to recognize one's self within the magazine's intimate and sororal public:

> You can't think how I've just been aching to get out of that prim corner headed "Brush Studies," into this chatty column for a real cosy [*sic*] visit with you and my Journal friends. I want to tell you how much I enjoy the good letters, and sage advice, and encouraging words which come to us every month, as also to express my cordial interest in the Journal and its readers.
>
> During the past year many have come to me with their troubles and perplexities, and how sorry I have felt always, when it chanced to be beyond my power to help such correspondents.... Sometimes, perhaps, in consequence of these very appeals to my sympathies, I have been in need of cheering words myself, and at such times your friendship, and kindly interest have been fully appreciated. Now, if I had arms long enough to go way around the U.S., from California to Maine, and from my own Empire State, to the Gulf of Mexico, I would give you all one big hug this very minute.[6]

Clarkson positions the *Journal's* editor and readers within a mediated attachment, predicated upon their shared reading experience, infused with mutual sympathy, and imagined as a gendered, "cosy" space inhabited by "friends." In her image of a coast-to-coast embrace, she crystallizes the identification readers felt with the *Journal* and its familiar signifiers of women's culture. Explicit in her account also is the sense that the *Journal* and its community of readers eases her burdens, providing relief from an existence plagued by dispiriting hardships. Nancy Glazener argues that any given periodical "provokes...interpellating identifications for its readers," which is to say that it calls upon readers to accept and internalize the periodical's values and cultural ideals as their own.[7] Clarkson experiences this interpellation as a source of comfort and confirmation in her own burdened life and, by extension, in the burdened lives of white women more generally, one that provides a mirror for recognition and a window into thousands upon thousands of other readers' similarly lived experiences. Within these feelings of attachment, individual existence and social convention circled one another with centripetal force and created a normative framework for social belonging.

Such assumed sameness allows the *Journal* and its readers to couch their relationship explicitly as kinship—as a sisterhood. In one 1888 letter, for instance, reader M.M.M. writes,

> I am more in love with the Home Journal every day. We have long felt the need of just such a bright little paper to help lift the burdens and cheer the ladies of this busy world. And it is such a help; telling of the trials, failures, and success of so many of the sisters, it helps lighten each other's burdens wonderfully. There is nothing in this world like sympathy, and to feel that some one, although unknown to ourselves, cares for our welfare enough to drop a few roses in our pathway of thorns.

The letter then continues as M.M.M. drops her own rose by telling "the sisters, how I made a pretty and inexpensive basket for waste papers."[8] The writer's use of "the sisters" constitutes a phrase that, along with "Journal sisters," repeats time and again in the *Journal's* pages, deployed both by readers in their frequently published letters and by editors and contributors in their direct addresses to readers. Such a sisterhood helps to explain how M.M.M. can move so quickly from her subjective feelings of love for the *Journal* into her communal identification with the shared need for relief from burdened existence. She sees her experience fundamentally aligned with her fellow readers. The *Journal* and its sisterhood speak for her just as readily as she speaks for them.

Two conventions—the formal device of relayed correspondence and the stylistic device of a self-consciously intimate tone—encouraged this sense of sororal intimacy. The *Journal* used readers' letters as far more than an occasion to respond and talk directly with individual subscribers. More significantly, it published letters in order to craft a mediating node for communications between readers, turning itself into what we might even identify as an early, textual instance of a social media platform. This letter from H.L., published in October 1887, is one of dozens upon dozens exactly like it and illustrates how such a relay operated:

RAVENNA, July 21st 87.

EDITOR JOURNAL:—I have been thinking for some time of writing to you and telling you how very much pleased I am with the JOURNAL. I am a new subscriber, but as the years roll on, shall become an old one, for I mean never to be without it again. The chat of the Sisters is very interesting, and I always feel that I must talk with them.

I want to tell Addie not to give her baby boy too many new playthings. He will be more contented if he is taught to play with the old ones, which can easily be done if he is not left with them too long at one time.

I should like to shake hands with "Harry's Wife" and tell her "that is just the way I did." She has such pleasant words for us old ladies that we shall like to hear from her often.

Alice can make her old walnut furniture look quite like new by using black varnish plentifully diluted with kerosene. Can any of the sisters tell me how to prevent black ants from getting into my pantry. H.L.[9]

H.L. responds to queries published in February 1887, May 1887, and July 1887 before then making one of her own, which subsequently gets picked up by Mrs L.W.S. in January 1888. She calls upon her own experiential knowledge of household labor, revels in the opportunity to give strangers her advice, and enters into a relay of communication that circles readers around one another. Significantly, neither H.L. nor the *Journal* feels the need to contextualize originating letters beyond brief markers signifying their intended readers. Both expect *Journal* subscribers to recall Addie, "Harry's Wife," and Alice and to be familiar with their enquiries. Through such familiarity, the *Journal* provided a network of social interaction, bringing readers into contact with one another and promoting their sense of greater attachment to a common identity. Unlike the advice column, a media genre that takes root during the early twentieth century and revolves around the personality of a single figure, the *Journal's* relay technology creates lateral relationships among its subscribers, linking them into chains of familiarity and intimacy.[10]

The *Journal's* many contributors additionally encouraged deep identification between writer and reader by incorporating what feminist critic Helen Damon-Moore, in her crucial *Magazines for the Millions*, terms a "sisterly, peer-to-peer tone."[11] This tone—or, perhaps more accurately, house style—consisted of direct address, informal asides, and frequently self-deprecating humor. One recurrent column responding to readers' letters, for instance, came under the heading "Just Among Ourselves," as though writer and readers were sitting together sharing coffee or tea.[12] Another referred to its style as "A Talkative Way."[13] The *Journal's* contributors deployed this intimate, chatty aesthetics across a wide range of content. Consider, for instance, "Whooping Cough, Etc.," part of "Talks with the Doctor," a feature by Laury MacHenry that ran from June 1889 through May 1890. I quote at length from the opening and conclusion in order to underscore just how unrelentingly this style guided the *Journal's* prose:

> I find I have a great increase in my mail since commencing these talks with the
> JOURNAL sisters, and I like it! The letters and queries come "from all over" I answer
> by mail those which seem to be merely personal, but others, which relate to mat-
> ters of general interest, I shall, as I find opportunity reply to through these "Talks."
> Wasn't it Mr. Shakespeare-Bacon who said something about "One touch of
> nature" making "the whole world kin"? I was reminded of it when in one mail
> I received letters from mothers in Maine, Oregon and Georgia, asking what to do
> for their little ones who had whooping cough. Of course, I answered them direct;
> but as more young mothers would doubtless like some points, I will try to help
> them out. In the first place—*Let 'em whoop!* When the child once catches it, you

needn't try to stave it off or break it up. You have a three months' siege before you, and all you can do is to watch and guard against undue exposures to cold and draughts, give such care and medicines as will make the attack as light as possible, and be thankful that you haven't a dozen children to nurse through it instead of one or two; although I do remember the case of one poor "sister" who engineered five through at once!

...

I have received letters asking for advice about diseases and ailments which, judging from the auto-diagnosis (new word—copyrighted!) I should despair of relieving by making half a dozen personal calls a day at four dollars per visit! I am glad, however, to receive letters (care of this JOURNAL) referring to everyday trials and tribulations, and I will answer all as fast as I can find the time, either by mail or through the JOURNAL.[14]

The passage produces intimacy by insisting that it is participating in a mutual dialogue, a "talk" that at least implicitly generates back-and-forth exchange. In addition, MacHenry shifts between the specificity of actual women (the readers in Maine, Oregon, and Georgia along with the "poor 'sister'" who nurses five children at once) and the abstraction of other "young mothers" whose children will face a similar illness. In so doing, she places her advice into an imagined conversation in which readers can feel directly addressed while also understanding themselves as part of a nationwide sorority of mothers nursing sick children. Simultaneously, MacHenry incorporates a deliberately informal tone through the imprecision of the quotation ("said something about") and its fuzzy attribution ("Shakespeare-Bacon"), the enthusiastic frequency of her exclamation marks, the shift into dialect ("*let 'em whoop!*"), and the light touch of humorous asides ("*new word—copyrighted!*"). Like the institutionalized informality we find in campus novels' banter and gaiety, the *Journal's* loose intimacy hails its readers into a fast, effortless sense of connection with each other, extending their feeling of utter familiarity across geographic and social distances.

Together, the *Journal's* mediating function as a social platform between sisters and its "sisterly" house style collaborate as generic conventions on behalf of social belonging. In large part, they do so in order to fulfill a palliative role in their readers burdened existences. Indeed, if we return to the frequency with which women like Lida Clarkson and M.M.M. described the *Journal* as a reprieve from burdened existence—or, as M.M.M. puts it "a few roses in our pathway of thorns"—then we can begin to see how the *Journal's* very style addresses the material, social, economic, and cultural limitations placed on white women's lives, turning those limitations into a resource for the production of kinship among similarly burdened readers. Despite its occasional moralizing injunctions against expressions of burden ("Let us cease this tiresome, this inconsiderate, this unnecessary talk about our ailments"), it is rare for an issue to go by that doesn't attend to the serious hardships placed upon women.[15] Laury MacHenry writes, for instance, "I think you will agree that most of our headache trouble arises from our neglect of ourselves or from over-working ourselves in some way." Similarly, in one of her "Heart-to-Heart Talks with Girls," "The Lady from Philadelphia" notes the frequency with which readers send the *Journal* letters describing their "troubles," "sorrows," and "discontent," while also identifying themselves as "anxious-minded," "depressed," and "'low-spirited'". Such troubles served, of course, as an asset for advertisers, who exploited white women's hardships by proposing their products as ameliorants. One advertisement for Hood's Sarsaparilla, for instance, includes a testimonial from Mrs M. A. Scarlett in Northville, Michigan: "I say this for the benefit of all the tired, run-down, hard-working women. Hood's Sarsaparilla is not only excellent as a blood purifier, but for all other female complaints, even if of long standing."[16] Yet more crucially, these expressions of burdened existence, even in the context of advertising, took the antagonisms and pressures of individual experience and redirected them into the emotional attachments of belonging—and suffering—together as women.

At the same time, readers were expected never to take their expressions of suffering too far. Belonging to the *Journal's* mediated intimate community required women to perform themselves as close as possible to conventional domesticity, and, above all, conventional domesticity required keeping gripes close to the vest. The "Lady from Philadelphia," for instance, advised her depressed readers to seek their joy and satisfaction by pleasing others: "A woman's supreme joy is to be loved.... If you are cross hide it as you would a crime." Likewise, "As a Physician Sees a Woman," the first in a series of articles "in which women will actually see themselves as men...see them," blames women for "eighty percent of the nervous troubles" that face them: "In her natural career and environment—the home—there is no excuse for her to mope, complain, bury herself in introspection, and bring upon herself an imaginary illness that is a nuisance to everyone around her, including the annoyed and disgusted physician."[17] Undoubtedly, the *Journal's* responses to these realities in their readers' lives contributed to the underlying conditions creating burden, isolation, and depression: sisterly identifying with readers' burdens on one page before then excoriating them for the expression of burden on the next. Yet even disciplined expressions of the burdens facing daily existence provided key contributions to women's understandings of their lives under patriarchy. They offered a forum for women to interpret, analyze, and describe their gendered selves. Indeed, Helen Damon-Moore argues that white women's desire to understand their experience in relation to each other and to men constituted an overriding emphasis of the *Journal's* first three decades: "[T]he *Journal* embodied the process of gender construction. Women in the *Journal's* pages were always in the making."[18] And, moreover, as I've been arguing, these descriptions provided a fantasy of belonging that at least partially staved distress: "the gender-marked texts of women's popular culture," as Berlant puts it, "cultivate fantasies of vague belonging as an alleviation of what is hard to manage in the lived real."[19] White women may have been pressured to hide their crimes of crossness, but the *Journal* allowed them to be criminals together.

## Women's Culture and White Supremacy

The *Journal* had at hand an additional resource it could call upon to ease readers' burdens: expressions of antiblackness affirmed white women's belonging to the national community of "*Journal* sisters," sanctioned their rightful membership within the white nation, underwrote the psychological and material compensations of racial supremacy, and, in so doing, diminished the pressures produced through heteropatriarchy and gender conflict. When "a Plain Country Woman" contrasts the black servants "I have found truly faithful and kind-hearted in time of confusion and trouble" with the hired help she alternately calls "white girl" and "American woman," who "will leave me in a pinch or demand higher wages," the *Journal* turns conflict between a white employer and her white employee into an affirmation of their underlying racial affinities, highlighting a racial kinship that transcends class tensions (both employee and employer equally unfit for servitude) and directs attention away from intra-white differences.[20] When Emmy Cummings, in one of her dispatches from Washington DC, describes the city's "rich colored people," notes their multilingual accomplishments and professional successes, interrupts herself to "wonder if, as a race, they are as happy as when they were slaves," and then quotes, in dialect, the contempt her "old Lem" holds toward "'de high-toned quality' of his race," the *Journal* doubles down on such black inferiority and servility, downplaying interracial class similarities, nurturing contempt against the black middle class, and affirming the preeminence of its white women readers' racial affinities with one another.[21] When the *Journal's* anecdote and joke columns turn antiblack humor—particularly that focusing on black porters and black sermons (a mode of popular literature I take up in Chapter 4)—into a conventional source of merriment; when it includes jocular blackface characters in the Christmas plays it invites its readers to perform at home; when it describes the joys of an after-dinner minstrel show in a nostalgic piece enjoining its readers "Let Us Go Back"—in all of these cases and more the *Journal* renders white supremacy part of its readers' ordinary lives, offering antiblackness as a payment, a premium, to bolster its white women readers' sense of their own positions in the world.[22]

According to W. E. B. Du Bois's well-known argument, antiblackness provides white laborers with a "public and psychological wage" that "compensated in part" for low monetary wages. Yet when Du Bois elaborates on the dispensation of that wage, it quickly becomes clear he's talking primarily about the wages white supremacy affords to white men: "They were given public deference and titles of courtesy because they were white. They were admitted freely with all classes of white people to public functions, public parks and the best schools. They were drawn from their ranks, and the courts, dependent upon their votes, treated them with such leniency as to encourage lawlessness."[23] White women were, of course, afforded "public deference and titles of courtesy," but the *Journal* additionally suggests that they collected their wages through more casual mechanisms and frequently within domestic settings: laughing at a racist joke around the dinner table, merrily staging a racist play on Christmas afternoon, chuckling softly while reading "darky" sketches in between domestic tasks. All of these practices were designed to please, gratify, and flatter whites in general, while also, by virtue of their location within a vehicle for white women's culture, vouching for white women's rightfully superior position over black men and women within white supremacist racial hierarchy. The *Journal* offered antiblackness to its white women readers as no less of a wage than the one offered to white male laborers, one capable of at least partially compensating for the gendered burdens, patriarchal double standards, and exploitation that characterized their shared existence.

Moreover, the *Journal's* explicitly reconciliationist agenda avers the ability for its sorority—bound together through familiarity, mediated through stylized intimate and informal address, uplifted through white supremacy—to link white women of the North with their sisters of the South, forging American womanhood into a distinctly white nationalist disposition. The magazine expressed this agenda through, among many other instances, the publication of reconciliationist genres, such as the Lost Cause reminiscences of Laura Spencer Portor's *Those Days in Old Virginia: A Picture of the South Before the War*, advertisements for The Blue and the Gray Civil War tales ("bound in the two colors which supply the title"), a feature titled "Where Southern Memories Cluster" that boasts showing "for the first time in any Magazine the Confederate Museum at Richmond," and Mrs Thaddeus Horton's celebratory story of pistol-toting Confederate women who successfully defended their home front during the war before being "wooed and won by erstwhile Federal soldiers": "In this way the blue and the gray were at last united."[24] The magazine also called upon the strategy of freed people's testimonial, a device through which African Americans serve as character witnesses for slavery's benevolent side. Hence the story about Charles Dudley Warner who, during a national tour, expresses the desire "to see a real, typical negro" and is then met with silent hostility from the "loquacious old 'aunty'" presented to him. When questioned about her silence, "[w]ith as much dignity and scorn as a grande dame 'Aunty' replied, 'Ugh! I wa'n't gwine talk to dat Yankee. I knowd him soon's I seed him. He's de very one dat stole mistiss' silver du'in' de wah.'"[25] The *Journal* additionally overlays urgency to the push for white nationalist affinities and reconciliation by invoking the specter of "race suicide" in content ranging from advertisements for infant formula to descriptions of President Roosevelt's initiatives, all of which despair, in the words of one contributor, "the pathos of having good old families represented in the next generation by smaller numbers than in this, and still worse of having them run out entirely."[26] The cohesive force exerted by this collection of white nationalist sentiment established citizenship as first and foremost a mode of racial belonging. As in campus novels, such citizenship emerges as an outgrowth of humor, asides, amusements, and merriment, an informal and ordinary web of practices underwriting citizenship's formalization of racial hierarchy.

## The Racial Politics of Friendship

The next step in my argument, which shifts from the racial politics of women's culture and sorority to the racial politics of intimate friendship, may seem jarring. This is in part because contemporary criticism—particularly that influenced by queer studies, postcolonial studies, and American studies—so frequently idealizes friendship as an exception to aggregate and normative social arrangements, a jarring threat to the reproduction of the status quo. In these arguments, which frequently build on Michel Foucault's interview "Friendship as a Way of Life," friendship becomes a radical break with the nation and history: an escape from "readymade formulas" and a way for the "tying together of new alliances and unforeseen lines of force."[27] Hence, to highlight two frequently cited examples, Jack Halberstam claims that friendship enables queers "to open up new life narratives and alternative relations to time and space," and Leela Gandhi claims that friendship enables anticolonial radicals to imagine utopic communities marked by "[a]ffective singularity, anarchist relationality, and other-directedness."[28] My aim here is not to overturn critical investment in friendship's capacity for instigating ruptures in dominant social patterns. Instead, I want to ask how the singular, small-scale, and potentially disruptive practice of intimate friendship can sit so easily within the general and large-scale practice of white supremacist sorority. Indeed, it's not only contemporary literary and cultural theory that espouses the radical potential for intimate friendship to undo solidified social patterns. We see early strains of Foucault's, Halberstam's, and Gandhi's arguments developed in the *Ladies' Home Journal* itself, as when the President of Smith College argues against secret societies on the ground that they cloister students in a "confined atmosphere" of sameness, limiting the possibility for transformative "intimate friendships" between women "with so many dissimilar minds and temperaments," or when Alice Preston extolls the virtue of cross-class and heterosocial friendships on the ground that they break women and girls free from the "merest prejudices" and enrich them through "uplifting and ennobling association" across difference.[29]

To examine the ways these intimate friendships interacted with the white supremacy of women's culture, it helps first to step back from the *Ladies' Home Journal* in order to consider the racial politics of friendship within the postbellum US more generally. During this period, the phrase "friend of the negro," which had shifted in and out of favor from the 1830s through the 1850s, became a commonplace expression. The phrase described a set of specifically white commitments, referring not to a reformist stance but to a realm of feeling, philanthropy, and missionary work that applied to sentiments across the political spectrum. So in 1868, powerful Louisiana congressman and later Speaker of the House, Michael C. Kerr, could, without any contradiction, vilify African Americans as "the most inferior and ignorant and corruptible races of the earth" and, in the very same speech, insist that he and the entire "Democratic party is to-day, and has been throughout the whole history of this country, the truest and best friend of the negro."[30] As a phrase, "friend of the negro" thus organized whites' rhetorical positioning of black subservience in the postbellum United States. Like paternalism, that meeting ground for white abolitionist and pro-slavery thought, white friendship assumed black dependence upon white benevolence and denied even the possibility for black political agency. It expressed the "white man's burden" as a form of intra-national colonialism that nevertheless lent whites an aura of good will.[31]

Simultaneously, intraracial intimate friendship came to be a cherished social form, the ideal for an "authentic" and "real" interpersonal connection. At first glance, these two modes of attachment may seem unrelated, a mere coincidence of terms. Yet their overlap signals an affective and social economy of race: a white supremacist politics of friendship in which the racial exclusivity of intimate friend-ship served to bolster the paternalism behind "friend of the negro." Whites could be a "friend of the negro" because they would never, as it were, be friends with a negro. Put differently, the meaningfulness of intraracial friendship justified and naturalized the hierarchy of interracial friendship. In this way, friendship in the postbellum US became a way for whites to conceptualize their personal relation-ships to the color line and to manage their structural and hierarchical position vis-à-vis African Americans.

We can clarify this process by looking briefly at Walt Whitman's postbellum sentiments toward white Southerners, which link the racial politics of friendship to the history of white reconciliation. In an 1888 conversation transcribed by his friend and personal archivist Horace Traubel, Whitman describes himself as "warmly disposed towards the South: I must admit that my instinct of friendship towards the South is almost more than I like to confess: I have very dear friends there: sacred, precious memories: the people there should be considered, even deferred to, instead of browbeaten."[32] In an unpublished comment from late in his life, he clarifies such friendly instinct as a deep-seated, intensely meaningful, and somatic intraracial attachment:

> I know not how others may feel but to me the South—the old true South, & its succession & presentation the New true South after all outstanding Virginia, the Carolinas, Georgia—is yet inexpressibly dear.— To night I would say one word for that South—the whites. I do not wish to say one word and will not say one word against the blacks—but the blacks can never be to me what the whites are[.] Below all political relations, even the deepest, are still deeper, personal, physio-logical and *emotional* ones, the whites are my brothers & I love them.[33]

As Ed Folsom notes, Whitman kept these statements and those like them private, "unpublished, excised from the book versions of the essays, or recorded only in conversations."[34] Nevertheless, as the century came to a close, even public Whitman came to be closely associated with the agenda of white sectional recon-ciliation: "In his reminiscences of the Civil War," reports an 1899 *Ladies' Home Journal* article on the secrets of happiness, "Walt Whitman tells us how a kind word turned a rebel into a patriot."[35] The private conversations therefore don't reveal Whitman's motivations so much as they reveal the white supremacy inherent in those motivations. Whitman gestures toward a set of "political" feelings he maintains regarding black progress; he is, he might very well tell us, a "friend of the negro." Yet in an altogether different register, he feels "warmly disposed" toward the whites—an "instinct of friendship" justified in part because he counts "very dear friends" among white Southerners. The phrasing here is tricky, with friendship serving to signal two distinct yet related forms of intraracial attachment: one between intimates ("dear friends") and another between complete strangers ("that South—the whites"). These two attachments coexist in a cyclical and self-enclosed economy. The "dear friends" seed the "deeper, personal, physiological and *emotional*" instinct toward whites in general, even as that same warm disposition toward white strangers creates the possibility for those intimate friendships to emerge in the first place. Whitman thus describes an affirmative and almost innate impulse toward intraracial friendship, an intensity of feeling so precious and unique it could never cross the color line ("the blacks can never be to me what the whites are").

These white supremacist politics of friendship imagine the world as a division separating the whites (friends and potential friends) from all others. Hence Whitman's comments—signaled by the continuity he sees between "the old true South" and the "New true South"—provide one lens through which to understand the history of Civil War reconciliation, in which actual and potential intraracial affections bound together the previously warring enemies, positioning white supremacy as a natural and logical outcome that foreclosed emancipationist alternatives and radical, interracial politics. In this cycle where race, nation, and friendship reinforce one another, racial hierarchy takes on inevitability. Such a political function links the politics of postbellum friendship less to Foucault's radical creativity and more to an Aristotelian, nativist organization of racialized affinity and national belonging that, as Ivy Schweitzer and Caleb Crain argue, has prevailed within Anglo North America since the 1600s. In this model, political friendship constitutes the bond between citizens, defined as those who meet the criteria for actual friendship.[36] For Aristotle, this included all non-slave men; for Whitman, it meant "the whites." Political friendship produces national stability because it excludes those rendered ineligible for intimate friendship, those who might produce tension and conflict by introducing dissimilarity into the *polis*. Hence, Aristotle writes in the *Nicomachean Ethics*, "friendship would seem to hold cities together, and legislators would seem to be more concerned about it than about justice."[37] Of course, as Crain notes, "because women were not full citizens, the political implications of their friendships were different."[38] The *Ladies' Home Journal's* emphasis on women's friendships allows us to qualify precisely the nature of this difference, revealing how white women's friendships constituted a potent sublayer affirming and undergirding the racialization of national belonging.

From the 1880s through the early twentieth century, the *Journal* repeatedly worried about a crisis in conditions conducive to "real friendship."[39] Its pages treated intimate friendship as a social form under siege by more easily achieved and hence fraudulent forms of social connection. Trivial, widely distributed, and superficial attachments, argued *Journal* contributors, threatened to overtake heartfelt, meaningful, and, above all, *authentic* intimacies. "Great women," writes advice columnist Ruth Ashmore, "have most of them been fortunate in having about them women friends who were as true as steel," and they therefore know how to ascertain "real friendship" from the "foolish, ecstatic, miscalled friendship of today." Encouraging her readers to resist fast "weeds" of relationships ("real friendship takes years to form"), Ashmore entreats, "I beg of you be careful in your choice of a friend, and be more than careful in the conduct of your friendship," for, she continues, "that woman is happiest who has a true, honorable woman friend who is companionable, lacks inquisitiveness, and is always considerate and always true."[40] Only through such friendship could the social world attain authenticity and truth. "There is too little human love in the world," complained Fannie L. Fancher in an 1889 *Journal* column. "Love and friendship, that divine form of love, should be assiduously cultivated."[41] Intimate friendship appears in the *Journal* as not simply another intimate form, still less a generalizable vehicle for mass identification, but a precious rarity that alone could rescue women from the deferred promises of group affinities, the pettiness of superficial ties, the overly fast intimacy of being-in-common, and the shallowness of large-scale belonging. Friendship, for Ashmore, enables ways of living that remain "true" to one's self and to others, both in the sense of being faithful and in the sense of being authentic.

Ashmore's anxiety stemmed in part from the new prevalence of fraternalism during the so-called Golden Age of Fraternity (another contributor does complain that "women nowadays are clubbing themselves to death").[42] It also stemmed from the sense that the Civil War had hastened modernity, putting into motion what Alan Trachtenberg famously terms an "age of incorporation."[43] Men and women experienced the 1870s, 1880s, and 1890s as a period of inexorable aggregation—a congealing of time into linear teleology; of space into flat homogeneity; of economic production into corporate industry; of towns into metropolitan centers; of professions into professionalism; and of the state into a federalized apparatus.[44] This set of transitions led to what historian T. J. Jackson Lears describes as a craving for "authenticity" and what the *Journal* frequently expressed as an aspiration to simplicity.[45] Such craving helps to explain the sense that friendship was under attack and the urgency felt around efforts to nurture it as a cherished and uniquely *authentic* social form.

Yet friendship also lent its semblance of realness and authenticity to more aggregate forms of belonging, providing a meaningful and highly valued interpersonal practice that directed warmth of feeling back onto white women's culture. White women could see their *Journal* sisters as metonymic extensions of their "real" friends—each a reinforcing reflection of the other. Just as friendship in Aristotle's political model works to strengthen and justify the exclusivity of the polis, so too did the *Journal's* idealization of white women's intimate friendships help to transform whiteness into a natural, common-sense prerequisite for belonging.

## Befriending and Reading

The racial politics of friendship and sorority extended past social ties linking one white woman to another. They entered as well into the affective and even intimate ties linking white women readers to the white characters they encountered in literature. This is because, for the *Journal*, literary reading constituted a vital practice in the art of befriending, one that could teach women how to appreciate one another across intraracial difference and provide them with experience in doing so.

The *Journal's* coupling of friendship and reading grew out of the nineteenth century's close connection between reading and sociality. As Gillian Silverman argues in *Books and Bodies: Reading and the Fantasy of Communion in Nineteenth-Century America*, men and women alike used leisurely, literary reading to offset the forces of industrialization and the isolation of the nuclear household: "Historically tied to the emergence of the privatized liberal subject, the book nonetheless offered its nineteenth-century readers an alternative model of identity—a sense of wholeness based not in autonomy and terminal existence but in accretion, correspondence, and extensivity."[46] By emphasizing the value such social expansion might have for friendship, the *Journal* invited its readers to practice literary reading and intimate befriending as complements to the sisterhood of their intimate public.

From the 1880s through the early twentieth century, the *Journal* explicitly and extensively advocated literary reading as an apprenticeship in befriending. In an article titled "Neighborly Confidences," for instance, the author cites a "Chinese maxim"—"There are plenty of acquaintances, but few real friends"—and then concludes on the necessity for analysis of character: "But these facts should not produce a wholesale cynicism and reserve regarding neighbors; for in them are often found as true and tried friends as one could wish; but they should teach us to study and analyze character—to know if back of the pleasing, friendly manner there exists integrity of heart and a fair measure of common sense."[47] The magazine's use of "character" here refers to the neighbor's moral and mental qualities, as well as to the features that provide her distinctiveness and depth. Hence the passage takes advantage of *character's* doubled reference to literature—to print and writing as well as to literary personages—telling its readers that they should learn to become careful, astute, and critical readers of each other, distinguishing between the surface performance and the potentially cloaked inner drive, outlook, and motivation. For the *Journal*, there's but a thin line between this sort of interpersonal wisdom and the close reading of literature. Our ability accurately "to study and analyze character" among neighbors amounts to a skill learned through our ability to study and analyze literary texts.

The *Journal* articulated its most thorough elaboration of this reading formation in popular novelist Adeline D. T. Whitney's series of letters on reading. Initially announced in its November 1892 issue as "The World of Reading," the series promised readers in-depth exploration of "the most interesting and entertaining authors and books."[48] Thirteen months later, when the series' first letter finally appeared, "The World of Reading," had been replaced with a new title altogether: "A Friendly Letter to Girl Friends."[49] This substitution of titles, which the *Journal* left entirely unremarked, together with the doubled friendliness of the ultimately successful title (friendship as both a quality and a subject position), signal the guiding principle of the *Journal*'s literary reading formation: the distance between reading and friendship is at most negligible. The two entail practices of discernment and engagement that develop complementary proficiencies; engaging with fictional worlds ushers us into the best possible apprenticeship for constructing meaningful—and, hence, also laborious—social intimacies.[50] Defending literary style and imaginative storytelling, Whitney calls for fiction that is "an imaging of the true," sufficiently removed from its immediate, empirical context to open a deeper hermeneutic space in which the reader can interpret and engage.[51] For Whitney, texts that simultaneously refract and represent reality facilitate an ideal reading practice that at once expands and regulates the self by "either confirming and developing, or checking and denying ... proclivities," thereby exposing readers to the full range of "human possibilities."[52] Fiction mediates between private and social life. It "fits" readers for interpersonal relationships. For, indeed, Whitney insists, "most of us do have to be fitted, in taking ourselves—if there is anything of us—out of our separate life into the world."[53] To be thus "fitted" is to cultivate the skills necessary to enter into "genuine friendship," a social form Whitney contrasts to the "little, frittering, life-exhausting etiquettes," the "show and pretense," and the fraternalism or "clubbing" that characterize "artificial society."[54] "[I]magination," Whitney writes, "is founded on all the realities we have: it is the mirrored reflection." Therefore books "are for far more than amusement. They are for vital sympathies and understandings; human thought to human thought, hope to hope, motive to motive."[55]

Bridging these gaps between human thoughts, hopes, and motives requires a set of skills that correspond neatly to those required, in the words of *Journal* editor Hamilton Mabie, to "enjoy books and gain their friendship."[56] Reading of this sort allows us to understand the "relations of thought and word" and therefore to discover what Whitney calls "the deepest reality."[57] It requires, moreover, an intimacy at once intellectual and corporeal, inviting readers to feel language in their mouths and understand its effects through movement in their fingers.[58] By learning to read with such affection, we see where "hides a meaning of true nobility" in both language and people.[59] Though such simultaneously punctilious and affective practice, readers enter into what, in a series of autobiographical essays published in the *Journal*, Helen Keller refers to as the "sweet, gracious discourse of my book-friends."[60] In so doing, women become closer readers and slower readers, forging, in Mabie's description, a "habit of mind" that turned them into more astute participants in both fictional and social spheres.[61]

Indeed, *Journal* book reviewers gave their highest praise when claiming that a text enabled its readers to befriend its characters. As one reviewer notes of Jewett's

*Strangers and Wayfarers* (1890), "the characters whom we meet...are so admirably introduced that the 'Strangers' become our friends, and the 'Wayfarers' find hearty welcome on their way."[62] Likewise the same reviewer praises Mary Wilkins Freeman's *A Humble Romance and Other Stories* (1887) because it produces a "feeling [that] gains upon the reader...and one lays this delightful volume aside with the thought that many friends dwell beneath its covers, and that it will be pleasant to revisit them from time to time."[63] Similarly, for the *Journal*, books that we give to our friends are companions who come to commingle within the emotional life of the friendship. "Droch's Literary Talks," a column that ran briefly during the 1890s, therefore warns readers to take more care in their literary gifts than in all others: "The flowers soon wither and the perfume passes, but the book remains not only on the shelves but in the memory—and the perfume of it is indissolubly wedded to the giver. If we realized how often we walk through the memories of our friends, attended by the strange company who have stepped out of the books that we have given them, we should certainly shudder—and choose better next time."[64] Friendship is, for the *Journal*, an essentially *literary* phenomenon, one thick with previous reading experiences, shared reading histories, and the literary characters who circulate, like perfume, in and out of friends' selves.[65]

## White Readers and Nonreaders of African American Literature

This intimate or social reading formation provides the background we need to understand the *Journal's* aversion to African American literature and African American writers. From its 1883 inception through the turn of the century, the *Ladies' Home Journal* managed an exceptional feat of omission. It published only a smattering of works by writers of color; included virtually no commentary on race, race relations, or segregation; and, with the exception of Lost Cause plantation sketches or blackface characters in plays, entirely excluded literature centered on characters of color. This was not merely the result of being a white magazine with white editors and a white audience. As Kenneth Price and Heather Tirado Gilligan have shown, other postbellum magazines—including the *Atlantic Monthly*, *Harper's New Monthly Magazine*, the *Century*, the *Arena*, and the *Independent*—frequently published fiction and essays by writers of color and featured race, racism, and race relations as explicit, recurrent themes.[66] So, for instance, the *Atlantic Monthly* published four of Charles Chesnutt's sketches during the 1880s and 1890s and a favorable survey comparing his work to, among others, Mary Wilkins Freeman and Sarah Orne Jewett. The *Ladies' Home Journal*, on the other hand, left Chesnutt wholly unmentioned.[67]

While we cannot know the precise reasoning behind the *Journal's* systematized publication decisions, we do have evidence that it viewed its approach to literature and literary reading as a distinct alternative to the approach of the *Atlantic Monthly* and its highbrow cohorts. It's through this differentiation that we can better understand the *Journal's* exclusion of black writers. As the *Journal* developed a more consistent approach to literature, it refined a system of generic differentiation and evaluation that derided the overly literal realism it associated with the *Atlantic Monthly*. Such "realism carried to the extreme," the *Journal* argued, left readers stifled, cramped by too many details and too little characterization, and denied entry points through which to develop experiential knowledge about fictional characters and worlds.[68]

Consider an 1890 book review comparing the latest novels by William Dean Howells and Charles Dudley Warner, which allows the *Journal* to articulate its aesthetic criteria while simultaneously positioning itself and its approach to literature as a distinct alternative. In it, Annie R. Ramsey contrasts Warner's imaginative realism to Howells's technical realism: "Mr. Howells photographs those who pass before his camera, and makes a study of their inconsistencies, being just as much interested in any one point, as in any other." Warner, on the other hand, brings to the same "studied details... a sentiment, a poetic feeling which Mr. Howells does not, will not, allow himself to believe in."[69] Howells's camera fixes its representations into still images; he leaves the reader no possibility to interact with his subject because he presents her with an empirical and undistinguished "study" of reality rather than an aesthetic engagement with contemporary experience. The "sentiment" and "poetic feeling" Ramsey identifies in Warner's fiction enables a more fluidly interactive reading experience. Where we observe the way Howells's types "put on their hats," take note of their "certain trick of speech," and nod in recognition at their "habit of shrugging the shoulders," we join in with Warner's characters: "we go with them through every phase and detail" of their daily lives.[70] For Ramsey, Warner's fiction by contrast is valuable for its expression of "poetic feeling" its capacity as a medium that enables reading to become a playful, engaged social experience. The ambitions of Ramsey's review thus exceed simple evaluation of two recently published novels. She works to construct an alternative program for evaluating literature and reading, one that positions the *Ladies' Home Journal* against Howells, Howells's criteria for realist fiction, and the entire genre of *Atlantic*-style magazines through which Howells and his peers sought to influence American literary history.[71] Later reviewers and contributors amplify these criteria, praising fiction above all when it allows readers and characters to interact and develop bonds akin to friendships.

Briefly comparing the two publications' approach to a single author both admire, Mary Wilkins Freeman, illustrates the distinction. Howells's 1891 admiration of Freeman—that her sketches depict "just the expression of that vast average of Americans who do the hard work of the country, and live narrowly on their small earnings and savings"—contrasts sharply with the kind of praise found in the *Ladies' Home Journal*.[72] There, for instance, Freeman is celebrated precisely because she avoids typology and enables a reading experience that cannot fall back on previously held knowledge: "She leaves us to meet her people very much as we should, if we went to visit... a friend who could give us the history and ancestry of her neighbors, but is forced to allow us to follow their lives, to find out their minds and characters for ourselves."[73] This praise uses repeated first-person plural signs ("us," "we," "our") to link Freeman's regionalist fiction to the mass audience that enacts white women's culture, and it therefore might at first seem to replicate Howells's emphasis on regionalism as an encounter between a familiar "us" and a foreign "them." Yet it elaborates by defining the value of Freeman's fiction through that mass audience's innumerable set of distinct, irreplaceable encounters with specific friends, neighbors, minds, and characters. It thereby links the reading of fiction with intimate friendship and the non-appropriative knowledge of others (in this case, figured as the friend's neighbors).

Such a distinction between reading as ethnographic study and reading as imaginative befriending provides the most compelling explanation for the *Journal's* decision to segregate its pages. By incorporating an ethic of engagement across interpersonal difference into its reading formation, the *Journal* encouraged white women to understand literary settings and characters as extensions of their intimate world.[74] Characters were not, as they were for the *Atlantic Monthly*, figures to study at arm's length. They were friends to cherish and embrace. The *Atlantic Monthly*, with its ethnographic approach to reading, could integrate its pages without threatening the racial status quo. Indeed, doing so affirmed white supremacist hierarchy and its white readers' segregated subjectivity, figuring whites as the purveyors of racial knowledge over and against the black character-objects they encountered in fiction.[75] Yet the *Journal* required print segregation in order to retain social segregation, screening its readers from a mode of interracial engagement that held out at least a potential for disrupting racial hierarchy. In this way, the *Journal's* decision to omit African American literature collaborated with its emphasis on the value of intimate friendship between white women, both of which provided compensations to women's burdened existences while justifying and defending the racial exclusivity of *Journal* sisterhood. The mediation of white women's sorority and the segregation of white women's friendships—over coffee as well as on the page—arose in the last decades of the nineteenth century as key players in securing white nationalist futurity, naturalizing the inevitability of white sectional reconciliation, and abandoning the prospect that whites would commit to an emancipationist outcome for the Civil War.

# Elegies, White Dissent, and the Civil War Dead

In Chapters 1 and 2, I looked at interactions between popular literature, popular culture, social convention, and the social patterns of white nationalism. I argued in particular that campus novels and the *Ladies' Home Journal* helped white Americans relate to one another and to understand their interactions as constituents of racial and national belonging. This chapter shifts to white nationalism's interior dimensions. Focusing on Civil War elegies published in Northern periodicals, newspapers, and anthologies from 1861 through the century's end, I probe Northern whites' sense of loss and misrecognition in the face of nationalism's inexorable momentum. How do elegies negotiate the competing scales of wartime loss: the intimate, inward torment of private grief (*my* son, *my* brother, *my* husband) and the public, outward abstraction of shared grief (*our* boys)? In their lines, what happens to mourning that cannot withstand the logic of substitution wherein individual pain becomes nationally meaningful and politically useful? What strategies did poets incorporate to guard their personal loss from collective appropriation? What of those insensible elegists who didn't fret, as Herman Melville did in the "Supplement" to his volume of Civil War poetry, that they might "be contributing to a bitterness which every sensible American must wish at an end"?[1]

In exploring these questions, I've come to think that Civil War elegies comprise the best archive we have for assessing the conflicted nature of Northern white feeling in response to North–South reconciliation and white nationalist belonging. If during this period, as Max Cavitch argues, "American elegy bids its long farewell to the soul and steps up its hailing of the unconscious," then these elegies capture the crisscrossing routes Civil War memory and loss passed between psychic life and intersubjective experience.[2] They mark the moments when whites complied or collided with the work of nation building: when they experienced comfort and consolation in racialized citizenship organized through what psychoanalyst Vamik Volkan names a "shared chosen trauma"; or, alternately, when they felt in some perhaps faintly perceptible way misrecognized and misunderstood by the wounded nation's projection of itself.[3] Mourning, as we know, consists of attitudes and feelings toward the dead; it also works to shape patterns of attachment among the living, requiring survivors to negotiate between intimacy and sociality, interior

*Genre and White Supremacy in the Postemancipation United States.* Travis M. Foster, Oxford University Press (2019).
© Travis M. Foster.
DOI: 10.1093/oso/9780198838098.001.0001

and exterior, proximity and distance, specificity and abstraction. While some Civil War elegies labored to facilitate links between individual hurt and social totalities such as whiteness and the nation, others highlighted the incommensurable qualities of some grief and some grievers within any such totalizing plots.

If we take the genre as a whole, with all of its contradictory and competing impulses, Civil War elegies thus reveal the complex attachments that coexisted for white Northerners from their position within nationalist belonging: not merely the rousing appeal of patriotic affirmation that comes from recognizing one's own membership in something worthy and grand, but also the desire to stand apart and give voice to individuality and misalignment. Highlighting precisely these complexities within the experience of recognition and normativity, Stephanie Foote argues we should think of white "interiority as precisely that secret consciousness of difference that is paradoxically the sign that one really belongs."[4] Such simultaneity of misalignment and alignment, difference and belonging, finds a comfortable expressive home within Civil War elegies. The genre thereby witnesses and archives the phenomenally incorporative and elastic characteristic of postbellum whiteness, which lays a claim at once to dominant centrality and dissenting marginality. By representing such a wide range of emotional and political attachments, Civil War elegies cast a democratic aura on the transition from Reconstruction to Jim Crow, helping even a rigidly segregated white nation to present and see itself as liberal, capacious, diverse, and open to dissent.

Working against perceptions within American literary studies that tend to discount conventional, nineteenth-century verse as too unvarying and predictable to merit sustained attention, this chapter proposes that we take Civil War elegies seriously as objects for critical and historical reflection.[5] To do so, I've compiled and closely studied as many Civil War elegies circulating in the North as I could find, including those published in *Harper's Weekly*, *Harper's Monthly*, the *Atlantic Monthly*, *Century*, *Godey's Lady's Book and Magazine*, and *Overland Monthly*; those published in nineteenth-century anthologies such as *Poems of the War* (1864) and *Bugle-Echoes* (1886); and those collected in more recent anthologies, especially Faith Barrett and Cristanne Miller's excellent *"Words for the Hour": A New Anthology of American Civil War Poetry*. While it's true that most Civil War elegies follow a nationalist template similar to that made famous in Julia Ward Howe's "Battle Hymn of the Republic" (1862), many others engage in substantial protean, intra-generic, intra-textual jostling. Whereas campus novels and *The Ladies' Home Journal* by and large aligned ideologically and remained stubbornly consistent, Civil War elegies prove a much roomier genre, incorporating wide-ranging dissent from their own reigning conventions.

I'll start my analysis by expanding on the role of mourning and loss within the cultures of Civil War memory, linked in ways historians and critics sometimes do not acknowledge to the politics of white supremacy and white national reconciliation. I then return to the methodological and historiographical questions informing so much of this book's project—questions concerning genre, convention, social history, and the ordinary—by specifying them to the particular scene of nineteenth-century verse, so often dismissed as uninspired and banal. My subsequent sections diversify our understanding of Civil War elegies by concentrating on three attitudes for mourning and remembering the dead: nationalist, antiwar, and melancholic. Making the case that these elegies deserve our sustained attention, for each attitude I analyze a handful of poems, chosen for their ability to serve as representative examples, that provide a sense of the genre's variable and seemingly conflicting ideological work. "Society stays alive, not despite its antagonism, but by means of it," writes Theodor Adorno, and Civil War elegies' expressions of nationalist, antiwar, and melancholic attachments reveal a white nation that takes solace in the peaceful coexistence of its divisions.[6]

## Pressures on Civil War Grief

Civil-War-era Americans treated elegies—their poems of death and dying, mourning and remembering—with substantial care and attention, incorporating them as valued articles within the phenomenology of bereavement culture. Elegies passed over people's tongues, entered into their ears, and were copied out by their fingers. Because they were so frequently read aloud in the immediate aftermath of death, for instance, anthology editors included sections of elegies within volumes of verse otherwise designed for the sick and dying. Likewise, elegies acquired a privileged position in the ritualistic practice of nineteenth-century copying, one of the literary forms most frequently transcribed into commonplace books. Elegies didn't simply stay on the surface: they were experienced by and through the body; they lent shape to the tempos and patterns of mourning's corporeal manifestations, as well as its spiritual and intellectual ones. They belong to literary history, of course, but also to a material history of grief and loss, as kin to mourning quilts, cemeteries, tombstones, post-mortem portraits, memorial lithography, and ritualized hair weavings.[7] Deeply enmeshed within the social practice of nineteenth-century mourning rituals, elegies taught American women and men how to grieve and then became crucial objects in the practice of that grief once its occasion arose.

For Civil War elegies, violence added to and complicated these broader aesthetic, intimate, and social functions. Historically, war elegies have faced the impossible task of transubstantiating the machinery of death—the very violence that occasioned the loss being mourned in the first place—into a pathway toward redemption. In the lines of war elegies, violence must appear not as the source of cruelty and suffering but as their improbable solution. Within Christian contexts, of course, influential theological interpretations of the crucifixion make this task less cumbersome and jarring. Hence the purple color of the lilacs in Walt Whitman's "When Lilacs Last in the Dooryard Bloom'd," which recalls the Passion, lending Lincoln's assassination a noble function within a larger narrative of redemption, martyrdom, and the alleviation of suffering. Hence too the most famous and ubiquitous Civil War elegy of all, "John Brown's Body," which puts into song and verse Ralph Waldo Emerson's prediction that Brown's hanging would "make the gallows glorious like the cross."[8]

The sheer scope of death during the Civil War, its efficient and unprecedented delivery of violence and disease to soldiers and civilians, meant that poets often saved their redeeming labors for representative, celebrity deaths like Lincoln's and Brown's. Most Civil War death—common, everyday, mass death—was rote and mechanical, rendering the war elegy's redemptive function even more difficult and paradoxical than it already had been.[9] When Diana Fuss argues that "the cataclysmic cultural changes ushered in by modern warfare, technology, and communications have ratcheted up the ethical burden of elegy," she refers to an era of mass death that the American Civil War in no small part inaugurated—death on a scale of brutality that outpaced and overwhelmed the nation's or the elegist's ability to remediate human violence.[10]

Yet everyday death could still withstand repurposing into something useful. The scale of Civil War death made grief even more ubiquitous than it had already been, turning the dead into a readily available resource for nationalist cohesion. After the Civil War, white Northerners (and, later, white Southerners) transformed the work of mourning into the emotional labor of nation building, calling upon shared grief to supersede sectional bitterness and provide a unifying sense of belonging to one citizenry. "The Dead," writes historian Drew Gilpin Faust, "became the focus of an imagined national community for the reunited states, a constituency all [whites] could willingly serve."[11] Simultaneously, grief tapped into reconciliationist and, by the 1890s, Lost Cause impulses that removed the nation from its recent history, paradoxically pursuing the chronology of national progress within non-teleological experiences of time and memory. Mourning, Dana Luciano argues in her study of nineteenth-century grief culture, enabled men and women to position themselves, even temporarily, outside the progressive time of industrial capitalism. It opened selves and souls to "sacred time," a Sabbath period of reflective devotion organized around life events and interpersonal relationships rather than calendric regularity.[12] By facilitating white " 'feeling-in-common,' " collective grief united "mourning's backward gaze and the progressive direction of patriotic nationalism."[13] Operating in similar fashion to the nostalgia we encountered in campus novels, a nation sutured together through white grief could smooth the edges of recent history and lend white national citizenship the gloss of timeless transcendence. Take, as an example, the bulk of Walt Whitman's Civil War elegies. As Adam Bradford argues, Whitman's predominant elegiac strategy, like that pursued by many of his lesser-known peers, is to recall specific dead soldiers in a nonspecific way that invites readers to project their own loved ones into his scenes of loss. Whitman thereby creates "a community of 'readerly' mourners united despite geographical, political, or ideological distances."[14] Or we might take Henry Timrod's "The Unknown Dead," published in the 1866 anthology *War Poetry of the South* and then reprinted in 1911 by Dodd, Mead, and Company as part of its popular anthology *Memorial Day: Its Celebration, Spirit, and Significance as Related in Prose and Verse, with a Non-Sectional Anthology of the Civil War*. Like many Civil War elegists, Timrod takes advantage of the war's rapid production of unknown graves and anonymous deaths to turn the dead into a collectivity, the shared loss of a nation trumping the particular loss of any individual. In this way, Whitman's and, though he may not have intended it, Timrod's elegies joined a reconciliationist grief culture that placed immense pressures onto intimate, private scenes of grief, driving them toward an increase in scale whereby they could become shared, dispersed, and atmospheric—adhesive agents for white nationalist belonging.

Yet mourning's resourcefulness did not come without risk for white reconciliationist agendas. Most obviously, how do you turn your profound grief over the loss of, say, a son into sympathetic and shared identification with those responsible for his death? How does grief produce amity toward former enemies rather than an intensification of bitterness and conflict? Grief—particularly when it assumed the long-term, unabating form of melancholia—threatened to nurture an affective memory bank in opposition to any agenda that would prefer to forget, rewrite, and move on.

Mitigating such a threat to national union, disciplinary forces and counterforces ensnared scenes of Civil War loss. In December 1864, for instance, Southern diarist Mary Chesnut recorded her husband's injunction against outward displays of bereavement: "Noisy, fidgety grief never moves me at all;" he tells her, "it annoys me. Self-control is what we all need."[15] Reconciliationist sentiments took advantage of these longstanding associations of mourning with weakness, irrationality, and femininity, casting overly externalized mourning or overly long melancholia as improper and pathological modes of Civil War memory. We need look no further than the famously satiric fun Mark Twain has with the interminable and extravagant mourning of the Grangerford women in *Adventures of Huckleberry Finn* (1895). Twain's humor works to quarantine the anti-reconciliationist risks of melancholia, first, by reenergizing differentiations between the healthiness of a short-lived grief and the pathologies of unadapting mourning, and, second, by underscoring the longstanding association between excessive melancholic feeling and the supposed waywardness of women. Recalling *Huckleberry Finn's* postbellum authorship allows us to take the episode as an allegory for those who would hold onto to their Civil War grievances and keep alive accompanying sectional tensions. Moreover, Twain's gendered structure, in which surviving women mourn the loss of dead men, mirrors that of the Civil War more broadly, reinforcing and, in the process, trivializing grief as the specific domain of women. The Grangerfords, in this sense, offer postbellum whites, men as well as women, a cautionary tale about the proper scale of mourning and memory alongside a reconciliationist nudge to forget and forgive.

We can locate a perhaps even more effective and widespread tactic for disciplining melancholia in popular discourses of heaven that render death familiar and even inconsequential. It's hard to mourn the dead, after all, when they don't exactly die. Popularizing a movement started with Emanuel Swedenborg's 1758 *Heaven and Hell*, Civil War-era Americans wrote poetry, newspaper articles, dozens of theological books, novels, and funeral sermons (often reprinted as widely circulating pamphlets)—all of which aimed to undo Calvinist notions of the afterlife as a distant, unknowable world in which heavenly spirits entirely leave behind earthly existence. Instead, in their pages, heaven became a familiar and proximate extension of mortal life, including its human bonds of friendship and family. One historian counts over 100 books published about heaven in a ten-year period following the Civil War.[16] Most famous of all, Elizabeth Stuart Phelps's bestselling Gates trilogy (appearing in 1868, 1883, and 1887 respectively), popularized what Cindy Weinstein calls "the joys of being dead, which are not unlike the pleasures of being alive."[17] The first novel in the trilogy, *The Gates Ajar*, details a slow and careful instruction in this view of the afterlife for its first-person narrator, Mary Cabot, and, by extension, for its readers. The novel begins shortly after the death of Mary's brother, Royal, on a Civil War battlefield, which puts her into a state of profound, lasting melancholia: "Something ails the voices of the children," she writes, "all the music has gone out of them, and they hurt me like knives."[18] By the novel's end, however, when Mary's spiritual teacher, beloved friend, and surrogate mother, Aunt Winifred, also dies, the proximity of heaven produces an altogether different emotional reaction: "I say it from my honest heart, I cannot grieve. In the place out of which she has gone, she has left me peace."[19] In this view, mourning itself, even seemingly healthy and short-lived mourning, constitutes an indecent emotional response to loss and a fundamental misunderstanding of the proximity between earth and heaven, life and the afterlife. So while Phelps intends her novels to provide consolation in particular to the hundreds of thousands of women experiencing loss after the Civil War, her trilogy simultaneously exacts a disciplinary price, propagating a social system that creates pathology out of grief.[20]

Given this complex and conflicted background, to write a Civil War elegy was never simply to remember or honor the dead. Elegists weighed in, explicitly and not, on which lives were worthy of grief and memory, which suffering ought to be included in national consciousness, which grief could be acknowledged, and which survivors, alternately, should be disparaged as overwrought or pathologically feminine. Doing so, elegists entered a fraught political field, full of contestation over the proper nature of grief, Civil War memory, white political relationality, and national futurity.

## Elegy, Genre, Method

During the last three decades, critics have soured on the elegy. They've read it against itself, as a genre estranged from its consolatory premise and promise. Exemplary among this work, Jahan Ramazani and R. Clifton Spargo separately use the term *anti-elegy* for modernist poets who take up the themes of loss and mourning while refusing their audience the twin comforts of consolation and sympathy with the dead.[21] "In becoming anti-elegiac," writes Ramazani, "the modern elegy more radically violates previous generic norms than did earlier phases of elegy: it becomes anti-consolatory and anti-encomiastic, anti-Romantic and anti-Victorian, anti-conventional and sometimes even anti-literary."[22] Ramazani's and Spargo's insistence on the newness and radically oppositional nature of their objects of study is, to be sure, an impulse in modernist criticism more generally. Yet in their tendency toward literary exceptionalism, or, the valuation of a text primarily according to its ability to stand apart, they reveal something about the longstanding and seemingly kneejerk critical predisposition to place immense value on individual difference at the expense of common and shared convention.

Part of the problem is that we—literary critics and literary historians—lack critical frameworks that value our objects of study precisely for their ordinariness or that might help us to apprehend the ordinary as something other than flat. Indeed, even outside of modernist studies, many of our assumptions about the value of literature rely upon disdain for generic consistency across texts, as we contrast our object's singular status with the generic humdrum. Michael Warner, for instance, offsets the isolated rarity of Melville's 1862 elegy "Shiloh," with its refusal to figure violence as redemptive and its distrust of "conviction's transcendent objects," by contrasting it with Howe's "The Battle-Hymn of the Republic," which figures violence "not as a program of cruelty, but as a redemption from cruelty."[23] The contrast implicitly sets Melville's canonical and exceptional Civil War elegy against Howe's popular, exemplary, and generic one. Likewise, critics frequently bundle generic literature through a shorthand phrase that serves to heighten the difference and, therefore, the value of their objects of study.[24] Ian Finseth offsets the value of canonical realist fiction by contrasting its representation of the Civil War dead with that found in "great quantities of conventional verse": Where we *most* see the failure to "reckon with the face of the dead," he concludes, "is in the various elegies, paeans to the dead, and memorial addresses that pay tribute to the dead while carefully controlling the meaning of their death."[25] In this, Warner and Finseth echo an earlier generation of Civil War literature critics such as Edmund Wilson, who bemoans the "mediocre level of the poetry of the Civil War," the scarcity of "poets with real distinction," and the absence of any verse that, "reflecting the idiosyncrasies of the writer, was likely to take on an unconventional form," and Daniel Aaron, who concludes that only the very rare and exceptional poet had anything meaningful or valuable to say about the war at all.[26]

I want to suggest instead that the hasty conclusions indicated in phrases like "great quantities of conventional verse," "various elegies," or even "the poetry of the Civil War" have more to do with critical assumptions about ordinariness than they do with the particular body of texts those phrases index. Rather than flat and transparent, *ordinariness* comprises what Lauren Berlant terms "an intersecting space where many forces and histories circulate and become 'ready to hand'... for inventing new rhythms of living, rhythms that could, at any time, congeal into norms, forms, and institutions."[27] Likewise, Stanley Cavell argues that we often fail to take into consideration "the extreme oddness of the everyday world" because our skeptical stances lead us either to repudiate the conventions of our shared life or to pass them by.[28] Hence, within literary historical methods, *ordinary's* antonyms—critical descriptions like *anti-elegy, anti-generic, distinct, idiosyncratic,* or *original*—often stand as sufficient justification for aesthetic and political value, repudiations of the ordinary, even though those same terms all too often overstate difference and underestimate play within the generic or conventional. Moreover, this pattern produces a stark implication for literary historical and critical work that views itself as politically motivated. In casting the objects we admire against conventional and generic patterns, we replicate one overriding ideology of the status quo: the heroic individual—or, as it were, the heroic text—as the primary agent through which to conceptualize social change.

Such literary exceptionalism cannot begin to apprehend Civil War elegies. To justify a certain poem more by positioning it *against* than *with* is to obscure the ways that elegists negotiated the aesthetic, ethical, historical, personal, and political pressures they faced. Likewise, to describe a dissenting elegy as an anti-elegy is to offer a blunt and misleading interpretation of that poem's role within its genre and the genre itself, particularly when attempting to account for the complicated, contradictory, and nuanced ways that Americans responded through verse to Civil War death. Indeed, my aim in this chapter is in part to bring recuperative motivations to unexceptional objects. Yet by *recuperative* I mean more than recirculating unstudied texts. The term also stands as a mark of value and, hence, a justification for applying close reading methods, in the sense that *close reading* identifies both a critical practice and a form of attention, care, and consideration. Giving even highly conventional nineteenth-century verse such attention reveals the complex political and emotional work performed within individual elegies. Simultaneously, precisely because of these elegies' conventionality, close reading reveals the multilayered work of genre within the history of Civil War loss.

## Nationalist Mourning and the Disciplining of Grief

In July 1866, the *Atlantic Monthly* published William Cullen Bryant's "The Death of Slavery." An apostrophe to slavery's still-fresh corpse, the poem condemns white Southern preachers ("meaner cowards, mingling with thy train, | Proved, from the book of God, thy right to reign"), white Southern rapists ("Thy inner lair became | The haunt of guilty shame"), and, of course, slaveholders and overseers ("Thy lash dropped blood; the murderer, at thy side, | Showed his red hands, nor feared the vengeance due"). In its final stanza, the poem claims that a robust historical memory of slavery should be the overriding legacy of the Civil War and demands ongoing witness to slavery's institutional and material remains ("The graves of those whom thou hast murdered," "The slave-pen," "the grim block"): "There, 'mid the symbols that proclaim thy crimes, | Dwell thou, a warning to the coming times."[29] As an early poem in the contestation over Civil War memory, "The Death of Slavery" speaks directly to its elegiac counterparts, proposing a vision of the war that competes with those that would neglect emancipation and normalize, minimize, or willfully forget the realities of slavery. The war, it declares, should be remembered first and foremost as the violent eradiation of a treacherous evil, a just redistribution of power from former slaveholders to those they enslaved, and a righteous punishment of white Southern sin. It should be held up as the victory of good over evil, and the antebellum white South should be cast through the ages as a warning against tyranny and cruelty.

Just fourteen months later, the same magazine published Francis Miles Finch's "The Blue and the Gray," a harshly, even perversely different account of the Civil War: one that called for forgiveness toward the white South and envisioned white sectional union as the war's foremost legacy. As the century progressed, Bryant's "The Death of Slavery" lingered quietly in the background of Civil War memory, appearing in collections of his poetry and anthologies such as Henry A. Ford's *Poems of History by the Most Famous Poets of All Ages* (1883). Finch's vision, on the other hand, quickly rose to fame and ubiquity, frequently cited at Decoration Day ceremonies and Blue–Gray reunions, recurring on lists of poems for elementary students to memorize, providing the title for multiple anthologies of Civil War poetry, and retaining influence even into the late twentieth and early twenty-first centuries, when it lent its title to a 1982 CBS miniseries, a 1996 illustrated children's book about white kids and black kids befriending each other, and a 2007 Wargame of the Year award winner jointly released by AGEOD and Matrix Games.

"The Blue and the Gray" in this way became a model for Civil War elegies, exerting normative pressure on poets and mourners to repurpose the dead for nationalist and reconciliationist ends. Because of this significance, I cite it here in its entirety, including the originally published epigraph:

The women of Columbus, Mississippi, animated by nobler sentiments than are many of their sisters, have shown themselves impartial in their offerings made to the memory of the dead. They strewed flowers alike on the graves of the Confederate and of the National soldiers.—*New York Tribune*

> By the flow of the inland river,
>   Whence the fleets of iron have fled,
> Where the blades of the grave-grass quiver,
>   Asleep are the ranks of the dead:
>     Under the sod and the dew,
>       Waiting the judgment day;
>     Under the one, the Blue,
>       Under the other, the Gray.
>
> These in the robings of glory,
>   Those in the gloom of defeat,
> All with the battle-blood gory,

In the dusk of eternity meet:
  Under the sod and the dew,
    Waiting the judgment day;
  Under the laurel, the Blue,
    Under the willow, the Gray.

From the silence of sorrowful hours
  The desolate mourners go,
Lovingly laden with flowers
  Alike for the friend and the foe:
  Under the sod and the dew,
    Waiting the judgment day;
  Under the roses, the Blue,
    Under the lilies, the Gray.

So with an equal splendor,
  The morning sun-rays fall,
With a touch impartially tender,
  On the blossoms blooming for all:
  Under the sod and the dew,
    Waiting the judgment day;
  Broidered with gold, the Blue,
    Mellowed with gold, the Gray.

So, when the summer calleth,
  On forest and field of grain,
With an equal murmur falleth
  The cooling drip of the rain:
  Under the sod and the dew,
    Waiting the judgment day;
  Wet with the rain, the Blue,
    Wet with the rain, the Gray.

Sadly, but not with upbraiding,
  The generous deed was done,
In the storm of the years that are fading
  No braver battle was won:
  Under the sod and the dew,
    Waiting the judgment day;
  Under the blossoms, the Blue,
    Under the garlands, the Gray.

No more shall the war cry sever,
  Or the winding rivers be red;
They banish our anger forever
  When they laurel the graves of our dead!
  Under the sod and the dew,
    Waiting the judgment day;
  Love and tears for the Blue,
    Tears and love for the Gray.[30]

The elements of the elegy collaborate with astonishing efficiency. From the epigraph's aspirational injunction toward the "nobler sentiments" of reconciliation; to the second stanza's indeterminate pronouns suspending the sectional identity of both the victorious and the defeated; to the pastoral and transcendent natural imagery harnessing the fantasy of a shared white agrarian past; to the progressively increasing indentation within each stanza leaning hopefully into the white future; to the ababcdcd rhyme scheme and perfectly regular iambs underscoring the rightness of unity; to the final couplet's chiasmic encircling of Blue and Gray into mutual embrace—through all of these the poem works to "banish" anger and memory in the service of a unified national future, rendering failure to do so a crime of spite and debased feeling. Moreover, each stanza's repetition of two lines drawing attention to the dead as both corpse and soul ("Under the sod and the dew, | Waiting the judgment day") shifts the burden of memory and accounting from humanity to God and suggests that a judgment day might also await those who fall short of the mercy inherent within reconciliation's "nobler sentiments." Finally, by taking white Southern acts of benevolence as its occasion, the poem hones its disciplinary attention primarily on Northern whites, like Bryant, inclined to hold the white South accountable for their slaveholding sins. This reconciliationist vision set out to make commonplace its own model for mourning the Civil War's dead, ultimately eclipsing the emancipationist sentiments in "The Death of Slavery" to the point, in 1890, that a black newspaper, *The Christian Recorder,* could refer to Finch's poem as a barrier to black well-being and interracial activism: "We do not forget that even in the North much greater consideration is shown the white man who attempted the dissolution of this government than to the black man who served it. The poetry of 'Blue and the Gray' is much more acceptable than the song of the black and the white."[31] Indeed, Finch's elegy depicts a frame for Civil War loss that became particularly desirable during the 1880s and 1890s, showing up, for instance, in almost all of the elegies published by *Century* magazine as part of its incredibly popular Civil War series, including "Between the Lines" (1887), "Over their Graves" (1889), "Thoughts on the Late War" (1890), and "The March of the Dead Brigade" (1898).

Yet even before the war's official end, the reconciliationist and nationalist weight of Finch's elegy had already started accumulating widespread influence. *Harper's New Monthly Magazine,* for instanced, featured Julia R. Dorr's "The Drummer-Boy's Burial," on its cover during the particularly deadly summer of 1864, underneath an illustration of the poem's depicted scene (Figure 1). Describing the ghastly aftermath of a deadly Civil War battle whose victor, as in "The Blue and the Gray," remains unspecified, the poem describes two white sisters "crushing back the pitying tears, | For they had no time for weeping, nor for any girlish fears." They encounter the corpse of the eponymous white Northern drummer boy—"a smile of wondrous sweetness lent a radiance to the face"—which they then proceed to robe and bury. Not until the poem's final couplet do we learn what the poem and geography have led us to expect all along: "And then the little maidens—they

FIGURE 1. *"The Drummer-Boy's Burial,"* Harper's New Monthly Magazine *(July 1864)*

were children of our foes— | Laid the body of our Drummer-Boy to undisturbed repose." Even as the wartime authorship and publication of the poem retain resonance through its first-person plural reference to the North, the poem itself already begins the work of depicting intra-white North–South kindnesses and compassions as among the noblest of Civil War era sentiments, a depiction the poem's illustration reinforces through the first Southern girl's sisterly embrace of the Northern boy's corpse, the similarity in her and his expressions, and the inclining, open posture of the second Southern girl. While the poem's sentiment in part captures Christian forgiveness—turning the other cheek—by underscoring the girls' "saintly hearts" and feelings "that Death was holy and it sanctified the deed" of burial, the poem also repurposes individual "holy work" and piety for a much larger scale, calling upon the sisters as models for a white national future and, hence, casting alternative sentiments as profane and dishonorable.[32]

Walt Whitman's "Reconciliation" makes even more explicit the racial stakes of this attitude toward the Civil War dead. A tribute to the capacity for death to ease internecine passions, Whitman first published the elegy as the penultimate poem in 1865's "Sequel to Drum-Taps." Later, when he revised his Civil War poetry for inclusion into the 1871 and 1881 editions of *Leaves of Grass*, the elegy shifted from the "Sequel" to the final third of the sequence, enabling the poems as a whole to tell a story of war that culminates in the overwhelming desire for peace and national unity:

> Word over all, beautiful as the sky,
> Beautiful that war and all its deeds of carnage must in time be utterly lost,
> That the hands of the sisters Death and Night incessantly softly wash again,
>     and ever again, this soil'd world;
> For my enemy is dead, a man divine as myself is dead,
> I look where he lies white-faced and still in the coffin—I draw near.
> Bend down and touch lightly with my lips the white face in the coffin.[33]

The poem finds comfort in the redeeming quality of beauty, here made transcendent through its association with the Word of God. It paints an almost infinitely transportable scene that could depict any pair of fallen and surviving soldiers—or, if we take this speaker to be a stand-in for Whitman, for any fallen soldier and any caretaking nurse. And it looks toward a future in which the shared experience of death cleanses and rebirths the white nation into a newly reconciled whole. Unlike many of its genre cohorts, "Reconciliation" makes the whiteness of its nationalism explicit. Lest we mistake its first reference to the white face as a sign of the dead's wan appearance rather than racial membership, the final line's repetition of "white face" leaves the matter decided, underscoring whiteness as an invitation for the survivor's kiss, an opening to intimacy between former enemies and across the mortal divide.

The poem, in its exceptional explicitness about its genre's unexceptional conventions, thus operates as a meta-commentary on the racial investments of the Civil War elegy more broadly. It suggests, as with the campus novels' dead-student plot lines, that white belonging nurtures its affective appeal in part through shared nostalgic relationship between the living and the abstracted, ahistorical dead. Indeed, before writing "The Blue and the Gray," Finch's fame had rested, as the *Indianapolis Sentinel* notes in its June 1, 1875 celebration of the poem, on his campus lyrics: "Some of his college rhymes, and especially one of his smoking songs, are great favorites throughout the country, and his poem on the chime and bells of Cornell University is the pet lyric of that institution." Like the reconciliationist fantasy of the campus, elegies like "The Blue and the Gray," "The Drummer-Boy's Burial," and "Reconciliation" called upon white men and women to overcome their grudges and embrace in fraternal union. So doing, they exerted a disciplinary pressure on opposing visions of the Civil War, such as Bryant's, stripping them of their political edge by rendering them ignoble and even petty.

Despite these pressures, many other Civil War elegies did dissent from their nationalist counterparts, expressing a set of alternative commitments to the dead and to the remembrance of the Civil War and revealing contested feelings about the shape and demands of national belonging. Yet, significantly, these alternatives were frequently not seen as oppositional or incommensurable. They more frequently coexisted more or less amicably within a network of nationalist sentiment, adding texture and complexity to white feelings about the Civil War dead, Civil War memory, and national belonging. Recall, for instance, the close proximity of "The Death of Slavery" and "The Blue and the Gray," appearing just over a year apart in the same publication. Or consider that Bryant himself included both "The Blue and the Gray" and "The Drummer Boy's Burial," two poems that seemingly repudiate his own vision of Civil War memory, in the second edition of his bestselling *The Family Library of Poetry and Song* (1878), a compilation he introduces by telling readers that "the words should be dwelt upon until they become in a certain sense our own, and are adopted as the utterance of our own minds."[34] Or consider editor Robert Haven Schauffler's decision to include "The Death of Slavery" in his *Memorial Day* anthology, whose subtitle promised a selection that would remain "non-sectional" and whose introduction praised North–South reunion as a symbol of "the sublime side of the Anglo-Saxon nature."[35] Or consider that Whitman's "Drum-Taps" sequences include not only "Reconciliation," but also poems like "The Artilleryman's Vision," which articulate trauma's repetitive reiteration of battle violence, gore, and death—a vivid reminder that forget and forgive names a set of frequently impossible demands. I want to suggest, therefore, that the two alternative attitudes toward Civil War death and memory that I turn to now play a role of dissenting companionship to their dominant, white nationalist counterpart. I begin with the starkly dissonant antiwar attitude before then shifting to the melancholic attitude that most frequently presented itself as a counterpart to nationalist elegies.

## Antiwar Mourning and Ugly Feeling

Civil War elegies that take a delegitimizing approach to the war refuse to think of violence as redemptive, describing it instead as a violation of nobility, heroism, patriotism, and legitimacy—precisely those things war proposes to couple with violence. They foreground the machinery of the state and undermine the affinities of the nation, breaking with sectional reconciliation's impulse toward white national belonging. In their lines, even the dying and the injured find their suffering irredeemable. Antiwar war elegies therefore operate primarily through irony, wedging themselves into the distance between how war is supposed to feel or what war is supposed to accomplish and the actual experience of those it forces to die and to kill.

Perhaps the sharpest and most cutting example, the anonymously published "The Song of the Drum," appeared in *Harper's Weekly* in November 1864, the same month as Sherman's March to the Sea. Over the course of six stanzas, the poem uses the forward momentum of repetition, iambic meter, rhyming couplets, and enthusiastic punctuation to drive the reader inexorably from the rallying call of men's ostensibly heroic enlistment to the irredeemable senselessness of their destruction. Here, to give a sense of this movement, I cite the opening and closing stanzas:

> Rataplan! rataplan! rataplan!
> Follow me! follow me! every true man!
> Hark to the sound of the rolling drum,
> Come with me! come with me! come with me, come
> Follow me! follow me! follow me, now!
> Come from the anvil, come from the plow;
> Don't think of the danger, which threatens your lives;
> Leave home, leave friends, leave your children, your wives
> Hark to the sound of the rolling drum,
> Come with me! come with me! come with me, come!
> Follow me! follow me! every one!
> To where the white camps shine in the sun!
> …
> Rataplan! rataplan! rataplan!
> Follow me, follow me, every true man!
> Follow me on through the fiery breath
> Of the vengeful cannon, scattering death;
> On through the battle's smoke and glare,
> Follow me, follow me everywhere!
> And hear the cries and the awful groans,
> The piercing shrieks and the feeble moans,
> And the ringing shout which goes up to the sun
> When a work is stormed, and a victory won;
> Rataplan! rataplan! rataplan!
> This is the death for every true man![36]

The opening stanza already suggests that its drumbeats toward war are not to be trusted, turning more sincere rallying sentiments, such as those found in William Ross Wallace's 1861 "A Psalm of the Union," into the Siren calls of an anxious and frustrated state. The repetition of demands accumulates a desperate edge, as though the state-speaker grinds out its line ending orders, "come" and "now!", through gritted teeth. The opening thus works to make visible the cynicism of the state, which calls for enlistment without thought, mocks the manhood of those who don't jump to its call, numbs soldiers into action through the trappings of patriotism, and attempts to turn certain death into the promise of heavenly reward "where white camps shine in the sun." The poem therefore highlights soldiers' willingness to be duped and turns fame and country into agents of deception.[37] By its final stanza, the poem has shifted from rallying call to elegy, and it works to reveal the indifference felt by its state-speaker towards the deaths of its intended audience, an indifference it takes to its bloody end in "piercing shrieks" and "feeble moans." Yet by coupling the state with the "me" of the personalized lyric self, the poem also draws attention to the wartime state as an agent with duplicitous desires and motives, making visible the nihilistic and amoral carelessness with which it makes machines of men and puts life to use. This is where the poem's irony comes into starkest relief, where it exposes the distance between the perspective of the state ("a victory won") and the perspective of the soldiers it has called to serve ("death for every true man"). Hence the cruel impossibility of the line—"Follow me, follow me every where!"—for the speaker, the state, like the Fox and the Cat in *The Adventures of Pinocchio*, has from the very beginning been leading its audience toward a fate that only it will survive.

Appearing in 1893, amidst a host of patriotic elegies within *Century Magazine's* Civil War series, S. R. Elliott's "With the Tread of Marching Columns" marks a rare antiwar elegy from the late nineteenth century. Likely depicting Sherman's strategy of "total war," the poem describes a mechanic series of "marching columns" that moves ceaselessly forward and then catalogs the wave of destruction toward which those columns remain wholly indifferent. The first stanza describes the reactions felt and experienced in the material and natural world—the stirred forests and hills, the dust that blurs fields, the shivering waters, the shuddering bridges—and the second describes the columns' effects on human life:

> With the thunder of cannon and shouting the valleys are flooded with sound,
> Till the church-bells are silent with terror, the peals of the organ are drowned:
> Hushed is the life of the village, stricken and palsied with dread;
> Closed are the shutters and doors—the village has closed its eyes,
> Like the helpless quarry when sudden and pitiless foes surprise!
> There is none to be seen, there is none to be heard—there is death, while the feet
> Of marching columns resound through the emptied and desolate street.[38]

Moving quickly from the thunder of battle to the silence of its aftermath, the poem depicts a mindless force that strips its victims of their senses, leaving nothing save death. Yet unlike "The Song of the Drum," it doesn't replicate that quick relentlessness in its form. Instead, through frequent use of feminine caesurae it at once retains the iambic meter we'd expect in a poem about marching and, strikingly, breaks its steady drumbeat. In the space of these pauses, it undermines the representation of violence as heroism so frequently found in *Century's* famous series, insisting upon consideration of exactly those effects of war that the marching columns ignore. The elegy doesn't spare its dead either. "There is none to be seen, there is none to be heard—there is death," its speaker tells us, describing the material destruction brought about in total war while also negating the useful narratives that either the survivors or the poem's 1893 readers might attach to the dead. There is no heroism; there is no nobility; there is no mutual sacrifice: "there is death."

Thomas Bailey Aldrich's sonnet "Fredericksburg," frequently anthologized from the 1880s through the turn-of-the century, describes one of the Union's most lopsided defeats in terms that likewise strip even the possibility for ennobling sentiments:

> The increasing moonlight drifts across my bed,
> And on the churchyard by the road, I know
> It falls as white and noiselessly as snow.
> 'Twas such a night two weary summers fled;
> The stars, as now, were waning overhead.
> Listen! again the shrill-lipped bugles blow
> Where the swift currents of the river flow
> Past Fredericksburg: far off the heavens are red
> With sudden conflagration: on yon height,
> Linstock in hand, the gunners hold their breath:
> A signal-rocket pierces the dense night,
> Flings its spent stars upon the town beneath:
> Hark!—the artillery massing on the right,
> Hark!—the black squadrons wheeling down to Death![39]

While the "shrill-lipped bugles" interrupt the "weary" and "waning" qualities of the natural world, they announce no heroism. Instead, the poem's initial set of human agents sit in passive anticipation—"the gunners hold their breath"—as the nonhuman forces of war, the "signal rocket" and "the artillery", fling themselves into violence. When, in its final line, the poem then presents its second set of human agents, "the black squadrons wheeling down to Death," it renders them ambiguously alive or dead, either the shadowed figures of soldiers running to their deaths or the shadowed figures of ghosts circling to their uncertain afterlives. Moreover, the verb "wheeling," instead of *running* or *marching*, firmly links the men to machines, creating an image either of men pulling a cannon, "[l]instock in hand," or men who have become more machine than human. The ambiguity makes its own ethical claims, as though to suggest that war undoes the distinctions between life and death, human and machine. Soldiers, in this vision of battle, wait passively to be taken over and controlled either by the violent machinations of the state or the totality of death or, more likely, both. Indeed, so stark and potentially off-putting was this vision of the Civil War that one editor of an explicitly patriotic anthology, *Our Country in Poems and Prose* (1899), felt compelled to add a Thomas Moore epigraph lacking in all other versions of the poem: "On, on to the combat, the heroes that bleed | For virtue and mankind are heroes indeed!"[40] The epigraph, however, primarily underscores the attitude toward war that Aldrich's elegy at first refuses to express and then represents as impossible and dishonest.

The mourning these elegies depict proposes to their readers a much more negative or even, in Sianne Ngai's useful term, *ugly* structure of feeling than we customarily associate with bereavement. Such mourning cannot fit within the nineteenth century's transformation of grief into something to cherish, as what Dana Luciano terms "the body's spontaneous and natural testimony to the importance of interpersonal attachment"; nor can we recuperate it within more recent efforts to cast mourning or melancholia as a source for alternative histories, producing what David L. Eng and David Kazanjian call "sites...for the rewriting of the past as well as the reimagining of the future."[41] Rather, antiwar Civil War elegies describe and enact an overwhelming docility that extends from the help-lessness of the soldiers who kill and who die in "The Song of the Drum" to the helplessness of the civilians who find themselves and their possessions trampled in "With the Tread of Marching Columns" to the helplessness of the soldiers who become first machines and then wraiths in "Fredericksburg." As Ngai argues, such an overwhelming experience of passivity when facing the unstoppable movement of the state and history remains "uniquely disclosed and interpreted by ignoble feelings," and the feelings produced and described in these poems—exhaustion, despair, and boredom in the face of a horror that has become at once relentless and mundane—disclose grief as the unremarkable effect of profound insecurity and helplessness.[42] Yet antiwar needn't also stand in for other forms of dissent from dominant social patterns. White nationalism and sectional reconciliation required Northern whites' inaction even more than their action, their passive consent more than their energetic selection. Thus while antiwar Civil War elegies enabled whites to channel their feelings of insignificance in the face of history, they did nothing to dislodge or undo the new structures of white supremacy to emerge following the so-called death of slavery. Feelings of aversion toward the war and expressions of antiwar hostility to the North's military victory over the South rested easily along-side reconciliationist sentiments binding white Northerners with their former enemies alongside an accompanying resurgence of antiblackness or, at the very least, alongside an apathy to the war's emancipationist prospects for the formerly enslaved.

## Melancholic Mourning and Disaffiliation

There is a good deal of crossover between antiwar and melancholic elegies, includ-ing the fact that some writers like Aldrich wrote both varieties, and the distinction I'm drawing is therefore more analytical than taxonomic. Yet, loosely, antiwar ele-gies focus on the experiences of those fighting and dying in the war, and melan-cholic elegies focus on the aftermath of those deaths, frequently capturing the grief of those left behind to mourn their losses. Most fundamentally, melancholic Civil War elegies remove mourning from its teleological momentum through grief toward consolation. So doing, they create openings within aggregate modes of white belonging—openings for dissent from national memory, national belong-ing, and the national insistence upon generalizing wartime loss.

Melancholia, as Freud describes it, names a process of irresolvable and there-fore ceaseless mourning; it occurs when a grieving subject internalizes the lost object, psychically protecting it from the evidence of its absence, evidence that would otherwise enable the mourner to re-enter so-called regular life.[43] By incorporating the dead into the grieving psyche, melancholia protects Civil War loss from abstractions of memorial and monument, and it safeguards recent history from the pressures of un-remembering and revision. This is not to say that it denies consolation altogether. Melancholia offers readers comfort in the space of refusal. By depicting sentiments found in nationalist war elegies as fraudulent, impossible, counterfeit, or obscenely obtuse, melancholic elegies provide a home for grief that misaligns with the available scripts; or, perhaps more accurately, they provide a mirror of recognition for that grief's necessary homelessness. In one sense, we might therefore see these poems as attempts to linger indefinitely in the pleasures of mourning, affirmations of stasis. Yet melancholic elegies simultaneously provide their readers with alternatives to treating the dead as a bland historical resource for white nationalist futurity, suggesting new ways to narrate, understand, and feel their grief. In so doing, they reveal a range of white affective responses to the Civil War dead that fit at best uneasily within the nation-state's model for itself.

Melancholic elegies operate primarily by deploying the conventions of their nationalist counterparts only to dispense with them as inadequate to the reality of the Civil War's death or the experience of mourning its losses. They engage in a self-consciously intrageneric conversation about the meaning of Civil War memory and the shape of national belonging. We see this perhaps in no place more clearly than in another one of Thomas Bailey Aldrich's sonnets, alternately titled "Accomplices" and "By the Potomac," which takes up the common trope that turns natural beauty covering graves into an image of hope and redemption. The Petrarchan sonnet's opening octave presents its readers with the expected scene:

> The soft new grass is creeping o'er the graves
> By the Potomac; and the crisp ground-flower
> Lifts its blue cup to catch the passing shower;
> The pine-cone ripens, and the long moss waves
> Its tangled gonfalons above our braves.
> Hark, what a burst of music from yon bower!—
> The Southern nightingale that, hour by hour,
> In its melodious summer madness raves.

The natural world here signals tranquility for the dead and lends comfort to the living while transcending the conflicts and violence of war. Yet even amidst this scene of tranquility, the sonnet begins to anticipate its coming turn, with the "tangled gonfalons" suggesting the proximity of violence and the nightingale's raving madness cutting through the ostensibly peaceful scene. The concluding sestet then recasts that same imagery as an accomplice to murder that would hide the Confederacy's "awful Crime" and the horror of the South's devastating rebellion:

> Ah, with what delicate touches of her hand,
> With what sweet voices, Nature seeks to screen

> The awful Crime of this distracted land,—
> Sets her birds singing, while she spreads her green
> Mantle of velvet where the Murdered lie,
> As if to hide the horror from God's eye.[44]

First appearing in *The Atlantic Monthly* in 1865, two years before "The Blue and the Gray," the poem speaks proleptically to the latter poem's use of nature as a "screen" and provides a justification for Reconstruction that the latter poem seeks to undo. Subsequently republished in 1874 by the *Atlantic* in a survey of Aldrich's work as "perhaps one of the few good poems which our late war produced," by *Century* in 1891, and in numerous anthologies such as Francis Fisher Browne's *Bugle Echoes* (1886) and A. Dallas William's *The Praise of Lincoln* (1911), the poem then returns to look back and, as it were, call foul on its better-known counterpart.[45] Yet its target is not merely the reconciliationist impulse to forgive and forget. Just as vehemently, it targets the familiar expressions and images used to assuage grief. Turning "Nature" into a false screen, it gestures at a thin fraudulence it sees in the conventions of nineteenth-century bereavement culture, and it hints at a form of mourning mixed with resentment that, it insists, constitutes a deeper, more heartfelt and realized emotional response to the war—a form of mourning that acquires its ethics precisely through stubborn duration and the refusal to abate.

In this way, melancholic Civil War elegies represent their grief as the authentic alternative to nationalist elegies' misrepresentations. Take, as another instance, F. A. Moore's "In the Hospital," published by *Peterson's Magazine* in February 1863. The poem features a dying soldier who is at once the lost object that the poem invites us to mourn and the mourning subject grieving the future he will not obtain. The soldier's grief takes the form of a dream that begins in childhood, then shifts into the future when he envisions himself putting to bed the child he will never have. The dream thereby idealizes the soldier and sentimentalizes his future even as it offers readers a scene of repose amidst violence. While other poems capturing soldiers' dreams—including "The Soldier's Wayside Dream" (*Godey's Lady's Book*, 1863) and "A Soldier's Dream" (*Harper's Weekly*, 1865)—represent soldiers' restful sleep disrupted by a call to battle resulting in their heroic demise, "In the Hospital" denies its soldier such a good death. It instead again and again demands that the soldier and the reader snap back into the tedious monotony surrounding his dying—the "warlike sound," the "groans and raving words," the "sting in his bandaged wound," and, in the poem's closing line, the "glare of the hospital walls." The soldier finds his desire to return to the dream, where he might die undisturbed, stymied: he "again would woo | The visions of love and home; | And drink, though only in fancied joy, | The waterfall's cooling foam."[46] While we can quickly see how the poem, like Emily Dickinson's buzzing fly, takes aim at mid- to late-nineteenth-century attempts to romanticize the dying breath and familiarize the afterlife, a second look also reveals it to take aim at the consolation of the living that "would woo" a whitewashed vision of their dead, minimize his (and, consequently, their) suffering, seek reprieve for their grief, and rapidly forget the material agony of the hospital scene. Refusing such consolation, the poem lyrically encases its dying soldier in this glaring space of the hospital walls, resituating the dead and, hence, Civil War memory aslant the nationalist urge to disembody and transfer the soldier into an anodyne mass of shared experience. Its task is to insist upon the phenomenological specificity of the dead soldier and the irredeemable particularity of his scene of dying, denying any allegorical national imagination from making use of him and, in so doing, freeing the survivors to grieve their loss apart from available scripts, assigned destinations, or, indeed, any destination at all.

In this refusal to provide reprieve from wartime horrors, "In the Hospital" recalls those few elegies published in remembrance of soldiers who died gruesome and bureaucratic deaths as prisoners of war rather than ostensibly heroic deaths on the battlefield. "Our Dead at Andersonville," published by *Harper's Weekly* in 1865, for instance, directs readers' attentions toward those who died of malnutrition, dysentery, and diarrhea in what was perhaps the war's most notorious prison. I cite here the first six of eight stanzas:

> Not in the fierce and frenzied shock of war,
>   Amid the raging battle's heated breath,
> And clash of arms, and deafening roar of guns,
>   Met they the Angel, Death.
>
> But in foul prison-pens, with stealthy tread,
>   He came, and took them slowly, one by one;
> And they that lingered saw their comrades' eyes
>   Close sadly on the sun—
>
> Saw their pale eyelids close, and felt the hour
>   Draw nearer to themselves, till Death became
> As one of them, and with each suffering day
>   Familiar grew his name.
>
> Sometimes the sentry's gun, with sharp report,
>   Would send some poor soul on his heavenward flight,
> Who, weary of his prison's gloom, stepp'd forth
>   Boldly into the light!
>
> Great God, within that book Thy Angel keeps
>   Are such things written—such unhallowed deeds?
> O blot them from our memories, and heal
>   Each sorrowing heart that bleeds!
>
> Our land is one vast sepulchre—see rise
>   The swelling mounds; the dust which in them lies
> Is the rich price which cherished Freedom claims,
>   Our Nation's sacrifice.[47]

The poem stresses the bureaucratic banality of state violence, manifested in a scene of disease, overcrowding, and putridity, where even suicide by prison guard becomes routine.[48] When it finally does attempt, in its fifth and sixth stanzas, a more generically typical call for healing ("heal | Each sorrowing heart that bleeds"), it does so by insisting on exactly that which its entire purpose it has been to refuse: blotting unhallowed deeds from Civil War memory. The sixth stanza therefore falters in the poem's refusal to meet its own precondition, its paradoxical insistence that readers forget the dead even as they witness that the land has become "one vast sepulchre," so that each of the three terms in its concluding phrase—"Our," "Nation's," and "sacrifice"—become open questions rather than reliable footholds.

Melancholic Civil War elegies hold close to their dead and even closer to their grief. They make an effort, always incomplete, to close off the circuit between the dead and the loved ones who mourn, to preclude substitution, to shut down appropriation. Another strategy for this involved simply naming the dead. Although I don't want to overstate its effectiveness (named dead, of course, can also enter into chains of substitution), doing so does stand in stark contrast to most Civil War elegies, which tend to depict the dead and their surviving loved ones in wholly depersonalized terms. We need look only at a handful of titles: "The Soldier's Wayside Dream" (*Godey's Lady's Book*, 1863), "The Soldier's Mother" (*Peterson's* 1863), "The Nation's Dead" (*Peterson's*, 1864), "The Fallen" (*Century*, 1890), or Walt Whitman's "Adieu to a Soldier" (1871). So when an elegy provides its dead with a name and a distinct identity, it stands out. This is precisely the point of Nathaniel Graham Shepherd's "Roll Call," published December 1862 in *Harper's New Monthly Magazine*, and then reprinted in at least nineteen different anthologies through the early twentieth century. The poem sets its eponymous event on a "crimson-dyed" field shortly after a particularly deadly battle: "'Twas a victory—yes; but it cost us dear; | For that company's roll, when it called at night, | Of a hundred men who went into the fight, | Numbered but twenty that answered, '*Here!*'"[49] By then specifying three names of those present (Corporal Green, Herbert Cline, Ezra Kerr) and three of those recently dead (Cyrus Drew, Hiram Kerr, Ephraim Deane), the poem refuses to aggregate the soldiers, dead or alive, instead holding onto the specificity of each death even in the face of mass carnage.

Even more explicitly and effectively, Mary H. C. Booth's "While God He Leaves Me Reason, God He Will Leave Me Jim"—published in the oft-reprinted 1865 anthology, *The Civil War in Song and Story*, and Frank Moore's 1866 *Anecdotes, Poetry, and Incidents of the War: North and South*—guards its singular, named dead soldier from patriotic use. The poem's speaker is a mother, all of whose sons but one have been killed, who has just discovered the death of her last remaining child, Jim. In its final stanza, the poem contrasts the singularity of "Jim" with the war's seemingly endless appetite for bodies: "'Hush, there is Uncle Abraham a-knocking at the door; | He calls for other mothers' sons, '*Three hundred thousand more!*' / Be still, Old Uncle Abraham; 'twill do no good to call; / You think my house is full of boys; ah, Jimmy was my all.'"[50] While the common name, Jim, allows this particular dead to function as a stand-in for other readers' grief, the poem works to pull the one out from the "three hundred thousand." So doing, the final stanza speaks to the limited number of soldiers "Old Uncle Abraham" might call into battle and to the ways Lincoln might put the dead to use. Given the metonymy between president and nation, its command, "Be still," operates in a quiet, minor tone as a plea for the dead and those mourning the dead to be left alone, as if to say, "you've taken all my children from me; don't now also take my grief." Booth and Shepherd insist upon the dead as individuals with histories and specificity, individuals who were known and loved. Against a poem like Maud Mornington's 1864 "The Nation's Dead," with its commentary that "A nation weepeth for the slain | All hearts are torn with mighty pain," Shepherd and Booth insulate their dead, wrapping them in the named specificity of personal history and sheltering their loss in the grieving memory of those who knew and loved them during life.[51]

Melancholic elegies specify their lost objects and grieving survivors while belittling the sham tropes found in so many of their peers, disclosing variation and detail within the incorporated "we" proposed in nationalism's elegiac imagination. Yet the grief they express is never completely private or antisocial. Like antiwar elegies, melancholic Civil War elegies suggest another kind of "we," a disaffiliated and minor assemblage of mourners who positioned themselves at least in part against the national community. As I turn to now, such self-fashioning must be understood from within both the generic conventions of the Civil War elegy and the generic conventions of white nationalism.

## Conclusion: Incorporating Dissent

Civil War elegies depict moments of vulnerability in the face of death and in the sometimes-excruciating survival of loss, and, as this chapter has aimed to show, they frequently refuse to sanitize their grief into all-purpose, standardized forms. Yet even in their dissenting varieties, elegies mourning the white Civil War dead affirmed their white readers' sense of belonging to the nation. While the privileges of such abstracted citizenship are in part, as Russ Castronovo argues, made possible through the hyperembodiment of nonwhite others, Civil War elegies additionally suggest white citizenship remains shot through with the memories, pains, and ghosts of the white dead.[52] Their loss produces an affective richness that invests the otherwise abstract and thin attachments of such large-scale belonging with a charged depth of feeling.

Simultaneously, dissenting from the dominant mode of response enabled whites to stand apart in a way that perhaps paradoxically affirmed racial and national belonging. As Judith Butler puts it, in her work on the collectivities made possible through loss, grief "furnishes a sense of political community of a complex order"; so tightly wound is this scene of belonging to each other, that "the 'we' is traversed by a relationality that we cannot easily argue against."[53] The coexistence of nationalist, antiwar, and melancholic elegies adds fluidity and depth to this community, giving that "we" a wider array of affective resources for group belonging and individual identification.

We can see this succinctly in Herman Melville's 1862 "Shiloh," a poem that combines nationalist, antiwar, and melancholic attitudes into a single compact form, propagating white nationalism's attempts to make stranger affinity appealing while also questioning and challenging its attempts to put violence to good use:

> Skimming lightly, wheeling still,
>     The swallows fly low
> Over the field in clouded days,
>     The forest-field of Shiloh—
> Over the field where April rain
> Solaced the parched ones stretched in pain
> Through the pause of night
> That followed the Sunday fight
>     Around the church of Shiloh—
> The church so lone, the log-built one,
> That echoed to many a parting groan
>         And natural prayer
> Of dying foemen mingled there—
> Foemen at morn, but friends at eve—
>     Fame or country least their care:
> (What like a bullet can undeceive!)
>     But now they lie low,
> While over them the swallows skim,
>     And all is hushed at Shiloh.[54]

Michael Warner and Randall Fuller have argued that Melville uses "Shiloh" to issue what at the time amounted to an iconoclastic warning against the evil made possible through belief in divinely sanctioned violence. Focusing primarily on Melville's startling and potent parenthetical—"(What like a bullet can undeceive?)"— Warner writes: "In the poem's scene of injury, abandonment, and impending mortality, he subsumes legitimate state violence under the more general heading of violence as a suspect category, an intrinsic evil."[55] Yet even as Melville's elegy undercuts the legitimacy of the state's power over life and death, it also bolsters the fictive kinship of the nation, previewing an emergent reconciliationist narrative about Civil War bereavement that "The Blue and the Gray" will later popularize: the story of how thousands of dying soldiers are "Foemen at morn, but friends at eve | Fame or country least their care." Melville's use of the word "friends" to describe the relationship sutures the poem to an Aristotelian and racial politics of friendship like that we find in the *Ladies' Home Journal*, in which the citizenry includes those whose gendered and racial similarities make them eligible for friendship and excludes those with whom friendship would be impossible. If we think about "Shiloh" as a poem directed as much toward the national future as it is toward the wartime past (a line of thought encouraged explicitly in the reconciliationist vision of Melville's "Supplement" to *Battle-Pieces*), then "Foemen at morn, but friends at eve" prescribes a model for national reunion based on the political friendship among whites across intraracial differences. Fame and country may be least the care of dying soldiers, but that needn't prevent their deaths from recirculation as an affective resource for white nationalist belonging. Ironically, then, while the poem undercuts the legitimacy of state violence against white soldiers, it contributes to a reconciliationist outcome of the war that will, particularly after the end of Reconstruction, justify and transpire specifically through state and paramilitary violence against black lives. It incorporates dissent from the use to which nationalism puts death and violence even as it affirms white nationalism's monopoly on violence against racialized others cast as internal enemies.

We might say, then, that the white nationalist Civil War elegy willingly and even eagerly made room for its antiwar and melancholic others as coexisting, complex, and paradoxical structures of feeling that emerge in the wake of unparalleled personal and national loss. In this sense, antiwar elegies affirm the priority of precisely that abstracted belonging, even if doing so requires temporary resistance to the state, and melancholic elegies affirm the crisscrossing complexities capable of being held simultaneously, traversing the relationality holding the white nation together. As Eva Cherniavsky points out, whiteness operates through an appropriative capacity, incorporating a multiplicity of difference "that consolidates rather than prostrates white personhood."[56] While Cherniavsky focuses primarily on the incorporation of intrawhite racial alterity, Civil War elegies point also to those more psychic, social, and political incorporations that occur from within the white racial ordinary, such that the white subject can assert misrecognition without disrupting belonging, dissent from nationalism's projections without disrupting citizenship, and occupy several competing strands of attachment and particularity without disrupting white supremacy's defining claims on universality.

# Gospel Sermons, Christian Fellowship, and the Conventions of Freedom

Bishop Campbell preached to a large crowd. His text was "Run, speak to this young man." Those who do not like noise nor shouting must not be where the Bishop preaches, for before he gets through not only people, but the very stones will cry out. A sister cried out, glory, glory. We have such Holy Ghost preachers in our conferences, and if such were stopped Methodism would die.

*The Christian Recorder*[1]

... as a spark of fire will catch and kindle in dry stubble, so did the preaching and singing of this young woman, until not only the church, but the whole community was ablaze and vast crowds composed of all classes and denominations flocked to hear this princess of woman preachers.

"Revival—Woman Preacher [Miss. M. E. Taylor]," *Star of Zion*[2]

The old meeting house caught on fire. The spirit was there. Every heart was beating in unison as we turned our minds to God to tell him of our sorrows here below. God saw our need and came to us. I used to wonder what made people shout, but now I don't. There is a joy on the inside, and it wells up so strong that we can't keep still. It is fire in the bones. Any time that fire touches a man, he will jump.

-"Autobiography II: A Preacher from a God-Fearing Plantation," *God Struck Me Dead*[3]

To conclude his oft-delivered sermon "The Sun Do Move," John Jasper, the best remembered of all nineteenth-century black gospel preachers, tells the assembled worshipers: "Our eyes goes far beyond de smaller stars; our home is clean out of sight of dem twinklin' orbs."[4] The statement subtly informs worshipers that the point behind Jasper's famous conceit—an argument that the sun revolves around the earth—has not been to pit religious truth against scientific fiction, but rather to position a black imaginary "clean out of sight" of known existence. Speaking with a coded meaning that draws on the spirituals, Jasper uses his conclusion to signal both the promise of utopian afterlife and the prospect for an earthly home birthed through creation of new conceptual worlds, heretofore-unknown worlds, which

*Genre and White Supremacy in the Postemancipation United States.* Travis M. Foster, Oxford University Press (2019).
© Travis M. Foster.
DOI: 10.1093/oso/9780198838098.001.0001

establish their reference points outside the familiarities of the present. He thereby suggests how so-called freed people after the Civil War might assert themselves as free people, affirming forms of creative existence that pushed up against and past the edges of the present moment's structuring determination of reality.

Black congregations enacted John Jasper's alternative and determinedly irrational notion of freedom and entered into formally distinct patterns of being together in large part by hosting Jasper's chosen performative genre, the gospel sermon. Where the first three chapters of this book track how white popular genres made racism the underwriting feature of white life, this chapter tracks how a black popular genre facilitated collective experiments and practices of freedom. Because gospel sermons oriented worshipers "clean out of sight" of either white supremacist or capitalist logic, they acted as a generic engine for thinking and inhabiting modes of freedom otherwise unimaginable or unthinkable. And because they existed within the provisional temporality of the performative occasion, they developed modes of community irreducible to being-in-common. Gospel sermons made such experimentation possible through shared ecstatic experience and collective encounter with the unknowable, uncanny presence of the Holy Ghost, relocating worshipers outside of themselves into an enchanted, divine–human realm. These experiences shaped congregants' relationships along three intersecting axes: to their own subjectivity, rendering their selves permeable, multiple, and filled with the spirit; to the divine, affirming an attachment that empowered and sanctioned dissent; and to each other, enacting a fellowship of anti-fraternal and provisional feeling in which common life need not rest on the preexistence of similarity or likeness.

As Hortense Spillers defines them, gospel sermons constitute a ritualized, formal, and collective performance: they are "an oral poetry—not simply an exegetical, theological presentation, but a complete expression of a gamut of emotions whose central form is the narrative and whose end is cathartic release."[5] In content, they oriented their themes around a passage from scripture, telling stories rich in practical, political, theological, and social implications. In form, they fashioned religious enthusiasm into a durable and recurrent genre: at once regular enough to facilitate performative collaborations between worshipers and loose enough to allow unforeseen paths. In practice, they traveled between preachers and congregations, emerging as a widespread and ubiquitous—though not, as we will see, uncontroversial—source of homiletic organization within the postbellum era's national network of black churches and denominational institutions. If, following Spillers, we understand the gospel sermon as poetic performance, then this understudied form was also by far the most widely distributed, authored, performed, and experienced mode of African American literary expression during the late nineteenth century—an alternative mode of popular literature that twisted the logic of white supremacy and white nationalism through experimentation with forms of being and being together that neither social system could even begin to imagine.

This is to say that gospel sermons circulated a resistance to white supremacy that didn't allow white supremacy to call the shots, straying far off the pathways of mere opposition. They did so at a crucial time, emerging into popularity during an era when white supremacy was seeking to put constraints on the meanings, expressions, and practices of black freedom, reorganizing the racist status quo around servility rather than slavery. White employers, government agents, and former owners encouraged formerly enslaved people to cultivate a mode of proper conduct, defined as subservient, obedient, and humble. One mode of "encouragement" was, of course, juridical, and the coercive measures used to control black labor—the Black Codes, anti-enticement laws, vagrancy laws, convict labor, and breach-of-contract laws—transformed contracts and the growing state prison systems into de facto re-enslavement. Encroachments on freedom also came through demands that black women and men perform and understand their freedom on white terms. Whites attempted to fashion a newly normative sense of the proper black individual: a subaltern *homo economicus* driven by her own consent and rational self-interest to honor the continuation of white supremacy, abasing herself willingly to white authority, and freely entering into contracts that secured un-freedom. "The issue was not simply whether ex-slaves would work," Saidiya Hartman writes, "but rather whether they could be transformed into a rational, docile, and productive working class—that is, fully normalized in accordance with standards of productivity, sobriety, rationality, prudence, cleanliness, responsibility."[6] Freedom, thus defined, meant both comporting as a self-possessed individual who assented happily and rationally to the post-slavery social and economic order and entering into forms of belonging organized around stable and preexisting identifications.

Readers of Max Weber's *The Protestant Ethic and the Spirit of Capitalism* might expect the black church to align itself firmly on the side of the self-possessed, rational subject and its fraternal modes of being-in-common, for Weber aligns even the "emotional religion" of the shouting Methodists with the rationalism of the capitalist subject.[7] And, indeed, black Protestantism organized a vast network of civil institutions (what E. Franklin Frazier famously called a "nation within a nation") that enabled viable anti-racist movements capable of establishing legitimacy within rational, recognized legal frameworks.[8] As Evelyn Brooks Higginbotham describes it, "the church served as the most effective vehicle by which men and women alike, pushed down by racism and poverty, regrouped and rallied against emotional and physical defeat."[9] This process transpired in no small part through "the public dimension of the black church," predicated as it was on being recognizable and knowable. But careful examination of the gospel sermon reveals that it transpired too through a much less predictable religious, spirit-filled dimension, and, moreover, that the institutional and sacred fields of action frequently entailed profoundly different gestures toward freedom.

I make this case by examining the gospel sermon's emergence as a distinctly black homiletic form from the Civil War through the rise of Jim Crow. My first two sections engage the methodological questions that emerge when we place into literary and social history a performative form like the sermon. From there, I turn to the gospel sermon's formal conventions and reception histories, which together provide evidence for its effects within congregations and within the larger postbellum world. I conclude by turning to the question of fellowship, using worshipers' descriptions of their experiences to better understand the social forms and possibilities enabled through the collective performance of gospel sermons.

## Oral Poetry: Method and Genre

How do we conduct literary history in the absence of what literary historians typically take as our primary texts? What Hortense Spillers names "oral poetry" cannot be captured in an anthology or replicated on the page. As James Weldon Johnson writes in the introduction to *God's Trombone*, his 1927 volume of sermon adaptations, "There is no way of recreating the atmosphere—the fervor of the congregation, the amens and hallelujahs, the undertone of singing which was often a soft accompaniment to parts of the sermon; nor the personality of the preacher, his [*sic*] physical magnetism, his gestures and gesticulations, his changes of tempo, his pauses for effect, and, more than all, his tones of voice."[10] Hence scholars who study the gospel sermon form tend to use methods drawn from performance studies, anthropology, and "folklore" studies rather than—or in combination with—close reading and textual interpretation. The most widely cited studies rely on nontextual archives: personal experience, ethnographic observation, and either commercial or personal recordings.[11] More recently, literary critics have drawn on this body of research in order to trace the relationship between gospel sermons and other forms of what Houston A. Baker calls "Afro-American expressive culture," finding elements of gospel sermon content and form in writers from Frederick Douglass and Frances Ellen Watkins Harper to Langston Hughes, James Baldwin, and Gwendolyn Brooks.[12] Their work complicates any strict opposition between speech and writing, "oral poetry" and written poetry, sermon and literature; "the relations of orality and literacy," writes Marcellus Blount in an article on "preacherly" literature, "are continuous."[13] These critics thus undo any attempt to contain oral "folk" tradition as the past against which African American literary or expressive modernism asserts itself, demonstrating the gospel sermon's ongoing capacity to cultivate what Kimberly W. Benston calls "the revolutionary potential of idiomatic resources."[14] To study the gospel sermon is to appreciate the performative and the literary as interactive forms of expression that, over time, have given each other resources and maintained each other's vitality.

While the sermon, as embodied performance, occasioned an irreproducible aura in excess of any archive's potential to capture and retain knowledge, the remarkable body of scholarship I've just cited also points us toward the performance's durable qualities: its conventions, its tropes, its genericness. That is to say that we can apprehend those conventions of the gospel sermon genre that provided preachers and congregants with a set of expectations for how the worship experience would look, sound, and feel.[15] What this chapter assembles, therefore, is a diverse set of materials that pass alongside and through the sermon, indicating its formulas, its poetry, its embodiment, its music, its scene, and even, to a point, its presence. These include representations of late-nineteenth-century gospel sermons that appear in twentieth-century literary texts; sermon transcriptions; sermon adaptations into poetry; Works Progress Administration oral autobiographies, along with those conducted by Fisk University graduate students; arguments about the aesthetics of the sermon form appearing in denominational newspapers, such as the African Methodist Episcopal Zion's weekly *Star of Zion*; critiques of the gospel sermon form by African Americans concerned with a politics of respectability; white first-hand accounts, themselves regular enough to comprise a genre, that use the sermon as evidence in favor of white supremacy; and childhood reminiscences by black writers such as Johnson and Hurston who grew up in the postbellum church. Taken together, these materials record impressions created by the postbellum gospel sermon and allow us to track it as a popular, dominant genre.

I'm arguing in part that the sermon rewards such attention because it was unfailingly repetitive and *generic*, yet that term here needs to be understood apart from its pejorative associations with blandness, mass production, and reactionary politics. Genres need not, as Franco Moretti argues, simply "make individuals feel 'at ease' in the world they happen to live in...[and] reconcile them in a pleasant and imperceptible way to its prevailing cultural norms."[16] We can locate an alternative trajectory for genre's entrance into the social world in Paul Gilroy's distinction between "politics of fulfillment" and "politics of transfiguration." Where the former works within the unfolding potential of the existing world, striving to complete the projects of Enlightenment and modernity, the latter emerges extra-discursively, through play and performance, in order "to conjure up and enact new modes of friendship, happiness, and solidarity."[17] Just as Henry Louis Gates locates an affirming black literary tradition in "the repetition and revision of shared themes, topoi, and tropes," Gilroy finds greatest potential for a politics of transfiguration within common—and, hence, conventional or generic—"folk knowledge."[18] In this sense, genericness enabled the gospel sermon to emerge as a collectively pursued form of what Gilroy, paraphrasing Ralph Ellison, calls "politics...on a lower frequency."[19] The genericness of the sermon lent it the mobility of collective knowledge, and the gospel sermon form, as well as individual gospel sermon narratives, thus traveled widely between churches, preachers, and regions. As James Weldon Johnson puts it, sermons "passed with only slight modification from preacher to preacher and from locality to locality."[20] So doing, they spread "folk knowledge" horizontally and rendered the potential for transfiguration widespread.

At the same time, Gates's emphasis on "repetition and revision" suggests the instability that always attends the relationship between the generic iteration (a single text or performance) and the categorical grouping. As we know, the paradox of repetition is such that no event ever occurs the same way twice, and the gap between one iteration and another can occasion unpredictable effects even when the two remain wholly similar. Hence Jacques Derrida's argument that texts participate in generic categories more than they belong to them; the individual performances that accrue into genre play out with varying degrees of distance from that genre's ostensibly defining conventions and, as they emerge, alter the genre by adding, subtracting, or refiguring characteristics. Moreover, it would be a mistake to think of any given generic iteration as a static entity made up of fixed conventions. Genres and generic performances move: they move, on the one hand, externally, as modes of expression encountering social forms and institutions; and they move, on the other, internally, as intra-generic conventions jostling with and against one another. Genres, as Frederic Jameson argues in *The Political Unconscious*, are thus at once constant and fickle; they satisfy our expectations while remaining internally variable, such that in any given genre a plurality of conventions interact with and shape one another.[21]

## Genealogies, Networks, Movements

On the face of it, generic genealogies follow more-or-less linear paths. American writers, encouraged by the popularity of British schoolboy narratives, crafted campus novels. *The Ladies' Home Journal*, attempting to fashion its readers into a distinctive public, turned the anthology content of women's magazines into a coherent, corporate, and generic identity. Poets of all stripes, responding to mass death and loss during the US Civil War and working with well-known conventions in the poetics of death and grief, wrote Civil War elegies. Yet if we heed Jameson's observation that genres consist in interacting parts, then we begin to see the need for plural or conjoined genealogies—heeding for instance not simply the campus novel's indebtedness to schoolboy tales, but also to the picaresque and the Bildungsroman, each of which suggest a longer, more geographically and temporally dispersed mapping.

More than the other genres I've looked at, gospel sermons foreground this plurality of influences. When I've presented versions of this chapter, audiences invariably bring up roots and analogs, asking about presumably white antecedent forms and Africanisms. Yet in its plurality, the gospel sermon also points to a more fundamental problem with genealogy, even plural genealogy, and, hence, to the difficulty we face when addressing these sorts of questions. Genealogy cannot help but falsify a set of singular, pure, unmixed origin points that, in combination, arrive at a given form. This is Foucault's fundamental point in "Nietzsche, Genealogy, History": "the body," or, in this case, the genre, "sustains the origin"; the form gives rise to the appearance of its beginnings.[22] Such an observation becomes particularly vexed with any history of the gospel sermon, where desire for genealogy too often presupposes a set of racially pure origins leading to a racially mixed form: a fusion of, on the one hand, black or West African modes of worship (including call-and-response, rhythmic dance, ring shouts, singing the word, and a belief that spiritual forces make themselves present to collectives), and, on the other, white traditions of enthusiastic preaching and religious emotionalism (such as George Whitefield's evangelical revivals, John Wesley's Methodist insistence on "the witness of the Spirit," or John Edwards's highly dramatic and moving conversion sermons, perhaps extending even as far back as medieval mysticism and *gratia lacrimarum*, the grace of tearful response).

Yet such distinctly white or distinctly black religious expressions remain hard to come by in the history of North American Christianity. "It is important to recall," writes historian David W. Wills, "as it often has not been by historians of North American religion, that the British settlement of North America took place both against the backdrop of the Puritan Revolution and its transformation of British religious life and also in relation to the creation of a British Atlantic-world empire in which the practice of racial slavery—and therefore the presence of a multitude of Africans—was an essential constitutive reality."[23] Hence Africanisms untouched by Anglo-Americanisms remain just as rare as Anglo-Americanisms untouched by Africanisms, and drawing any strict line between Anglo- and Afro-Protestantism remains a historical fiction. As the black preacher Zilpha Elaw put it, when describing an 1821 camp meeting in New Jersey: "high and low, rich and poor, white and coloured, were all melted like wax."[24] Similarly, the white, mid-eighteenth-century iterant preacher, Freeborn Garrettson, describes a racially mixed prayer meeting in Maryland as a space of mutual influence: "I suppose about twelve whites and blacks were present. The power of the Lord came among us: Mrs Airey was so filled with the new wine of Christ's kingdom, that she sunk to the floor, blessing and praising the Lord. And many of the blacks were much wrought upon."[25] Indeed, one primary argument used by white anti-revivalists during the period cited enthusiasm as a black influence on white worshipers. In *Methodist Error: Friendly Christian Advice to Those Methodists Who Indulge in Extravagant Emotions and Bodily Exercises* (1819), for instance, John Fanning Watson complains that, despite the racially segregated nature of revivalist camp meetings, worship practice in the "*blacks'* quarters"—"short scraps of disjointed affirmations, pledges, or prayers, lengthened out with long repetitious *choruses*"— "has already visibly affected the religious manners of some whites."[26] Even in the deeper South, where African American church attendance was highly restricted and where sermons often dwelled on the sanctity of obeying one's master, enslaved people frequently constituted the majority of church membership.[27] Considering the degree to which Baptists and, in particular, American Methodists welcomed what Claudia Stokes terms a "populist reconstitution of religious authority," it's difficult to imagine that influence in these spaces flowed only from the white pulpit to the segregated pews.[28] In short, religious enthusiasm traveled widely across the multiracial scene of North American religious practice, and the gospel sermon traces its disparate origins to roots dispersed and racially mixed.

We might do better, then, to replace questions about the origins of the gospel sermon with questions about its postemancipation movements through new networks of black churches and its remarkably fast emergence as a popular form. If Christianity remained a non-dominant religion among black people in the US well into the nineteenth century, then emancipation facilitated the public emergence of the black church as a prevailing institution and belief system.[29] While emancipation created at best highly suspect modes of freedom, it did largely remove worship from the control and surveillance of whites, who had remained especially jittery in the wake of Gabriel Prosser's planned uprising in 1800, Denmark Vesey's revolt in 1822, and Nat Turner's rebellion in 1831, all of which arose in part within the context of black Christian practice. Emancipation meant the cherished right to worship what one pleased and, just as importantly, how one pleased. Elizabeth Kilham, a white New England teacher working among black Southerners, recorded one woman's testimony to this freedom: "I goes ter some churches, an' I sees all de folks settin' quiet an' still, like dey dunno what de Holy Sperit am. But I fin's in my Bible, that when a man or a 'ooman gets full of de Holy Sperit, ef dey should hol' dar peace, de stones would cry out... dey tells us we musn't make no noise ter praise de Lord. I don't want no sich 'ligion as dat ar. I wants ter go ter Heaben in de good ole way."[30] Responding to these new freedoms of worship, African Americans both fled their white churches and converted to Christianity, ultimately establishing black houses of worship at such a rate that by 1890 there was at least one for every sixty families.[31] This new density constituted a series of overlapping networks—an infrastructure for the intermingling of preachers and congregants as well as sermons and forms, linking churches and denominations, regional camp meetings and national conferences—all of which facilitated the movement of the genre, providing "noise ter praise de Lord" with the gospel sermon's generic regularity of form and frequency.[32]

This, indeed, constitutes the defining feature of the gospel sermon. While it shares conventions of traditional sermons dating at least as far back as the Puritans, its distinctness as a genre arises from its racialization (by century's end, gospel sermons were seen and, as we shall see, derided as a distinctly black homiletic form) and its intended emotional effect. Gospel sermons transformed the "cathartic release" Spillers describes as their defining feature into a regular, recurrent pattern; they made emotional response to the spirit a repeated feature of the sermon's performance—hence the common reference to gospel sermon preachers as Holy Ghost preachers. Some readers might therefore object that the genericness of the gospel sermon undercuts my argument that it occasioned a unique form of freedom outside the confines of liberal organizing or familiar notions of personhood and community. For doesn't genericness exert a neutering force that regularizes and structures "noise," relocating congregants from spontaneous, enchanted contact with the Holy Ghost to mundane and rote worship? Indeed, historically, some opponents of religious enthusiasm have viewed frequency and regularity in precisely these terms. Schoolteacher Elizabeth Kilham, for instance, complains about the regularity of "religious expressions" among African Americans and concludes that enthusiastic worship and even regular church attendance stem "from habit," leaving both forms of religious experience as benign performances "without thought or meaning."[33] Likewise, some religious authority figures working to rein in the enthusiasms of white Christians in North America and England hoped that frequency would, as historian Leigh Eric Schmidt puts it, bring an "order and discipline" that would inure worshipers "to a Protestant vision of steady devotion Sabbath after Sabbath."[34] Yet more often, others found the regularizing—or putting into genre—of religious enthusiasm to constitute a threat to the social order. Hence, as Ann Taves argues, though leaders like Jonathan Edwards and John Wesley sometimes invited bodily and vocal expressiveness during worship, they also sought to confine those instances to a single moment in a believer's religious life: conversion. In like mind, when a new form of recurrent public worship began to emerge among Methodists around the beginning of the nineteenth century, one influenced by the singing and dancing found at racially mixed Virginia camp meetings, reformers opposed not the acts themselves, but what minister George Roberts called "forming jumping, dancing, shouting, &c. into a system, and pushing our social exercises into those extremes."[35]

In the end, we need not pick sides between those who argue that genre tames enthusiasm into steady habit and those who claim it elicits radically non-normative social exercises. Certainly, it would be hard to believe that some congregants didn't, as it were, go through the motions. But, as we will see, when we listen to the claims of worshipers themselves, it is equally hard to believe that many congregants, likely most, weren't moved by their experiences to imagine and inhabit ruptures within the rote scripts of social reproduction. Ultimately, our inability to fix and universalize congregants' responses to gospel sermons suggests an interpretive challenge to think about the meanings and effects of the genre as a product of movement as well as content and form. Recall, for instance, Johnson's description of sermons "pass[ing] from preacher to preacher and from locality to locality." Given this network of motion, we might think of gospel sermons as comprising what Bruno Latour calls "flows" rather than "fixed entities."[36] "[T]he sermon," as Hortense Spillers puts it, "not only catalyzes movement, but *embodies* it, *is movement*."[37] Such a scene of dispersed and shifting agency—with congregants and preachers and sermons and the Holy Spirit all acting continually on and through each other—does not preview ahead of time what form its social effects will take. We must instead, as Latour suggests, "follow the actors themselves," that is try to catch up with their often wild innovations in order to learn from them what the collective existence has become in their hands "… [and] to collect anew the participants in what is not—*not yet*—a sort of social realm."[38] If movement constitutes a key defining characteristic of each iteration of the gospel sermon, as Spillers suggests, and the defining characteristic between different iterations, as Johnson suggests, then even within its highly scripted and regularized ritual fellowship among worshipers never settled down. It too moved. In its elastic, provisional structure, it remained ever open to what it had not yet become. With this perspective in mind I now want to shift from the history and movement of the gospel sermon genre to how the playing out of its conventions invited imagination of what we might, echoing the spiritual, call *something new*.

## Conventions for Freedom

This section elaborates the many ways that gospel sermons facilitated *something new*, first, by analyzing their generic and spatial framing and, second, by working through sermons' aesthetic and performative conventions. By adhering so closely to these conventions, gospel sermons operated according to what John Ashbery, in reference to the pantoum verse form, names the "paradoxically liberating effect" of "restraints."[39] Just as adherence to rules of rhyme and meter creates a tactical confinement that forces writing outside the norms of conventional language use, so too the gospel sermon's conventions, along with its spatial framing within a church or other scene of worship, enabled an experimental reality. Carving out a physical, sacred, and aesthetic space apart, the gospel sermon was at once an everyday piece of postbellum black life and a glimpse over the horizon; at once a regular, recurrent part of people's routines and a break with the rhythms of everyday life; at once the repetition of something familiar and an event imagined and lived as something profoundly other. Remarking on an 1874 sermon preached by Bishop T. M. E. Ward, for instance, Reverend W. M. D. Johnson described worshipers suspended into mystery: "It was a gospel sermon, pointed, bold and elaborate. The very text itself was heavy, and the Bishop it seemed, blended all his powers of thought and language into the one mighty effort, lifting and suspending the vast audience, trembling and electrified into the awfully mysterious regions of the sublime."[40] This sense of suspension apart from everyday life also comes through in Toni Morrison's *Beloved* (1987), which contains what has become literature's most famous representation of a nineteenth-century gospel sermon. Morrison locates her preacher, "Baby Suggs, holy," in "the Clearing—a wide-open place cut deep in the woods."[41] As both gerund and noun, "Clearing" indicates in a word how the sermon's restrictions in place and form actively worked to open up new possibility (clearing the way) while also framing worship within differentiated space (in Morrison's case, symbolized and actualized by an opening in the thick Ohio forest).

In part, Reverend Johnson and Morrison represent the scene of worship as a space of reprieve from the postemancipation movement toward Jim Crow segregation and resubjugation. For James Baldwin, this function of the preacher and the sermon, which he dates to slavery, constituted an urgently needed source of spiritual solace and political countermovement: "The Black preacher ... was our first warrior, *terrorist*, or *guerrilla*. He said that freedom was real—that *we* were real. *He* told us that *trouble don't last always*. He told us that our children and elders were sacred, when the Civilized were spitting on them and hacking them to pieces."[42] Yet

Baldwin's description of the preacher as a "warrior, *terrorist*, or *guerilla*" also points to the sermon's potential to transfigure reality. Within the space of "the Clearing," the unfolding performance of the sermon worked to open fissures in the foreclosed world, inviting participants into what Ashon Crawley, in reference to black Pentecostalism, calls an "irreducible openness...toward "the movement of the Spirit," or what we might simply call "change."[43]

Like most homilies, gospel sermons commenced with the introduction of a theme, typically organized around a line of scripture that then also constituted an approximate title or an identification mark. For instance Reverend Johnson introduces Bishop Ward's aforementioned sermon by noting that "[h]e took the text, Gen. lix. 10. 'The scepter shall not depart from Judah &c.'"[44] This theme became a touchstone that allowed the preacher to combine allegories, biblical hermeneutics, morals, and proverbs, collapsing biblical times, contemporary strivings, and the millennialism of end times. It provided a fixed point around which the congregation could orient itself while also departing from linear, ordered, teleological chronologies. The sermon thereby created a particularly thick spatiotemporal atmosphere that altered the experience of time's passing, calling upon worshipers' heightened sensitivity to the palimpsestic past, the prophetic future, and the resonances between events. We might call this the time of prayer, for it united two simultaneous experiences of human–divine interaction: one in which worshipers temporarily inhabit God's temporal perspective of the world not as a chain of events but as an unfolding of concurrent processes; and one in which worshipers invite that ineffable and ungraspable potential that lies outside conscious presence to cross into the familiar and knowable world, where it can be shared and dispersed, opening into alternative futures.

At their outset, sermons frequently shifted from the announcement of a theme to a prayer aimed at summoning God's transfiguring presence. Take the opening stanza of "Listen, Lord—A Prayer," James Weldon Johnson's adaptation of a sermon invocation familiar to him from childhood:

> O Lord, we come this morning
> Knee-bowed and body-bent
> Before thy throne of grace.
> O Lord—this morning—
> Bow our hearts beneath our knees,
> And our knees in some lonesome valley.
> We come this morning—
> Like empty pitchers to a full fountain,
> With no merits of our own.
> O Lord—open up a window of heaven,
> And lean out far over the battlements of glory,
> And listen this morning.[45]

The invocation invites the Spirit to enter through "a window of heaven," and it reorients the congregation toward such an experience through the insistence on supplication to divine presence. "Like empty pitchers," the worshipers stand ready to be transformed into instruments, to be made agents for purposes and possibilities beyond the capacities of human thought or consciousness. Moreover, the invocation multiplies and layers the spatiotemporal ground of the worship scene by relocating parishioners to "some lonesome valley"—a site that is, on the one hand, an open and vast elsewhere, a stage for potential, and, on the other hand, an echo of the black spiritual, "I Must Walk my Lonesome Valley," in which "valley" signals a site and a period of Lenten trial that worshippers share with Jesus and his forty days resisting temptation.[46] The sermon's opening thereby operates as a temporal, imaginative, and performative transition between mundane and sacred worlds, simultaneously generating the performative grounds that will become a clearing and ushering worshipers into its potential.

With an opening that thus pushed against the normative pull of secularism's rationality and clock time, the sermon then invited worshipers into enthusiasm for the Spirit, incorporating what Johnson calls "a progression of rhythmic words" delivered by a preacher "who was above all an orator, and in good measure an actor":

> He was a master of all modes of eloquence. He often possessed a voice that was a marvelous instrument, a voice he could modulate from a sepulchral whisper to a thunder clap. His discourse was generally kept at a high pitch of fervency, but occasionally he dropped into colloquialisms and, less often, into humor. He preached a personal and anthropomorphic God, a sure-enough heaven and a red-hot hell. His imagination was bold and unfettered. He had the power to sweep his hearers before him; and so himself was often swept away. At such times his language was not prose but poetry.[47]

These swelling crescendos and decrescendos, sudden shifts from "sepulchral whisper" to thunder, fervent discourses put into relief by colloquialism and humor, and invitations to be familiar with the divine—all expanded the range of behaviors permitted within the sermon's performative space. They provided collective permission to move outside self-monitoring frameworks for emotional display. To be swept away here is thus to realize an open vulnerability to the presence of others, human and divine, as well as to the otherness within. It is to be in ecstasy, outside of the self. Consider the example of the shout: the preacher's "thunder clap" in Johnson's description and the urge that "wells up so strong that we can't keep still" described in this chapter's epigraph. Johnson calls his preacher's voice an "instrument," a term that speaks to the preacher's ability to be the source of praise, but also to the preacher's capacity to be used for and by another—to be made into an instrument—through which the Holy Spirit exerts agency. The shout that wells up rapidly and uncontrollably is made by the self and comes from outside of the self, exceeds the self; it is an expression of being given over, implicated in lives and agencies that cannot be contained or possessed.

What any focus on the role of the preacher's performative powers leaves out, however, is the collective aspect of this ecstatic experience and the sermon's open invitation for parishioners to join in and even overtake the preacher's eloquence—the ways, that is, that congregants' shouts and enthusiasm respond to the Holy Spirit or the preacher and, simultaneously, to other congregants' shouts and other expressions of joy or possession. Shouts by their very nature rise above the soundscape of the sermon, demanding to be heard and known. They assert the Spirit's presence. Others' expressions of God's immediacy thus become, within the performance of the sermon, texts in their own right, authorizing parishioners' experience and bearing witness to divinity. Simultaneously, they produce an alternative literacy, a grammar and vocabulary of kinesics, affects, and enunciations that join worshipers into fellowship and mutual understanding. Such collectivity comprised a built-in convention for the sermon's performance. The preacher's repetitions in phrasing, regularity of intoning, and syncopations between enunciations gave the sermon a predictable rhythm, a meter pulsating through breath that opened space for the performances of others.

Such predictability thereby derailed binaries between speaker and audience, preacher and worshiper, because they made even the newest of sermons predictable, enabling collective, seamless, and seemingly rehearsed participation in which the "audience" could become a louder, more ostensible "performer" than the preacher. In *Jonah's Gourd Vine* (1934), Zora Neale Hurston's novel of Southern black life from emancipation through the Great Migration, one character defines a successful sermon by the degree to which the preacher's voice is but one of many: "Man, you preached!... so many folks wuz shoutin' Ah couldn't half hear whut you wuz sayin'."[48] This approbation describes something more than antiphony; while call-and-response certainly played a role in the sermon, Hurston's character gestures also to those moments when shouting, dancing, and counter-preaching— parishioners incorporating their own testimonies to the presence of the Spirit— emerge to displace the preacher as the sermon's central figure. Hurston thus underscores the capacious generosity of a performative art form that depends upon a central performer's gifts of eloquence, oratory, drama, poetry, and vocalization, yet also succeeds most when those gifts shift from foreground to background. So doing, the gospel sermon, even more so than other performative genres, undoes what Foucault identifies as "relationship between text and author and...the manner in which the text points to this 'figure' that, at least in appearance, is outside it and antecedes it."[49] Hence Johnson's observation that the preacher was often swept away by a performance that has come to exceed the performer. The preacher, like the parishioners, remains inside the performance, playing a pivotal role to be sure, but also one role among many, decentralized and frequently overcome.

The gospel sermon thus produced a uniquely dynamic mode of authority, an attribute that provided black women, who constituted a majority of church membership, outlets for dislodging the typically male preacher's centrality. Even though the African Methodist Episcopal denomination in particular was known for prominent and powerful women preachers and feminist activism (a piece in the AME's *The Christian Recorder* lamented, for instance, a "day of prejudiced" when "[a] woman preacher of Ohio has had some difficulty in securing the license to perform the marriage ceremony"), it wasn't until 1894 that the denomination ordained their first female deacon, Julia Foote, and women preachers remained a distinct minority.[50] Black Baptists, meanwhile, by far the largest denomination of African American Protestantism, entirely refused to ordain women, although black Baptist women did achieve great success entering other leadership positions and developing, in Evelyn Brooks Higginbotham's words, "a distinct discourse of resistance, a feminist theology."[51] Yet by organizing conventions for the pulpit and the parishioner to enter what Spillers calls "a common ground of inquiry," the gospel sermon at least partially destabilized patriarchal gender hierarchies.[52] To be sure, the feminism of this gesture hardly manifested without complexity or contradiction. For one, religious enthusiasm confirmed a cultural belief that women, particularly black women, were inherently more emotional and expressive than (white) men.[53] At the same time, however, the gospel sermon occasioned a venue that created value out of the ostensibly devalued—that, indeed, made the emotional enthusiasm associated with black women the very sign of performative success and authorized that enthusiasm as an effect of divine agency and approval.[54]

The gospel sermon thereby disrupted normative conventions of performance, self-conduct, and gender; it also, strange as it might sound, disrupted itself. The sermon's form paradoxically resisted stability, so that even the sermon's genericness refused to become static. Gospel sermons operated in ceaseless flux, allowing them a nimble flexibility that evaded easy or stable categorization and that, even from within the generic fulfillment of expectations, resisted rote performance. Johnson's description above points at the sermon's movement between the worldly and the otherworldly, the familiar and the strange: on the one hand, the comfort of colloquialisms, the collective affirmation of shared laughter, and the affirmation of a God that invites intimacy and identification; on the other, the "high pitch" of fervent possession, the crack when whisper shifts to thunder, and the awful unknowability of a God who vastly exceeds the horizon of human thought and possibility. Hence Hurston's *The Sanctified Church*, a collection of essays in part built on her recollections of the late-nineteenth-century sermons preached by her Baptist father, stacks contradiction upon contradiction in order to get as close as possible to the crux of gospel worship in practice. "Beneath the seeming informality of religious worship," Hurston writes, "there is a set formality. Sermons, prayers, moans and testimonies have their definite forms." She then elaborates that her observation extends even to "hums," which "are formal and can be found unchanged all over the South." Yet without flagging any seeming contradiction in her descriptions, Hurston also calls the service "loose and formless" and claims that "the congregation is bound by no rules." In like fashion, she hails the sermon as a "conscious art expression," yet just two sentences later notes the moment of "emotional pitch" when the preacher "loses all self-consciousness." And finally, she claims in one paragraph that "shouting is a community thing" and that "it thrives in concert," yet in the very next writes that shouting "is absolutely individualistic."[55] Hurston uses paradox to resist ethnography's propensity for fixing its objects of analysis, a project she deftly explores and enacts in *Mules and Men*, and to point toward the sermon's unique breed of formalism: in which generic conventions at once sustain stability from week to week and from congregation to congregation, yet also exist in an ad hoc capacity, ceaselessly under negotiation, because the gospel sermon form includes built-in antinomies to form—improvisation and spontaneity—that work to undo its stability.

## Racial Uplift and the Holy Ghost

I've been pursuing my argument through analysis of the gospel sermon's movements through the postbellum social world and its defining conventions. Now I want to look at the genre from a different angle by attending to the sermon's controversial reception. Indexing the gospel sermon's ability to bring profound and, for many, unfathomable scenes of worship into the postbellum social world, white and black detractors of the sermon's form merit our attention. Most of these detractors write from an ethnographic stance after observing the sermon in performance, and they thus provide a rather odd history of reception—not a history of those who experienced and enacted the sermon (as we'll see in the next section), but a history of those primarily interested in turning their observations into evidence for political beliefs about race, class, and respectable conduct. I present them here, then, as a secondary reception: a way of uncovering the dominant understanding of a scorned form and, hence, for assessing the stakes of the gospel sermon's interventions into postbellum social worlds and politics. Moreover, white detractions, in particular, link this chapter's emphasis on black generic collectivity to my previous chapters' emphases on white national affiliation, for, as we saw in the *Ladies' Home Journal*, denigrating responses to black cultural productions infused white popular culture with a sense of rightfulness and ascendancy.

Whites—including reformers, carpetbaggers, philosophers, missionaries, and travel writers—emphasized what, for them, comprised the preacher's and congregants' foolishness and the sermon's inscrutability. The "negro preacher" jokes found in the *Ladies' Home Journal*, for instance, depicted black sermons as frivolous affairs, replete with the misreading of scripture and the twisting of parables for personal gain.[56] Similarly, in *The Cotton Kingdom* (1861), Frederic Law Olmsted begins his description of a gospel sermon with faltering praise ("much of the language was highly metaphorical; the figures long, strange, and complicated, yet sometimes, however, beautiful"), but he quickly moves into complaint that the preacher's poor "grammar and pronunciation" made him "incomprehensible," particularly when overtaken by the congregation's deafening shouts and "indescribable expressions of ecstasy." "I can compare them," he writes of these sounds, "to nothing else human I ever heard."[57] Likewise, James Bissett Pratt, a Williams College philosophy professor, describes a black Mississippi revival sermon thus: "merely a concatenation of misquoted, irrelevant Bible verses, quite detached; but the result was considerable. If he had spoken in Chinese and used the same intoning or singing method, his results would probably have been about as great."[58] Whites like Olmstead and Pratt drew their readers' attentions to the expressive, enthusiastic style of the preacher delivery and the "considerable" or "great" response of the parishioners—both of which, they intimated, stood outside the bounds of the human or, perhaps for them amounting to the same thing, the West. Their disciplinary descriptions thus worked to define the boundaries of acceptability and indicated black nonassimilability into normative social life.

Before the Civil War, white and black abolitionists frequently used Christianity as a measure of enslaved people's humanity and a critique of slavery's inhumanity (think, for instance, of *Uncle Tom's Cabin* (1852)). During and after the war, as Olmstead and Pratt suggest, black religiosity became instead a measure of unfitness for self-government, leadership, family life, and conscience-driven, internalized discipline.[59] As historian Curtis J. Evans writes in *The Burden of Black Religion*, religious "feelings became unruly emotions, and innate religiosity now meant the possession of a primitive or culturally inferior form of bodily religious expression."[60] One paradigmatic example of this comes in a white missionary's 1872 account of black life in the South: "it is my solemn conviction that......twenty-five years from to-day will find the schools and all Northern appliances for the regeneration of the freedman, swamped and swept entirely out of sight, by the fearful waves of social vice engendered and taught by the *religion* of the *Southern negroes*."[61] We can thus compare the treatment of postbellum African American religiosity—particularly as performed through gospel sermons and other enthusiastic practices—to the treatment of Mormonism and, to a lesser extent, Shakerism earlier in the century, both of which led to social and political exclusion because of religious practices considered incommensurable with national belonging.[62] So powerful was this argument when applied to black religion that white liberals, nominally devoted to black inclusion, treated the gospel sermon as an unfortunate holdout from slavery in dire need of reform. Howard University president Jeremiah E. Eankin, for instance, praised the "great progress" of the "Negro preacher" who, by century's end, has become "less emotional, more logical more thoughtful," and he reassured the white readership of *The American Missionary* that Howard's guest preachers are "without a single exception...free from boisterous utterance."[63] As the nineteenth century came to an end, white religious enthusiasm increasingly came under the disciplinary apparatus of psychology (personalizing enthusiasm as an individual defect); black religious enthusiasm, meanwhile, came under an anthropological gaze (generalizing enthusiasm as a group defect).[64] This racialization of enthusiasm depicted black worship as a practice that evinced black inferiority and primitivism.[65]

The debate over gospel sermons' worthiness occurred also between African Americans. Although the limited sources available do not support generalization, they do reveal vocal, pronounced, and prominent discomfort felt by some middle-class African Americans toward gospel religious practice.[66] Take, for instance, two educated property-owning characters at the beginning of Frances Ellen Watkins

Harper's *Trial and Triumph* (1888–9). Both speak fervently on behalf of "earnest thoughtful Christly men, who will be more anxious to create and develop moral earnestness than to excite transient emotions." They understand the "pitiful and weird" shouts and moans of gospel worship to comprise an unfortunate outgrowth of slavery, born of the desire to communicate "thoughts and feelings…which they [the formerly enslaved] did not dare express when they were forced to have their meetings under the surveillance of a white man."[67] (Several of Harper's poems celebrating fervent religious expression, such as "Church Building," mean that we should be careful not to equate Harper's characters' opinions with those held by Harper.) Similarly, in his travel narrative *My Southern Home* (1880), William Wells Brown inveighs against "outward demonstrations," "boisterous noise," and "revival meetings" as "injurious to both health and morals," and he calls for an "educated ministry" even as he condescendingly worries that it may be impossible to induce "the uneducated, superstitious masses to receive and support an intelligent Christian clergyman."[68] Likewise in his short story "Of the Coming of John" (1903), W. E. B. Du Bois's eponymous character returns home from college and immediately speaks out against his town's religious practices, which, he announces, stall the progress toward "human brotherhood" and racial "unity." The town responds with a spontaneous gospel sermon in defense of gospel sermons, after which John "felt himself held up to scorn and scathing denunciation for trampling on the true Religion, and he realized with amazement that all unknowingly he had put rough, rude hands on something this little world held sacred."[69]

These emphases on the unfitness of black gospel worship reveal the urgency behind John's observation that the gospel sermon constituted something to nurture and keep close, "something this little world held sacred." We might wonder, then, whether *fitness*—as a moral, social, and political aspiration to normative life—binds black aspiration too firmly to the constitutive elements of white supremacy. And, hence, we might ask whether fitness preemptively reinforces a racist outcome. In this respect, criticism of the gospel sermon indexes the genre's very success. Descriptions of inscrutability, weirdness, and boisterousness highlight the sermon's accomplishment, its ability to work aslant the foreclosure of black possibility and manifest through what Gilroy calls the "unsayable" expressions through which a politics of transfiguration takes hold.[70]

Certainly, the gospel sermon drew heartfelt defense when its critics became more prominent from the 1880s through the 1910s. Its defenders saw the gospel sermon as a religious and aesthetic form that enabled a uniquely active relationship between congregants and God and that appealed to a wide array of people: Northern and Southern, male and female, young and old, middle class and poor. Our best source for this side of the aesthetic debate comes from the *Star of Zion*, an AME weekly newspaper highly invested in scenes of worship. Time and again, the paper's editors included editorials, guest opinion columns, preacher obituaries, and accounts of revivals. These sources almost universally decry what they term "fops and dude preachers" who, to cite an 1897 editorial, do away with "the class and prayer-meetings and with these jubilee clap-hands and pat-feet religious songs that the old and many of the young people love...and in their places are substituting weekly lectures on the topics of the day and solos, duets, trios, quartettes, which have no place in these meetings."[71] Against both the gospel sermon's African American and white detractors, contributors to the paper emphasize the significance of religious feeling and collective improvisation. "We must have a live, wide-awake and spirit-endued ministry," says Bishop G. W. Clinton.[72] Likewise, the Reverend W. S. Meadows of Alabama complains in 1899 that "one of the great, if not the greatest defects, of the preaching of today is its tameness":

> The trouble is not so much with the matter as with the manner: the gesture, the tone of voice, the expressionless eye. By this I do not mean mere eloquence and gracefulness, nor the position of the feet, the attitudes of the body, or movements of the arms, such things as are taught by the elocutionst, for these are not to be despised, but highly esteemed and observed. But what I speak of is life, action. Preaching cannot be positive, at least cannot appear to be positive, and so impress the hearer, unless the preacher out of a warm and surcharged heart throws life, spirit and soul into his sermon.[73]

Emphasizing the significance of form over content and spirit over worldliness, the *Star of Zion* contrasted sermons to lectures, ministers or dudes to "Holy Ghost preachers," merely intellectual effects to those that spark new life and new action. Gospel preaching occurs, they argue, "when the minister is full of the Holy Ghost and the people are becoming alive to his presence": it creates, that is, a space for transcendence, and it enables a community of feeling oriented toward those possibilities and value systems that can only just begin to assert themselves within the field of representation.[74]

Congregants valued and defended gospel sermons for making them vulnerable to a spiritual presence that crossed human boundaries, and they therefore understood their very selves to be porous, integrated inextricably into currents or ecologies that included their fellow worshipers and the divine. This porousness meant, in the words of one *Star of Zion* column, laying "aside a pile of your stiff and starch nonsense called 'dignity.'"[75] Such a magnificently *un*dignified self differentiated religious from secular experience—or, what an editorial called "secular lectures" and "concert styles of singing" from "knee praying" and "jubilee religious singing."[76] Arguing that secularism asserts an active, formal presence that threatens to alter religious experience, the editorial anticipates anthropologist Talal Asad and philosopher Charles Taylor, who argue that secularism authorizes certain religious subjectivities while also making others the subject of reform: constituting, for instance, ecstatic worshipers as unruly subjects who must be tamed or marginalized. Nineteenth-century secularism, Taylor argues, came to constitute a new set of norms, oriented around "expressive individualism," for what it meant to embody and possess a self.[77] In this way, secularism—and the forms of religious subjectivity it sanctioned—played a direct role in the re-subjugating disciplinary project

I describe at this chapter's outset, supporting forms of belief that would transform formerly enslaved individuals into "rational, docile, productive laborers." As an unruly, heterodox, and widely scorned religious form, gospel sermons worked to undo this "buffered self" and linked congregants instead into unpredictable networks of connection suffused with divine presence and, as we will now see, love.[78]

## Fellowship & Electric Belonging

What did this collectivity feel like? What energies, connections, and relationships did it facilitate between worshipers? What configurations of community and fellowship? The men and women who describe their religious experiences in *God Struck Me Dead: Religious Conversion Experiences and Autobiographies of Ex-Slaves* provide, of course, many different answers to these questions. Yet a clear pattern emerges: many free people experienced freedom more urgently and more palpably in the context of the gospel sermon than they did during any other time; this experience connected them into fellowship with their fellow worshipers and, more broadly, with their fellow human beings; and this fellowship emerged not through the stability of a preexisting, singular identity but via the shared feelings enabled through mutual possession by the otherworldly presence of the Holy Ghost.

Time and again, the men and women interviewed describe an outpouring of love—a sense of deep affection that leads them to feel responsibility and care over their own lives and also over the sustenance and quality of life writ large. "I felt burdened down and that preaching was my only relief," reports one man: "When I was finished I felt a great love in my heart that made me feel like stooping and kissing the very ground."[79] "Whenever I hear the Gospel preached," explains another, "I just get a feeling of gladness and happiness that makes me lose all worldly cares. I just feel like running away somewhere. I have a deep feeling of love for everybody."[80] Another worshiper connects the intensity of this love to the unfathomable nature of intimacy with God: "The love of God is beyond understanding. It makes you love everybody."[81] A preacher narrates one particular morning during which he experienced this movement between personal encounter with God and intimacy with fellow beings:

> I felt awful bad when I first got to church and took my place on the stand waiting for the congregation to gather. And then the spirit lifted me up. I forgot all about the pain and just lost sight of the world and all the things of the world. When the spirit begins to work with one it don't have any cares for pain or anything of the world. My mind gets fixed on God and I feel a deep love, joy and a deep desire to be with God. We shout because we feel glad in the heart. At times I feel like I could just kiss the very feet of man and I had rather hear the voice on the inside cry out "Amen" when I do something than to have all the money in the world. We rejoice because the spirit makes us feel so good and makes us forget all worldly cares.[82]

Even though the spirit's grip constitutes a highly personal encounter requiring individual display ("when the spirit begins to move one"), the form of the service expands religious experience such that intimacy with God also becomes a grid of affection crisscrossing the entire congregation. Hence the preacher's easy movement between the first-person singular and plural: "I forgot" and "I feel" give way to "we shout because we feel glad in the heart" and "we rejoice because the spirit makes us feel so good."

Yet these affinities do not merge into an identity-based community ready to itemize political demands within the known, secular public sphere. They therefore differ from the very form of white nationalist and fraternal or sororal sociality I've described in previous chapters. While the anonymous preacher's description underscores an intensely collective experience binding the congregation into fellowship, his "[a]t times" also reveals fellowship's necessarily tentative nature. In this sense black fellowship is neither a stable affinity nor an organization of black communitarianism: it does not and cannot bind large-scale racial or nationalist belonging. Certainly it constitutes a form of racial community, a form of black community. But its performance neither relies upon nor produces stable racial identity, and its form of community does not exist as any kind of romanticized, feel-good site of easy commonality (as, for instance, would campus novels' communities of campus friendships: of Harvard men, say, or Smith women). It therefore brings into being a collectivity suited more to the accommodation of difference than to the coherent articulation of shared belief.

Where campus novels, the *Ladies' Home Journal*, and Civil War elegies helped whites to imagine themselves as part of a capacious national community based on racial similarity and supremacy, gospel sermons facilitated a fellowship closer to what Leela Gandhi names an "anti-communitarian communitarianism" or what Lloyd Pratt calls "stranger humanism": a non-fraternal form based on congregants' irreducible singularity and collective performance.[83] Such a collectivity, as Pratt describes it, occurs when "parties to the encounter never reach a concluding moment of full mutual intelligibility," but instead "participate in recognition predicated on emerging difference."[84] Gospel sermons facilitated such an unfolding and dynamic experience of coming together through an improvisational and ecstatic performance that invited the uncanny and destabilizing presence of the Holy Ghost.[85]

Such a communal form enabled a politics oriented toward experimental openness. To be recognized and known is to lodge one's being and one's future hopes firmly within existing possibilities. Fellowship instead occasioned glimpses toward the horizon of possibility itself by removing congregations from predictable, transparent forms of recognition or affinity—to the point where, as Du Bois's John discovered, congregations exhibited a constructive hostility toward the merging of worship with racially unifying strategies of organization. A second example makes the point with even greater precision. When the congregation in Hurston's *Jonah's*

*Gourd Vine* auditions Reverend Felton Cozy as a possible replacement to their current preacher, Cozy introduces himself as a "race man," introduces his theme as the "race problem," and then delivers a sermon expounding on race pride. Yet the congregation resists. Reverend Cozy frequently has to order his subdued audience to "say, 'Amen'!" and one woman later castigates the performance as generically inappropriate: "Sermon?...dat wan't no sermon. Dat wuz uh lecture."[86] Although the Reverend performs at least somewhat in the style of the gospel preacher, he errs when he, like Du Bois's John, attempts to replace the uncertainty of the mysterious, sacred world with the certainty of the concrete, mundane one. He assumes that the congregation's responsiveness will flow from a preexisting fellowship—a racially organized fraternity—that can be ignited into excitement through eloquent exclamations on its organizing feature: racial pride, racial solidarity, or even racial nationalism.

Du Bois's and James Weldon Johnson's own experiences in scenes of black gospel worship offer a useful corrective to Reverend Cozy's false assumptions. Reporting on their participation in gospel sermons, both men describe the fellowship within congregations as a process achieved through the unstable, provisional work of possession, madness, and electricity. For each, the gospel sermon enables affinities that begin with transformational confrontation between the individual and the unknown, and that then become charged with energy and potential through the intermingling emotional responses of the worshipers. Approaching the scene of his first gospel sermon, Du Bois initially seems to keep his distance, describing himself struck by "the air of intense excitement that possessed that mass of black folk." Immediately, though, he finds that he too is not immune: "A sort of suppressed terror hung in the air and seemed to seize us,—a pythian madness, a demoniac possession, that lent terrible reality to song and word."[87] Likewise, Johnson describes attending a gospel sermon that produced "an electric current [that] ran through the crowd" and infected him: "I was, perhaps against my will, deeply moved; the emotional effect upon me was irresistible."[88] The descriptors of madness, possession, and electricity redirect the organizing mode of black fellowship from identity, as Reverend Cozy would have it, to energy, movement, sensation, and impression: from what people have in common to the feelings and energies that circulate among them. As binding agents, madness and possession maintain the seeming absence of choice that describes so many varieties of identitarian belonging, yet they nevertheless refuse to substitute identity with any similarly durable or singular ontological form. Du Bois and Johnson experience a contagion spread through both collective feeling and, within the congregation's understanding of itself, the touch of non-human divinity.[89]

This inclusion of divinity remains essential for the constitution of congregational affinities and, by extension, for the politics of black fellowship. The gospel sermon's infectiousness collectivizes experiences of possession, turning fellowship into a hybrid form of community such that expressions of love and affinity fit easily alongside submission to the Holy Spirit. Thus one formerly enslaved woman's transition from a passive to an active participant in the gospel sermon's performance occurs precisely through the experience of being possessed:

> I used to see people shout a lot at meetings but I didn't want to do it. I tried to hold my peace and just rejoice inwardly but one day while I was attending a meeting a voice said to me, "Before you shall hold your peace the very rocks and mountains shall cry out against you." Since that day I have been praising God just as the spirit moves me. If it moves me to shout, I shout and I believe He is pleased with me.
>
> I saw in a vision a snow-white train once and it moved like lightning. Jesus was on board and He told me that He was the Conductor. I believe He is the conductor in my soul and when He moves, I move and I am not afraid of my journey.[90]

The vision of a train metaphorically links spiritual possession to the Underground Railroad and the promise of freedom.[91] Doing so, it sharply distinguishes between submission and enslavement while expanding conceptions of freedom into something more than mere sovereignty or self-ownership. Submission thus becomes an act of extension, the first step in a risky and potentially generative openness to all that is, in the words of one worshiper, "past finding out," thus enabling what another praises as "wisdom and knowledge that the world can't find out."[92]

Gospel sermons invited congregants in thousands upon thousands of churches collectively to experience alternate realities and to envision alternate futures in which the self might not survive at all—at least, not in any recognizable form. Through homiletic performances, congregations thus embraced a mode of freedom celebrated by Hannah Arendt, which emerges only through the kind of collective exertion able to "call something into being which did not exist before, which was not given, not even as an object of cognition or imagination."[93] Not self-expression, but world-transfiguration: "clean out of sight of dem twinklin' orbs." Working aslant the strains of white supremacy and amidst the crumbling rubble of emancipation, congregations linked their politics with impossibility itself, entering provisional forms of existence that severed investment in the known world.

## Coda: The Form of "God Damn America!"

The first three genres described in this book have long since faded from prominence. Novels about the frivolities of college students stopped appearing with any frequency by 1910. The *Ladies' Home Journal* of course still exists, but it no longer organizes a national public and has not referred to its community of subscribers as a sisterhood since the first years of the twentieth century. And World War I quickly replaced the Civil War in Americans' desires to remember and elegize fallen soldiers. Gospel sermons, however, remain an active, prominent, popular generic form. I turn in this coda to a recent though seemingly distant historical moment, the 2008 US presidential election, when white condemnation of gospel sermon form became as much of a national preoccupation as it was during the late nineteenth century—implicitly giving voice, just as it did then, to gospel sermons' lasting power for organizing and collectivizing alternatives to white supremacy.

During the spring of that campaign, Barack Obama's opponents turned the sermons of his pastor, Reverend Jeremiah Wright, into a measure of the candidate's patriotism, fitness for the presidency, attitudes toward white people, and Christianity. While initial focus remained on the liberationist and radical nature of Wright's message, criticism frequently undid any distinction between homiletic content and form. Commentators chided Obama for sitting through "mad lines," "ravings," and "hysterical pronouncements," perpetrated by a preacher who "fulminat[es] in front of a raucously enthusiastic congregation": "no sane person would sit through his gibberish, certainly not for 20 years."[94] Even white defenders of Reverend Wright came under an attack that focused primarily on the performative practices of gospel sermons, as when columnist Jonah Goldberg complained that during Wright's appearance on Bill Moyers's PBS talk show, "Moyers all but shouted 'Amen' every time Wright took a breath."[95] Critics targeted Obama for his association with Wright, but also for being an African American worshipper attending services in a black gospel tradition. Wright noted this later when he said: "This most recent attack...is not an attack on Jeremiah Wright; it is an attack on the black church."[96] Obama too knew that his political peril stemmed, at least in part, from participation in an enthusiastic religious tradition associated with black worship. When asked during a press conference following his resignation from Trinity United Church of Christ whether he would join another black church, he responded curiously and with characteristic reserve: "there is a different religious tradition or a worshipping style in some of the historically African American churches."[97]

Obama's detractors pursued a clear and, as we now know, rather preposterous agenda to paint the neoliberal senator as a radical socialist rooted intellectually in a Black Nationalist tradition. Such an argument, however, required no more than choice citation of Wright's words ("No, no, no. Not 'God Bless America'; God Damn America!"). By additionally foregrounding the performance of those words and the congregation's "raucously enthusiastic" response, white detractors further attempted to link the famously unflappable Obama to worship practices that have, since at least the early 1700s, been associated with social disruption. In this vein, Obama's twenty years attending Wright's church offered white supremacists a unique opportunity to associate him with enthusiasm's so-called disorders and, consequentially, to situate him within a racializing project that places blackness outside Enlightenment norms.[98] How, they intimated, could Obama be taken seriously as a presidential candidate when his long association with Jeremiah Wright aligned him so wholly with that mode of blackness against which the projects of US modernity—including constitutionalism, freedom of the market, secularism, reason, and self-possession—define themselves?

These reactions to Reverend Wright's sermons help us to see white supremacy's longstanding and, apparently, still potent fascination with black worship traditions as it confirms its own beliefs and propagates its ideology. Yet the Wright moment hints too at the "field of force relations" through which regulatory projects never operate along a singular repressive axis and instead contain multiple strategies, including strategies of dissent.[99] "[B]lackness," as theologian J. Kameron Carter reminds us, "is a disruption or disturbance from inside modernity's social logic and organization."[100] We see abundant evidence of this disturbing potential in the long and ongoing history of the black gospel genre, which continues to disrupt the epistemological monopoly of reasoned enquiry and fashion alternative models for knowledge, expression, and fellowship.

# Epilogue

On June 27, 2015, ten days after the massacre at the Emmanuel African Methodist Episcopal Church, Claudia Rankine published an essay on black loss in the *New York Times'* Sunday magazine: "the white liberal imagination likes to feel temporarily bad about black suffering," Rankine writes; yet "[w]e live in a country where Americans assimilate corpses in their daily comings and goings. Dead blacks are a part of normal life here."[1] Most obviously, Rankine stresses the central axiom of the Black Lives Matter movement, a simple truth that "All Lives Matter" naysayers would have us ignore: some lives, white lives, matter more than others, some suffering stands more worthy of attention and redress, some death qualifies more readily for grief and remembrance. Reframed in Rankine's register of black suffering, "Black Lives Matter" signifies in a phrase the racialized distribution of grievability—the parceling of lives lost into the noteworthy and the forgettable—and the consequent distribution of precarity among the living.

Yet Rankine, along with the activists and theorists of Black Lives Matter, also makes claims about scale, perspective, historicity, and form. If antiblack violence is, as the adjectives of Rankine's essay makes clear, "regular," "normal," "quotidian," "everyday," "everywhere," "commonplace," and "ambient," then what frame can possibly render it noteworthy and significant? What vantage point might enable a "sustained state of national mourning for black lives"?[2] Rankine's provocation in relation to these questions is that the killing of black people is part and parcel of everyday life and, for that, only rarely qualifies within the temporal framing of the spectacle; amidst so much violence, black claims to sanctity are rarely sufficient to summon public witness and response. Such an argument challenges how we represent and bear witness to the present and also how we narrate, understand, and remember the past. Rankine tasks us not, or not exclusively, to raise black suffering to the spectacle of eventfulness that it might become remarkable, but also to find methods for jarring the ordinary out of its complacency and making it newly problematic.

Readers of the *New York Times* print or digital editions would be forgiven if they missed Rankine's central claim, for editors chose to introduce her article under a misleading sub-headline: "The murder of three men and six women at a church in Charleston is a national tragedy, but in America, the killing of black people is an unending spectacle."[3] On the one hand, this paratext registers just how

*Genre and White Supremacy in the Postemancipation United States.* Travis M. Foster, Oxford University Press (2019). © Travis M. Foster.
DOI: 10.1093/oso/9780198838098.001.0001

enduring and intractable is the struggle to apprehend precisely the ordinary nature of antiblack violence. Like Albery Whitman's 1891 "A Bugle Note" with which I begin, the *New York Times's* language registers the difficulty faced when confronting crisis in the tempo and scale of the mundane, forcing the newspaper to settle on the paradox of "unending spectacle," in which the inaccurate noun belies the forceful reality of the qualifying adjective. On the other hand, the *New York Times's* editorial decision registers the stubbornness of historically white institutions to value black life (and the paper of record divulges its own devaluing of black lives through daily practices of inclusion, exclusion, framing, and describing). Its recourse is to the paradox of "unending spectacle" because it simply cannot assimilate Rankine's thesis—that there's nothing *spectacular* about the killing of black people—into its worldview and cannot bear the self-scrutiny it may have to face were it to acknowledge how frequently it fails to treat the killing of black people as newsworthy at all. It is true that Dylan Roof's murderous actions drew remarkably rare national and white attention to the killing of black people. Yet more than anything else, such frequently self-congratulatory attention implicitly made visible everyday white failure to account for antiblack violence and for all of the ways that such violence, along with the white supremacist hierarchy on which it depends, is reproduced, naturalized, and dismissed in the ordinary patterns of white spaces, white social norms, and white institutions.

In the face of the *New York Times's* misreading or misapprehension of her article, Rankine's argument becomes at once more tenuous and farther reaching than it otherwise might have been, calling for a shift away from the event-driven historical chronologies, media agendas, and critical attentions that fail to account for the ordinariness through which antiblackness takes its most pernicious and persistent hold. For literary critics and literary historians, this book has suggested, such a provocation means redirecting attention to the temporality of ongoingness and the scale of the everyday, valuing the generic for precisely its conventionality and unoriginality. Doing so requires no small shift in how literary critics determine what texts—and what aspects of texts—demand and reward analysis. Taking genre seriously reorients our attention to those repeated conventions that render even new texts normal and familiar. At this scale of attention, we might elect to study literature for its intersections and enmeshing with everyday social and habitual circumstances rather than merely for its ability to stand apart. Such a shift, I've argued, is vital for the critical study of white supremacy, making it possible to identify antiblackness (an initial step at which too often literary histories conclude), and, more significantly, to analyze its patterns and to trace the complexities of its social reproduction. We need better methods for seeing and describing the habitualness of violence directed against black lives; the merging of such violence into white common sense worldviews where it slips away from attention or accountability; and the collectivities, bound together in part through the conventions that make up shared life, which can blossom into antiracist alternatives. Genre, this book has ventured, provides a key approach.

{ ACKNOWLEDGMENTS }

It is a pleasure to acknowledge in print the many, many people—over the many, many years—whose support and kindness have made this book possible. At the United World College of the American West, Hannah Tyson and Patty White first showed me how culturally and politically inflected literary interpretations can produce life-changing knowledge. To this day my thinking and teaching benefit from my Amherst College professors, including E. Patrick Johnson, Andrew Parker, Michele Barale, Jay Grossman, and Robert Gooding-Williams. In between college and graduate school, my writing benefited greatly through the feedback from two demanding bosses/editors: Catherine Hanssens at Lambda Legal's HIV/ AIDS Project and Richard Burns at New York's Lesbian, Gay, Bisexual, and Transgender Community Center.

I couldn't have asked for a more rigorous and genuinely kind environment that the English Department at the University of Wisconsin—Madison. Our profession needs a Mentors' Hall of Fame, and Russ Castronovo needs to be among its first inductees. From line editing job letters (while my then-toddler son played on his living room floor) to challenging me to think more carefully about a topic (really: all the topics) to providing the most incisive of feedback—I can only hope to pay forward a fraction of his generosity. He, Rebecca Walkowitz, David Zimmerman, Cherene Sherrard-Johnson, and Stephen Kantrowitz constituted an ideal committee, merging both rigor and patience, and I continue to be grateful for their advice and generosity. My project also benefited from coursework and conversations with Caroline Levine, Henry Turner, Susan Bernstein, A. Finn Enke, Leslie Bow, Jeanne Boydston, Birgit Rasmussen, Jeffrey Steele, and Victor Bascara. Some of the best conversations within grad school happened on my porch during meetings of a dissertation writing group, and I will forever be thankful for the insights of Michelle Sizemore, Rebecca Entel, Rob Emmett, Michelle Gordon, Krista Kauffmann, and Ray Hsu. While living in Madison, I was blessed with wonderful friendships and countless conversations with my fellow graduate students and with the beautiful, odd, strong, and inspiring community of Wisconsin queers.

I'm fortunate to have spent time within two wonderful academic homes since leaving Wisconsin. I'm grateful for all the support I received during my three years at The College of Wooster, especially from the leadership of then-chair Jennifer Hayward, the mentorship of Debra Shostak and Thomas Prendergast, and the friendship of Leslie Wingard. I'd also be remiss not to mention the generous research support Wooster lent to the project, which funded a trip to the Schomburg Center for Research in Black Culture. Villanova University has also generously supported this project with research funding and leave time, as well as a subvention program that paid for the index. (Speaking of: thanks go to Dr. Cathy Hannabach of Ideas on Fire for such a fantastic index.) Each and every day, I am thankful for my Villanova colleague's warmth and support, and I owe special thanks to my two department chairs, Evan Radcliffe and Heather Hicks, respectively, who so doggedly worked to provide the space and time that are the lifeblood of Humanities research. I also thank my fellow Americanist, Michael Berthold, who welcomed me with extraordinary warmth and taught me huge amounts about teaching. I owe a special thanks to all my amazing junior colleagues (some no longer junior)—Joseph Drury, Brooke Hunter, Kamran Javadizadeh, Yumi Lee, Mary Mullen, Adrienne Perry, Megan Quigley, and Tsering Wangmo. At Villanova, I've also been wonderfully supported by some incredible graduate assistants, including Brendan Maher, Elena Patton, Julia Walls, Lee Nevitt, and Corey Arnold. Finally, I can't imagine this project ever seeing the light of day were it not for the warmth, humanity, and brilliance of Jean Lutes, whose expert suggestions and intellectual energy are reflected on each and every page.

The number of people who have read drafts of this book, helped me work through its ideas, and provided suggestions is greater than I could ever have imagined. For their time, care, and friendliness, my heartfelt thanks goes to my writing group: Angie Calcaterra, Greta LaFleur, Abram von Engen, Michele Navakas, Wendy Roberts, Kacy Tillman, and Caroline Wigginton. For reading drafts and/or listening to me struggle with ideas, I'm grateful to Laura Fisher, Ashon Crawley, Nancy Bentley, Amy Kaplan, Bethany Schneider, Lara Cohen, John Pat Leary, Hamilton Carroll, Colleen Glenney Boggs, Jed Esty, Meredith McGill, Nasser Mufti, Greg Laski, Todd Carmody, John Funchion, Gus Stadler, Jordan Alexander Stein, Julia Dauer, Elizabeth Maddock Dillon, Elizabeth Duquette, Claudia Stokes, Bert Emerson, Dana Luciano, Don James McLaughlin, Martha Nell Smith, and many, many others.

At Oxford University Press, Aimee Wright has been with this project from the very beginning, and her smarts and care have brought enjoyment to the work. The book's inclusion in the Oxford Studies in American Literary History series meant that I had the tremendous benefit of working with its editor, Gordon Hutner, who saw the book's promise early on and patiently guided it through its many phases. Gordon is the kind of editor who pays attention to writing as much as ideas. In a sentence or two, his suggestions identify patterns that provide inestimable improvement. The two anonymous readers for Oxford University Press gave the project careful, sharp, and hugely constructive feedback. The time and attention they put into their reports was nothing short of awe-inspiring, and they modeled the very best of the peer review process. Since that process ended, Samaine Lockwood outed herself as one of those readers, and I'm particularly happy to thank her by name for her insights and suggestions.

This book also benefited from readers' suggestions at *American Literary History*, which published a version of the first chapter. Over the years, I've given versions of the introduction, first chapter, and final chapter as part of the job application process, and the feedback and questions I've received from those departments and search committees have made this a much better project than it otherwise would have been. You know who you are; please also know how grateful I've been.

Work on this book has been progressing as long as both my kids, Miles Mikal Ethan Foster and Ada Regina Foster, have been alive, and through it all they've never stopped becoming ever more hilarious and inspiring and beautiful. The inclusion of their names here won't, I'm afraid, make them famous (as they recently insisted), but I do hope it serves as a reminder to them both that they fill me love and admiration. My parents, Carrita and Bob Foster, nurtured in me a love of books and learning from the very beginning. They were the least surprised people in the world when I announced I'd be pursuing a Ph.D. in literature, and they've never hesitated in their support. Mom and Dad, here's my love and gratitude in print: thanks for everything. Along with my parents, my in-laws, Darlene and Tom Freker, lent not only their tremendous emotional support and care but also their labor (childcare, household maintenance, food preparation, etc.) when I needed time to work and to write. I feel unbelievably lucky for their love and friendship and support.

This book is dedicated to my best friend and partner, Joshua Freker, who puts up with my anxieties and helps me find words for my ideas. His strength, brilliance, kindheartedness, and care have made my work—and me—inestimably better, and the abundant life we've built with our kids fills me with energy and joy. Josh, I am so very grateful for you, and I love you more than I can say.

# { ENDNOTES }

## Introduction

1. For more on Whitman, see Ivy G. Wilson, "Introduction: Reconstructing Albery Allson Whitman," in *At the Dusk of Dawn: Selected Poetry and Prose of Albery Allson Whitman* (Boston: Northeastern University Press, 2009).

2. Albery A. Whitman, "A Bugle Note," *The Christian Recorder* (Mar. 19, 1891); emphasis mine. "Racial capitalism" is Cedric Robinson's term for what Whitman is describing: the large-scale emergence of industrial capitalism as a coextension of racism and nationalism (*Black Marxism: The Making of the Black Radical Tradition* (Chapel Hill: University of North Carolina Press, 2000)). See also Edward E. Baptist, *The Half Has Never Been Told: Slavery and the Making of American Capitalism* (New York: Basic Books, 2014).

3. A variation of the resubjugation narrative appears, for instance, in Frances Ellen Watkins Harper's 1871 poem "An Appeal to the American People," depicting the white North as treasonous to the memory of the black Union dead ("To ignore, on land and flood, | All the offerings of our blood, | And to write above our slain | 'They have fought and died in vain'") (Frances Ellen Watkins Harper, "An Appeal to the American People," in *The Complete Poems of Frances E. W. Harper*, ed. Maryemma Graham (New York: Oxford University Press, 1988), 82). It shows up again in "The Color Question," Frederick Douglass's 1875 speech to a black Washington DC audience, which famously asks, "If war among the whites brought peace and liberty to the blacks, what will peace among the whites bring?" (Frederick Douglass, "The Color Question," in *The Frederick Douglass Papers, Series One: Speeches, Debates, and Interviews*, ed. John W. Blassingame and John R. McKivigan (New Haven: Yale University Press, 1991), 417).

4. Forty-four years later, in *Black Reconstruction*, W. E. B. Du Bois makes a similar observation, while also expanding Whitman's claim beyond the mingling of former enemies into white social practices writ large. Locating white racism in a new ordinariness, Du Bois describes what he terms a 'slowly evolved method' that affirmed and reaffirmed whiteness as the prerequisite for national belonging while compelling African Americans "almost continuously to submit to various badges of inferiority" (Du Bois, *Black Reconstruction* (New York: Free Press, 1998), 700, 701). As he put it in a 1907 address to students at the Philadelphia Divinity School: racism "is a problem not simply of political expediency, of economic success, but a problem above all of religious and social life" (Booker T. Washington and W. E. B. Du Bois, *The Negro in the South: His Economic Progress in Relation to his Moral and Religious Development* (Philadelphia: George W. Jacobs and Company, 1907), 185). For Whitman and Du Bois, the new color line comes into being continuously through an overlapping, interlinked series of social practices and commonsense understandings that enabled whites to negotiate their relationships to their selves, to one another, and to their nation, while also naturalizing their domination over black life. Saidiya V. Hartman echoes Du Bois in *Scenes of Subjection*, arguing that to historicize and understand intensified forms

of racist revulsion that replaced antebellum paternalism ("the revolution of [white] sentiment") we must focus our studies on the new "everyday sites and practices" of the postemancipation era (*Scenes of Subjection: Terror, Slavery, and Self-Making in Nineteenth-Century America* (New York: Oxford University Press, 1997), 121).

5. Whitman, "Bugle Note."

6. Variations of these questions have recently been explored through critical theory (e.g. Christina Sharpe's *In the Wake: On Blackness and Being* and *Monstrous Intimacies: Making Post-Slavery Subjects*), science fiction and fantasy (e.g. N. K. Jemisin's Broken Earth trilogy), poetry (e.g. Robin Coste Lewis's 2015 'Voyage of the Sable Venus'), and, as I elaborate in my coda, essay (e.g. Claudia Rankine's 2015 'The Condition of Black Life is One of Mourning' and 2017 'Was Charlottesville the Exception or the Rule?').

7. For a useful chronology of these developments, see *U.S. Popular Print Culture, 1860–1920*, ed. Christine Bold (New York: Oxford University Press, 2011), xviii–xxiii.

8. On the relationship between these technologies for the distribution of literature and the taste Americans developed for conventionality, see Thomas Augst, *The Clerk's Tale: Young Men and Moral Life in Nineteenth-Century America* (Chicago: University of Chicago Press, 2003).

9. As I elaborate later in the Introduction, these claims builds on a recent upsurge in critical attention to genre, all of which seeks to rescue it from both the rigidity of structuralist taxonomies and the extreme resistance to convention in deconstructionist sensibilities. Four recent monographs stand out particularly: Lauren Berlant, *The Female Complaint: The Unfinished Business of Sentimentality in American Culture* (Durham, NC: Duke University Press, 2008); Jeremy D. Lilley, *Common Things: Romance and the Aesthetics of Belonging in Atlantic Modernity* (New York: Fordham University Press, 2013); Theodore Martin, *Contemporary Drift: Genre, Historicism, and the Problem of the Present* (New York: Columbia University Press, 2017); and Jeremy Rosen, *Minor Characters Have their Day: Genre and the Contemporary Literary Marketplace* (New York: Columbia University Press, 2016).

10. On whiteness as a capacious and flexible hub of particularities, see Eva Cherniavsky, *Incorporation: Race, Nation, and the Body Politics of Capital* (Minneapolis: University of Minnesota Press, 2006); and Robyn Wiegman, *Object Lessons* (Durham, NC: Duke University Press, 2012).

11. I am indebted here to Stefany Harney's and Fred Moten's descriptions of the "the ordinary fugue and fugitive" fantasies that emerge from within the undercommons (*The Undercommons: Fugitive Planning and Black Study* (Brooklyn, NY: Minor Compositions, 2013), 94).

12. Claudia Stokes's history of the ways that "literary unoriginality had genuine value for much of the nineteenth century" traces the contemporary critical disdain of conventionality to our wholesale acceptance of "the New Critical regard for innovation as the distinguishing hallmark of literary achievement" ("Novel Commonplaces: Quotation, Epigraphs, and Literary Authority," 30 *ALH* (2018): 217, 202. Demonstrating precisely such an attitude in relation to genre and the value of genre criticism, Jonathan Culler argues that the point of genre analysis is primarily to offset the value of unconventional texts: "We are rich in theories about language, discourse, hybridity, identity, sexuality, but not in theories of the rules and conventions of particular genres, though such theories are necessary for understanding the ways individual works subvert these conventions—which, after all, is a major point of interest for interpretation" (*The Literary in Theory* (Stanford, CA: Stanford

University Press, 2007), 11). See also *Revisiting the Frankfurt School: Essays on Culture, Media, and Theory*, ed. David Berry (New York: Routledge: 2011).

13. For a significant analysis of dissent as a potent feature of ordinary black experience and aesthetics, see Paul Gilroy, *The Black Atlantic: Modernity and Double-Consciousness* (Cambridge, MA: Harvard University Press, 1995), an argument I take up further in Chapter 4.

14. Hannah Rosen, *Terror in the Heart of Freedom: Citizenship, Sexual Violence, and the Meaning of Race in the Postemancipation South* (Chapel Hill: University of North Carolina Press, 2009), 5.

15. Perhaps the most useful starting place for this historiography is the thirteenth chapter of Frederick Douglass's 1892 autobiography, titled "Vast Changes" (Douglass, *The Life and Times of Frederick Douglass*). Recent scholarship includes Frederick Cooper, Thomas Holt, and Rebecca Scott, *Beyond Slavery: Explorations of Race, Labor, and Citizenship in Postemancipation Societies* (Chapel Hill: University of North Carolina Press, 2000); Demetrius L. Eudell, *The Political Languages of Emancipation in the British Caribbean and U.S. South* (Chapel Hill: University of North Carolina Press, 2002); Eric Foner, *Reconstruction: America's Unfinished Revolution, 1863–1877* (New York: Harper and Row, 1988); Steven Hahn, *A Nation under our Feet: Black Political Struggles in the Rural South from Slavery to the Great Migration* (Cambridge, MA: Harvard University Press, 2003); Rebecca Scott, *Degrees of Freedom: Louisiana and Cuba after Slavery* (Cambridge, MA: Harvard University Press, 2005); and *The Materiality of Freedom: Archaeologies of Postemancipation Life*, ed. Jodi A. Barnes (Columbia: University of South Carolina Press, 2011). Historians also pursue 'postemancipation' as a useful category for Atlantic and comparative history. Readers may be interested, in particular, in Natasha Lightfoot's fantastic *Troubling Freedom*, which suggests many significant comparisons between the postbellum United States and post-1834 Antigua (*Troubling Freedom: Antigua and the Aftermath of British Emancipation* (Durham, NC: Duke University Press, 2015)).

16. I intend this emphasis on race and the ordinary as a complement rather than a challenge to projects that take up more visible objects in the history of American race relations. To cite one prominent example in this historiography, consider Colin Dayan's analysis of the gaping loophole carved out by Section 1 of the Thirteenth Amendment, which outlawed slavery "except for punishment of crime whereof the party shall have been duly convicted." The amendment, as Dayan argues, "marked the discursive link between the civilly dead felon and the slave or social nonperson," extending slavery's social status beyond both the historical border of emancipation and the geographic border of the South Legal history, literary history, and the history of everyday social experience intersect in this chiasmic knot tied around criminality and race ("[c]riminality was racialized and race criminalized") (*The Law is a White Dog: How Legal Rituals Make and Unmake Persons* (Princeton: Princeton University Press, 2011) 54). The amendment turned everyday, recurrent black social practices, such as the fellowship produced through gospel sermons (my topic in Chapter 4), into fodder for criminal misconduct, rendering African Americans unfit for civic belonging. Simultaneously, it extended roomy permissiveness around everyday, recurrent white criminality, such as the vandalism and carousing of college students enthusiastically celebrated in the pages of campus novels (my topic in Chapter 1), rendering them cause for national celebration rather than complaint.

17. Arif Dirlik, "Race Talk, Race, and Contemporary Racism" 123 *PMLA* (2008): 1367.

18. Charles W. Mills, *The Racial Contract* (Ithaca, NY: Cornell University Press, 1997), 3.

19. Toni Morrison, *Playing in the Dark: Whiteness and the Literary Imagination* (New York: Random House, 1992), 46–7.

20. Christina Sharpe usefully refers to antiblackness as a total climate (*In the Wake: On Blackness and Being* (Durham, NC: Duke University Press, 2016), 21, 13–14).

21. Whitman, "A Bugle Note."

22. Nina Silber, *The Romance of Reunion: Northerners and the South, 1865–1900* (Chapel Hill: University of North Carolina Press, 1993); David W. Blight, *Race and Reunion: The Civil War in American Memory* (Cambridge, MA: Belknap Press of Harvard University Press, 2001); Edward J. Blum, *Reforging the White Republic: Race, Religion, and American Nationalism* (Baton Rouge: Louisiana State University Press, 2005). I am indebted to two recent review essays published on sectional reconciliation scholarship: Robert Cook, "The Quarrel Forgotten?: Toward a Clearer Understanding of Sectional Reconciliation," *The Journal of the Civil War Era* 6 (2016): 413–36; and Nina Silber, "Reunion and Reconciliation, Reviewed and Reconsidered," *The Journal of American History* 103 (2016): 59–83.

23. Elizabeth Duquette, *Loyal Subjects: Bonds of Nation, Race, and Allegiance in Nineteenth-Century America* (New Brunswick, NJ: Rutgers University Press, 2010), 3, 5.

24. Ed Folsom, "'That Towering Bulge of Pure White': Whitman, Melville, the Capitol Dome, and Black America," *Leviathan: A Journal of Melville Studies* 16 (2014): 113.

25. Herman Melville, *Battle-Pieces and Aspects of the War* (1866; rpt New York: Da Capo Press, 1995), 267.

26. I am paraphrasing Folsom, "'That Towering Bulge of Pure White'", 116. See also Peter J. Bellis, 'Reconciliation as Sequel and Supplement: *Drum-Taps* and *Battle-Pieces' Leviathan: A Journal of Melville Studies* 17 (2015): 79–93; Thomas Kikant, "Melville's *Battle-Pieces* and the Environments of War," *ESQ* 60 (2014): 557–90; Zach Hutchins, "Miscegenetic Melville: Race and Reconstruction in *Clarel*" *ELH* 80 (2013): 1173–203; Edward Lybeer, "Whitman's War and the Status of Literature," *Arizona Quarterly* 67 (2011): 23–40; Tom Nurmi, "Shadows in the Shenandoah: Melville, Slavery, and the Elegiac Landscape" *Leviathan: A Journal of Melville Studies* 17 (2015): 7–24; Amy Parsons, "Desire, Forgetting, and the Future: Walt Whitman's Civil War" *Arizona Quarterly* 71 (2015): 85–109; Elizabeth Renker, "Melville and the Worlds of Civil War Poetry" *Leviathan: A Journal of Melville Studies* 16 (2014): 135–52; and Timothy Sweet, "Battle-Pieces and Vernacular Poetics" *Leviathan: A Journal of Melville Studies* 17 (2015): 25–42. For a dissenting view, arguing that Melville "refuses to erase, in the service of social consensus, persistent questions surrounding race," see Brian Yothers, "Melville's Reconstructions: 'The Swamp Angel,' 'Formerly a Slave,' and the Moorish Maid in 'Lee in the Capitol,'" *Leviathan: A Journal of Melville Studies* 17 (2015): 76.

27. Benjamin G. Cloyd, *Haunted by Atrocity: Civil War Prisons in American Memory* (Baton Rouge: Louisiana State University Press, 2010); Mark Elliott, *Color-Blind Justice: Albion Tourgée and the Quest for Racial Equality from the Civil War to Plessy v. Ferguson* (New York: Oxford University Press, 2006); Barbara A. Gannon, *The Won Cause: Black and White Comradeship in the Grand Army of the Republic* (Chapel Hill: University of North Carolina Press, 2011); M. Keith Harris, *Across the Bloody Chasm: The Culture of Commemoration among Civil War Veterans* (Baton Rouge: Louisiana State University Press, 2014); Robert Hunt, *The Good Men Who Won the War: Army of the Cumberland Veterans and Emancipation Memory* (Tuscaloosa: University of Alabama Press, 2010); Caroline Janney, *Remembering the Civil War: Reunion and the Limits of Reconciliation* (Chapel Hill: University of North Carolina Press, 2013); and John Neff, *Honoring the Civil War Dead: Commemoration and the Problem of Reconciliation* (Lawrence: University Press of Kansas, 2005).

28. Brian Matthew Jordan, *Marching Home: Union Veterans and their Unending Civil War* (New York: Livewright, 2014), 194–5.

29. Charles W. Calhoun, *Conceiving a New Republic: The Republican Party and the Southern Question, 1869–1900* (Lawrence: University Press of Kansas, 2006); Heather Cox Richardson, *The Death of Reconstruction: Race, Labor, and Politics in the Post-Civil War North, 1865–1901* (Cambridge, MA: Harvard University Press, 2001).

30. Cecilia Elizabeth O'Leary, *To Die For: The Paradox of American Patriotism* (Princeton: Princeton University Press, 1999), 203.

31. Timothy Sweet, "Introduction: Shaping the Civil War Canon," in *Literary Cultures of the Civil War*, ed. Timothy Sweet (Athens: University of Georgia Press, 2016), 2. See also Robert Levine on "the 'relative indeterminacy' of that which appears to be fixed and settled: the racial or racialized state" (Robert S. Levine, *Dislocating Race and Nation: Episodes in Nineteenth-Century American Literary Nationalism* (Chapel Hill: University of North Carolina Press, 2008), 7).

32. Colleen C. O'Brien, *Race, Romance, and Rebellion: Literatures of the Americas in the Nineteenth Century* (Charlottesville: University of Virginia Press, 2013), 157.

33. Pierre Bourdieu, *The Logic of Practice*, trans. Richard Nice (Stanford, CA: Stanford University Press, 1980), 56.

34. On biopolitics and race, see Kyla Schuller, *The Biopolitics of Feeling: Race, Sex, and Science in the Nineteenth Century* (Durham, NC: Duke University Press, 2018), Alexander G. Weheliye, *Habeas Viscus: Racializing Assemblages, Biopolitics, and Black Feminist Theories of the Human* (Durham, NC: Duke University Press, 2014); and Sokthan Yeng, *The Biopolitics of Race: State Racism and U.S. Immigration* (New York: Lexington Books, 2014).

35. Bourdieu, *The Logic of Practice*, 58.

36. Heather Love, "Critique is Ordinary," *PMLA* 132 (2017): 368.

37. Mills, *Racial Contract*, 19.

38. Charles Mills, *Blackness Visible: Essays on Philosophy and Race* (Ithaca, NY: Cornell University Press, 1998), 34.

39. George Yancy, *Look, a White! Philosophical Essays on Whiteness* (Philadelphia: Temple University Press, 2012), 17, 31. Emphasis in original.

40. Ibid., 3.

41. Aileen Moreton-Robinson, *The White Possessive: Property, Power, and Indigenous Sovereignty* (Minneapolis: University of Minnesota Press, 2015), xii. See also Jean M. O'Brien, *Firsting and Lasting: Writing Indians out of Existence in New England* (Minneapolis: University of Minnesota Press, 2010); and Patrick Wolfe, "Settler Colonialism and the Elimination of the Native," *Journal of Genocide Research* 8 (2006): 387–409.

42. Mark Rifkin, *Settler Common Sense: Queerness and Everyday Colonialism in the American Renaissance* (Minneapolis: University of Minnesota Press, 2014), 17. For recent work on the racial ordinariness that focuses not on the benefactors of white supremacy and the racial contract, but on those forced to negotiate its exclusions, see Ju Yon Kim's remarkably subtle *The Racial Mundane*. Kim tracks how, within the very ordinariness of racial existence, everyday bodily performances flicker as they mark the Asian American subject with stark racial distinction and then fade into a blurring of racial difference (*The Racial Mundane: Asian American Performance and the Embodied Everyday* (New York: New York University Press, 2015)).

43. Frequently cited texts within 1990s Whiteness Studies include Theodore Allen, *The Invention of the White Race, vol. 1: Racial Oppression and Social Control* (London: Verso,

1994); M. F. Jacobson, *Whiteness of a Different Color: European Immigrants and the Alchemy of Race* (Cambridge, MA: Harvard University Press, 1998); Ruth Frankenberg, *White Woman Race Matters: The Social Construction of Whiteness* (London: Routledge, 1993); and Noel Ignatiev, *How the Irish Became White* (New York: Routledge, 1995). By 2012, as Robyn Wiegman puts it in her critique of the field, "'Whiteness Studies as an autonomous field, listed on curricula vitae and supported by its own institutional initiatives, conferences, and publishing venues, has lost most of its critical appeal" (*Object Lessons*, 141).

44. Mat Johnson, *Pym* (New York: Spiegel & Grau, 2011), 31. Moreover, as historian Edward J. Blum notes in *Reforging the White Republic*, 1990s whiteness studies frequently left out the most elemental histories of antiblackness, including enslavement and its post-Reconstruction recapitulation. As just one glaring example, Blum notes that "studies of the making and transforming of whiteness in the nineteenth century...have largely neglected that the white republic fell, shattered, and was eventually put back together again," a critical absence that prevents them from seeing that, by the 1890s whiteness had "re-ascended and transcended sectionalism" (7).

45. Morrison, *Playing in the Dark*, 47.

46. Charles W. Mills, "Racial Exploitation and the Wages of Whiteness," in *What White Looks Like: African American Philosophers on the Whiteness Question*, ed. George Yancy (New York: Routledge, 2004), 32. Emphases in original.

47. See Cody Marrs, *Nineteenth-Century American Literature and the Long Civil War* (New York: Cambridge University Press, 2015); and Christopher Hager and Cody Marrs, "Afterword: Archiving the War," in *A History of American Civil War Literature*, ed. Coleman Hutchison (New York: Cambridge University Press, 2016).

48. Du Bois, *Black Reconstruction*, 124.

49. John Greenleaf Whittier, *The Letters of John Greenleaf Whittier, Volume 3*, ed. John B. Pickard (Cambridge, MA: Harvard University Press, 1975), 29–30.

50. John Greenleaf Whittier, "'Ein feste Burg ist unser Gott,'" in *Selected Poems*, ed. Brenda Wineapple (New York: Library of America, 2004), 90.

51. Isabella MacFarlane, "The Two Slave Mothers," *Continental Monthly* 4 (Nov. 1863). The poem also appeared in *The Anglo-African* 3 (Nov. 7, 1863): 1.

52. Hartman, *Scenes of Subjection*, 139.

53. Caroline Levine, *Forms: Whole, Rhythm, Hierarchy, Network* (Princeton: Princeton University Press, 2015), 56.

54. Marrs, *Nineteenth-Century American Literature and the Long Civil War*, 4, 6. See also Christopher Hager, Edward Sugden, Elizabeth Duquette, and Gregory Lasky, "Roundtable on The Long Civil War," *Common-place.org* 17 (2016).

55. Du Bois, *Black Reconstruction*, 670.

56. James Baldwin, *Just Above my Head* (New York: Random House, 1978), 292.

57. Sharpe, *In the Wake*, 12.

58. Northrop Frye, *Anatomy of Criticism: Four Essays* (Princeton: Princeton UP, 1957), 95–6.

59. Virginia Jackson, "The Function of Criticism at the Present Time," *Los Angeles Review of Books* (April 12, 2015).

60. My understanding of rhythm is indebted to Caroline Levine's *Forms*.

61. Berlant, *The Female Complaint*, 4. See also Lauren Berlant, *Cruel Optimism* (Durham, NC: Duke University Press, 2011), esp. pp. 6–9.

62. Judith Butler, *Gender Trouble* (New York: Routledge, 1999); Bourdieu, *The Logic of Practice*; Henri Lefebvre, *Introduction*, vol. 2 of *Critique of Everyday Life*, trans. John Moore (London: Verso, 1991).

63. Henri Lefebvre, *Foundations for a Sociology of the Everyday*, vol. 2 of *Critique of Everyday Life*, trans. John Moore (New York: Verso, 2002), 45.

64. Stanley Cavell, *In Quest of the Ordinary: Lines of Skepticism and Romanticism* (Chicago: University of Chicago Press, 1988), 154.

65. I'm building here on Franco Moretti, who applies a Darwinian understanding to the lifecycle of any particular genre: "A genre exhausts its potentialities—and the time comes to give a competitor a chance—when its inner form is no longer capable of representing the most significant aspects of contemporary reality" (*Graphs, Maps, and Trees: Abstract Models for Literary History* (New York: Verso, 2005), 17). My focus tweaks this claim in a small yet significant way. Where Moretti highlights genres' ability to represent their reality, I want to focus more their usefulness for their reality, a usefulness that cannot be reduced to representation. Moreover, as I'm describing it, genre operates as an agent in the present moment rather than as a tool for historical classification, and it therefore departs from taxonomy, as it is sometimes understood. That is, genre is not merely a device to be applied in retrospect through what Michel Foucault describes as "the history of the order imposed on things" (*The Order of Things: An Archaeology of the Human Sciences*, trans. Alan Sheridan (New York: Vintage, 1994), xxiv).

66. Bruce Robbins, "Afterword," *PMLA* 122 (2007): 1650.

67. Wai Chee Dimock, "Introduction: Genres as Fields of Knowledge," *PMLA* 122 (2007): 1377.

68. Jacques Derrida, "The Law of Genre," trans. Avital Ronell *Glyph* 7 (1980): 213.

69. I am thinking of Franco Moretti's argument in *Graphs, Maps, and Trees*. Rigorous critiques of Moretti's quantitative method are widespread. Two of these come with particularly useful insights about genre and genre criticism: Jeremy Rosen, *Minor Characters*, 15; and Wai Chee Dimock, "The Egyptian Pronoun, Lyric, Novel, the Book of the Dead," *New Literary History* 39 (2008): 620.

70. Dimock, "Introduction," 1378.

71. Rosen, *Minor Characters*, 17.

72. Eric Lott, *Love & Theft: Blackface Minstrelsy and the American Working Class* (New York: Oxford University Press, 1993).

73. Bill Brown, *The Material Unconscious: American Amusement, Stephen Crane & the Economies of Play* (Cambridge, MA: Harvard University Press, 1996), 216.

74. See Bruce E. Baker, *What Reconstruction Meant: Historical Memory in the American South* (Charlottesville: University of Virginia Press, 2007); K. Stephen Prince, *Stories of the South: Race and the Reconstruction of Southern Identity, 1865–1915* (Chapel Hill: University of North Carolina Press, 2014); Trent Watts, *One Homogenous People: Narratives of White Southern Identity, 1890–1920* (Knoxville: University of Tennessee Press, 2010); and *Thomas Dixon Jrvf and the Birth of Modern America*, ed. Michele K. Gillespie and Randal L. Hall (Baton Rouge: Louisiana State University Press, 2006).

75. See Karen A. Keely, "Marriage Plots and National Reunion: The Trope of Romantic Reconciliation in Postbellum Literature," *The Mississippi Quarterly* 51, no. 4 (1998): 621–48; and Silber, *The Romance of Reunion*.

## Chapter 1

1. Elizabeth Stuart Phelps, *Donald Marcy* (Boston: Houghton Mifflin, 1893), 28–9.

2. Ibid., 29.

3. Ibid., 29–30.

4. Ibid., 44

5. Ibid., 45.

6. Ibid., 32.

7. Ibid., 38.

8. Ibid., 137.

9. Ibid., 148–9.

10. On the post-1877 life of Reconstruction, see Heather Cox Richardson's *The Death of Reconstruction: Race, Labor, and Politics in the Post-Civil War North, 1865–1901* (Cambridge, MA: Harvard University Press, 2004).

11. William Tucker Washburn, *Fair Harvard; A Story of American College Life* (New York: Putnam, 1869), 20.

12. For a useful study of the role played by heterosexual marriage narratives in reconciliationist sentiment, see Nina Silber's *The Romance of Reunion: Northerners and the South, 1865–1900* (Chapel Hill: University of North Carolina Press, 1997).

13. Owen Wister, *Philosophy 4: A Story of Harvard University* (New York: Macmillan, 1903), 66.

14. See also Elizabeth Duquette, *Loyal Subjects: Bonds of Nation, Race, and Allegiance in Nineteenth-Century America* (New Brunswick, NJ: Rutgers University Press, 2010).

15. John E. Kramer, *The American College Novel: An Annotated Bibliography*, 2nd edn (Lanham, MD: Scarecrow Press, 2004). In addition to the campus novels cited or mentioned in this chapter, see also Ralph Henry Barbour, *The Land of Joy* (1903); Edward Tyler Blair, *Lloyd Lee: A Story of Yale* (1878); Flandrau, *The Diary of a Freshman* (1900); Hamlin Garland, *Rose of Dutcher's Coolly* (1895); Richard Thayer Holbrook, *Boys and Men: A Story of Life at Yale* (1900); Rupert Sargent Holland, *The Count at Harvard* (1906); Reginald Wright Kauffman, *Jarvis of Harvard* (1901); Shirley Everton Johnson, *The Cult of the Purple Rose* (1902); Jesse Lynch Williams, *The Adventures of a Freshman* (1899); Wood, *College Days: Or Harry's Career at Yale* (1894); Eleanor Dey Young, *Two Princetonians and Other Jerseyites* (1898); and Rida Young and Gilbert Coleman, *Brown of Harvard* (1907).

16. Very few literary critics focus on what I'm calling "campus novels." Historians of higher education, on the other hand, have occasionally turned to the genre. These include Michael S. Hevel, "Setting the Stage for Animal House: Student Drinking in College Novels, 1865–1933," *The Journal of Higher Education* 85 (2014): 370–401; and Christian K. Anderson and Daniel A. Clark, "Imaging Harvard: Changing Visions of Harvard in Fiction, 1890–1940," *American Educational History Journal* 39 (2012): 181–99.

17. Elaine Showowalter, *Faculty Towers: The Academic Novel and its Discontents* (Philadelphia: University of Pennsylvania Press, 2005), 4. On academic novels, see also *Academic Novels as Satire: Critical Studies of an Emerging Genre*, ed. Mark Bosco and Kimberly Rae Connor (Lewiston, NY: The Edwin Mellen Press, 2007); Ian Carter, *Ancient Cultures of Conceit: British University Fiction in the Post-War Years* (London: Routledge, 1990); Janice Rosen, *The University in Modern Fiction* (New York: St. Martin's Press, 1993); and Jeffrey J. Williams, "The Rise of the Academic Novel" *ALH* 24, no. 3 (2012): 561–89.

18. Hogwarth Press Bookshop, Advertisement, *New York Times* (Nov. 12, 1932): 3.

19. John O. Lyons, *The College Novel in America* (Carbondale: Southern Illinois University Press, 1962), 8.

20. Franco Moretti, *The Way of the World: The Bildungsroman in European Culture* (New York: Verso, 2000), 15; emphasis original.

21. Williams, "The Rise of the Academic Novel," 562. Like Williams, my research into the genre follows the bibliographic work of John E. Kramer, which identifies novels set primarily on or around college campuses, from Nathaniel Hawthorne's *Fanshawe* (1828) to William Hart's *Never Fade Away* (2002) (*The American College Novel: An Annotated Bibliography* (Lanham, MD: Scarecrow, 2004)).

22. Stephen Crane, *The Red Badge of Courage* (New York: Norton, 1994), 3.

23. Ibid., 26.

24. Henry James, *The Bostonians* (New York: Vintage, 1991), 221, 222.

25. Herman Melville, *Battle-Pieces and Aspects of the War* (New York: Harper & Brothers, 1866), 158–9.

26. F. Scott Fitzgerald's *This Side of Paradise* (New York: Penguin,1990), 30.

27. Michael Warner, "Uncritical Reading," in *Polemic: Critical or Uncritical*, ed. Jane Gallop (New York: Routledge, 2004), 15.

28. Wister, *Philosophy 4*, 23.

29. Ibid., 52.

30. Ibid., 83.

31. Cited in Helen Lefkowitz Horowitz, *Campus Life: Undergraduate Cultures From the End of the Eighteenth Century to the Present* (Chicago: University of Chicago Press, 1987), 51.

32. William James, "Letter to Henry James, 5 Dec. 1869," in *William and Henry James: Selected Letters*, ed. Ignas K. Skrupskelis and Elizabeth M. Berkeley (Charlottesville: University of Virginia Press, 1997), 61.

33. Kramer, *The American College Novel*, 3.

34. *Harvard Lampoon* (1876), 27; *William and Henry James: Selected Letters*, ed. Ignas K. Skrupskelis and Elizabeth M. Berkeley (Charlottesville: University Press of Virginia, 1997), 61; Kramer, *The American College Novel*, 3; William Tucker Washburn, *Fair Harvard* (1869), 14.

35. Lyman Baggs, *Four Years at Yale* (New Haven: Charles C. Chatfield & Co., 1871).

36. Rev. of *Hammersmith* by Mark Sibley Severance, "Literary Notes," *New York Times* (Aug. 24, 1878): 2.

37. "Books of the Month," *Atlantic Monthly 57* (1886), 718.

38. Rev. of *Harvard Episodes* by Charles Flandrau, "Notes and Comments," *New York Times* (Dec. 4, 1897): B10.

39. Rev. of *Yale Yarns* by John Seymour Woods, *Daily Inter Ocean* (June 29, 1895): 10.

40. See Michael David Cohen, *Reconstructing the Campus: Higher Education and the American Civil War* (Charlottesville: University of Virginia Press, 2012), Mark R. Nemec, *Ivory Towers and Nationalist Minds: Universities, Leadership, and the Development of the American State* Ann Arbor: University of Michigan Press, 2006), and Richard F. Teichgraeber, *Building Culture: Studies in the Intellectual History of Industrializing America, 1867–1910* (Columbia: University of South Carolina Press, 2010).

41. Teichgraeber, *Building Culture*, 106.

42. Noah Porter, *The American Colleges and the American Public* (New Haven: C. C. Chatfield & Co., 1870), 178.

43. Horowitz, *Campus Life*, 54.

44. George Santayana, "A Glimpse of Yale," *The Harvard Monthly* 15 (Dec. 1892): 93.

45. Horowitz, *Campus Life*, 23–55.

46. Ibid., 55. For a detailed and well-documented examination of this transition on Rutger's campus, including evidence of nonstudent enthusiasm for student culture, see Michael Moffatt, "Inventing the 'Time-Honored Traditions' of 'Old Rutgers': Rutgers Student Culture, 1858–1900," *The Journal of the Rutgers University Libraries* 47, no. 1 (1985): 1–11.

47. To my mind, the best history of this transition remains Laurence R. Veysey's *The Emergence of the American University* (Chicago: The University of Chicago Press, 1965). See, especially, 57–120 and 263–341. Veysey's text does remain, however, frustratingly blind to the tremendous growth in higher education for women, along with women's educational institutions and coeducation, during the nineteenth century. Barbara Miller Solomon's *In the Company of Educated Women: A History of Women and Higher Education in America* offers the best corrective ((New Haven: Yale University Press, 1985), esp. 43–114).

48. Thorstein Veblen, *The Higher Learning in America: A Memorandum on the Conduct of Universities by Business Men* (New York: Sagamore Press, Inc., 1957), 46, 51.

49. Veblen, *Higher Learning*, 87, 97.

50. Wister, *Philosophy* 4, 93–4.

51. For more on the role of college life, especially fraternities and athletics, in the production of a business class, see E. Anthony Rotundo, *American Manhood: Transformations in Masculinity from the Revolution to the Modern Era* (New York: Basic Books, 1993), 239–44; and Horowitz, *Campus Life*, 41–55.

52. Veblen, *Higher Learning*, 16.

53. Ibid., 12.

54. Michael David Cohen, *Reconstructing the Campus: Higher Education and the American Civil War* (Charlottesville: University of Virginia Press, 2012), 11.

55. My argument here has been influenced by Eva Cherniavsky, *Incorporations: Race, Nation, and the Body Politics of Capital* (Minneapolis: University of Minnesota Press, 2006), 49–70; George Lipsitz, "The Possessive Investment in Whiteness: Racialized Social Democracy and the 'White' Problem in American Studies," *American Quarterly* 47 (Sept. 1995): 369–87; and Robyn Wiegman, "Whiteness Studies and the Paradox of Particularity," *boundary 2* 26 (fall 1999): 115–50.

56. This focus on the praxis of social life distinguishes fraternity in campus novels from the imagined or fantastic fraternity that critics have so usefully analyzed in antebellum texts. See especially Dana Nelson, *National Manhood: Capitalist Citizenship and the Imagined Fraternity of White Men* (1998); and Peter Coviello, *Intimacy in America: Dreams of Affiliation in Antebellum Literature* (2005).

57. Olive San Louie Anderson, *An American Girl, and her Four Years in a Boys' College* (1878; Ann Arbor: University of Michigan Press, 2006), 48–50.

58. Ibid., 224.

59. Phelps, *Donald Marcy*, 65.

60. John Seymour Wood, *Yale Yarns: Sketches of Life at Yale University* (New York: Putnam, 1895), 22.

61. Helen Dawes Brown, *Two College Girls* (Boston: Ticknor, 1886), 50.

62. Washburn, *Fair Harvard*, 25.

63. Severance, *Hammersmith*, 479.

64. Washburn, *Fair Harvard*, 240.

65. Owen Johnson, *Stover at Yale* (New York: Frederick A. Stokes, 1912), 232.

66. Ibid., 320, 322.

67. Matthew Frye Jacobson's *Whiteness of a Different Color: European Immigrants and the Alchemy of Race* (1998), 42. See also David Roediger's *The Wages of Whiteness: Race and the Making of the American Working Class* (1991), and Matthew Ignatiev's *How the Irish Became White* (1995).

68. For arguments about whiteness as capacious rather than plural, see Cherniavsky, *Incorporations*; and Wiegman, "Whiteness Studies and the Paradox of Particularity."

69. Jacques Derrida, *Politics of Friendship*, trans. George Collins (New York: Verso, 1997), viii.

70. Novels set on campuses like Vassar or Smith largely refrained from presenting masculine or tomboy characters, preferring instead to have their characters participate in traditionally feminine social practices that replicate in form those found on the all-male campuses. This, I think, largely stems from their sensitivity to arguments, dating at least to Dr Edward L. Clarke's 1873 *Sex in Education: A Fair Chance for the Girls*, that all-women's campuses distorted femininity, damaged reproductive capacity, and turned women into spinsters, at best, and lesbians, at worst. Toward the turn of the century, the specter of white "race suicide" added to these pressures, with several influential thinkers blaming presumed declining white birth rates on the higher education of women. See Patricia A. Palmieri, "From Republican Motherhood to Race Suicide: Arguments on the Higher Education of Women," in *Educating Women Together: Coeducation in a Changing World*, ed. Carol Lasser (Chicago: University of Illinois Press, 1987), 49–64.

71. Caroline Fuller, *Across the Campus: A Story of College Life* (New York: Scribner's, 1899), 4, 3.

72. Joy Lichtenstein, *For the Blue and Gold: A Tale of Life at the University of California* (San Francisco: Robertson, 1901), 65, 66.

73. W. E. B. Du Bois, "The College Bred Negro," in *Proceedings of the Fifth Conferences for the Study of the Negro Problems* (Atlanta: Atlanta University Press, 1900), 34. I discovered the Du Bois document through Linda Perkins's remarkable history of black students at the Seven Sisters colleges ("The African American Female Elite: The Early History of African American Women in the Seven Sister Colleges, 1880–1960," *Harvard Educational Review* 67, no. 4 (1997): 718–57).

74. Du Bois, "The College Bred Negro," 34.

75. Washburn, *Fair Harvard*, 45.

76. William Faulkner, *Absalom, Absalom!* (New York: Vintage, 1990), 93, 253.

77. Brown, *Two College Girls*, 128.

78. Washburn, *Fair Harvard*, 19.

79. Lichtenstein, *For the Blue and Gold*, 7.

80. Severance, *Hammersmith*, 342, 341.

81. Brown, *Two College Girls*, 288.

82. Elisa Tamarkin, *Anglophilia: Deference, Devotion, and Antebellum America* (Chicago: University of Chicago Press, 2008), 302.

83. Svetlana Boym, *The Future of Nostalgia* (New York: Basic, 2001), 42.

84. David W. Blight, *Race and Reunion: The Civil War in American Memory* (Cambridge, MA: Harvard University Press, 2001), 4.

85. Tara McPherson, *Reconstructing Dixie: Gender, Race, and Nostalgia in the Imagined South* (Durham, NC: Duke University Press, 2003), 115–27.

86. My claims about the relationship between individual texts, genre, and history here draw on Frederic Jameson, *The Political Unconscious: Narrative as a Socially Symbolic Act* (Ithaca, NY: Cornell University Press, 1981).

87. Frederick Loring, *Two College Friends* (Boston: Loring, 1871), 92–3.

88. Ibid., 84.

89. Ibid., 36.

90. Excerpts of the novel have been anthologized in *Glances Backward: An Anthology of American Homosexual Writing, 1830–1920* (2006), ed. James J. Gifford; and *The Romantic Friendship Reader: Love Stories Between Men in Victorian America* (2003), ed. Mark Nissen. It has also been examined in Jonathan Katz's *Love Stories: Sex Between Men before Homosexuality* (2001); Nissen's *Manly Love: Romantic Friendship in American Fiction* (2009); and Chris Packard's *Queer Cowboys and Other Erotic Male Friendships in Nineteenth-Century American Literature* (2005).

91. Chris Packard, *Queer Cowboys and Other Erotic Male Friendships in Nineteenth-Century American Literature* (New York: Palgrave, 2005), 5.

92. Loring, *Two College Friends*, 130–1.

93. Ibid., 150.

94. Loring, *Two College Friends*, 161.

95. Ibid., 160–1.

96. W. E. B. Du Bois, *The Autobiography of W. E. B. DuBois: A Soliloquy on Viewing my Life from the Last Decade of its First Century* (New York: International Publishers, 1969), 135.

97. W. E. B. Du Bois, *Dusk of Dawn: An Essay Toward an Autobiography of a Race Concept* (1940; New York: Oxford University Press, 2007), 35.

98. W. E. B. Du Bois, *The Souls of Black Folk*, ed. David W. Blight and Robert Gooding-Williams (Boston: Bedford Books, 1997), 163, 165.

99. Ibid., 165.

100. Ibid., 166.

101. Du Bois mocks campus slang, for instance, in his Autobiography, where he says "I did not pick out 'snap' courses" and later remarks that most of the white students considered him a "'grind'" (*Autobiography*, 132, 139).

## Chapter 2

1. For more on late-nineteenth-century magazines as genres, see Jennifer Phegley, *Educating the Proper Woman Reader: Victorian Family Magazines and the Cultural Health of the Nation* (Columbus: The Ohio State University Press, 2004).

2. The *Journal* spent its first three years as *The Ladies' Home Journal and Practical Housekeeper*. For more on the *Journal's* history and influence, see Helen Damon-Moore, *Magazines for the Millions: Gender and Commerce in the* Ladies' *Home Journal and the* Saturday Evening Post, *1880–1910* (Albany: SUNY Press, 1994); and Jennifer Scanlon, *Inarticulate Longings: The Ladies' Home Journal, Gender, and the Promises of Consumer Culture* (New York: Routledge, 1995). In the late 1800s the *Journal* surveyed 100 randomly chosen subscribers, asking how many individuals read their issue every month and concluding that each issue counted seven distinct readers (Edward Bok, "The Magazine with a Million," *The Ladies' Home Journal* 20 (Feb. 1903): 16).

3. Lauren Berlant, *The Female Complaint: The Unfinished Business of Sentimentality in American Culture* (Durham, NC: Duke University Press, 2008), viii, x.

4. We don't typically think of a magazine like *The Ladies' Home Journal* as a genre. But we should. Magazines gather together such a wide range of materials—advertisements, advice columns, short and serialized fiction, jokes and anecdotes, news, opinion pieces, readers' letters—that they may seem too disparate to maintain the recognizable and reproducible conventions we associate with genre. Nevertheless, as serialized vehicles for distributing and arranging conventional content, magazines act as genres par excellence, regularizing promises and expectations into an utterly predictable delivery system and providing a new instantiation of a familiar cultural and aesthetic text every single month. Simultaneously, with organizing features such as an implicit house style, recurring columns and features, and a heavy editorial hand, magazines—and especially the early magazines of white women's mass culture—provided a frame that presented even highly disparate content as not merely proximate but interconnected and kindred. The *Journal's* success, we might say, hinged precisely on its ability to produce itself as generic, creating in readers the desires, expectations, and satisfactions genre at once produces and satisfies.

5. Lyman Abbott, "Just Among Ourselves," *Ladies' Home Journal* 10 (July 1893): 26; Michael A. Elliott, *The Culture Concept: Writing and Difference in the Age of Realism* (Minneapolis: University of Minnesota Press, 2002); and Nancy Glazener, *Reading for Realism: The History of a U.S. Literary Institution, 1850–1910* (Durham, NC: Duke University Press, 1997).

6. Lida Clarkson, "Letter 6," *The Ladies' Home Journal and Practical Housekeeper* 3 (May 1886): 6.

7. Glazener, *Reading for Realism*, 189.

8. M.M.M., "Letter 2," *The Ladies' Home Journal* 6 (Dec. 1888): 10.

9. H.L., "Letter 4," *The Ladies' Home Journal* 4 (Oct. 1887): 8.

10. For more on the advice column, see Jean Lutes's article, "Lovelorn Columns: A Genre Scorned," 91 *American Literature* (2019): 59–90.

11. Damon-Moore, *Magazines for the Millions*, 55.

12. The feature ran, with some breaks, from 1890 through 1907.

13. "Just Told In a Talkative Way," *The Ladies' Home Journal* 21 (Dec. 1903): 3.

14. Laury MacHenry, "Whooping Cough, Etc.: Talks with the Doctor No. 5," *The Ladies' Home Journal* 6 (Dec. 1888): 7.

15. "Talking About our Ailments," *The Ladies' Home Journal* 15 (Dec. 1897): 20.

16. Laura MacHenry, "Talks with the Doctor," *The Ladies' Home Journal* 7 (May 1890): 21; "The Lady from Philadelphia's Heart-to-Heart Talks with Girls," *The Ladies' Home Journal* 23 (Oct. 1906): 41; Hood's Sarsaparilla, Advertisement, *The Ladies' Home Journal* 8 (May 1891): 2.

17. "As a Physician Sees Women: A Frank View of Women from the Standpoint of a Successful Practitioner," *The Ladies' Home Journal* 24 (Mar. 1907): 16.

18. Damon-Moore, *Magazine for the Millions*, 37.

19. Berlant, *Female Complaint*, 5.

20. "The Ideas of a Plain Country Woman," *The Ladies' Home Journal* 24 (Sept. 1907): 38. In another column, Frances Kellor offers to help readers find "a helper" by directing them to local agencies, including those specializing in "negro help" (Frances A. Kellor, "The New Department: The Housewife and her Helper," *The Ladies' Home Journal* 22 (Sept. 1905): 17).

21. Emmy Cummings, "Tenth Letter," *The Ladies' Home Journal* 15 (Feb. 1898): 4.

22. For a black preacher joke, see "He Knew his People," *The Ladies' Home Journal* 23 (Apr. 1906): 2; for a black waiter joke immediately followed by a black preacher joke, see "The Game the Waiter Preferred" and "The Real Miracle," *The Ladies' Home Journal* 22 (Jan. 1905): 17; for a black porter joke, see "He Put Him Off, All Right," *The Ladies' Home Journal* 21 (Oct. 1904): 15; for a black sermon joke included in editor Edward Bok's own column, see "The Two Centuries and this Magazine," *The Ladies' Home Journal* 18 (Jan. 1901): 16. For one of several plays published by the *Journal* featuring blackface characters, see Ednah Proctor Clarke, "Of Santa Claus," *The Ladies' Home Journal* 18 (Dec.1901): 19. For one of many celebrations of blackface minstrel humor, see F. Hopkinson Smith, "Let Us Go Back," *The Ladies' Home Journal* 22 (Sept.1905): 7.

23. W. E. B. Du Bois, *Black Reconstruction in America, 1860–1880* (New York: The Free Press, 1992), 700

24. Laura Spencer Portor, "Those Days in Old Virginia," *The Ladies' Home Journal* 19 (Feb.–May 1902); The Blue and the Gray, Advertisement, *The Ladies' Home Journal* 9 (Jan. 1892): 32; Edith Carter Beveridge, "Where Southern Memories Cluster," *The Ladies' Home Journal* 23 (Sept. 1906): 34; Mrs. Thaddeus Horton, "The Story of the Nancy Harts," *The Ladies' Home Journal* 21 (Nov. 1904): 14.

25. "After-Dinner Stories: A Budget of Bright Anecdotes Told of Famous Folk," *The Ladies' Home Journal* 15 (May 1898): 3.

26. "The President: Mr. Roosevelt's Views on Race Suicide," *The Ladies' Home Journal* 23 (Feb. 1906): 21. See also Sanipure Milk, Advertisement, *The Ladies' Home Journal* 24 (Oct. 1907): 34; and "Mothers' Monuments," *The Ladies' Home Journal* 20 (Oct. 1903): 16.

27. Michel Foucault, "Friendship as a Way of Life," trans. John Johnston, in *Essential Works of Foucault 1954–1984, Vol. 1: Ethics: Subjectivity and Truth*, ed. Paul Rabinow (New York: New Press, 1997), 137, 136, 139.

28. Jack Halberstam, *In a Queer Time and Place* (New York: New York University Press, 2005), 1–2; Leela Gandhi, *Affective Communities: Anticolonial Thought, Fin-De-Siècle Radicalism, and the Politics of Friendship* (Durham, NC: Duke University Press, 20.

29. L. Clark Seelye, "The Influence of Sororities," *The Ladies' Home Journal* 24 (Sept. 1907): 12; Alice Preston, "A Girl and her Prejudices," *The Ladies' Home Journal* 24 (Nov. 1907): 40.

30. "Record of the Democratic Speaker" *The Republic: A Political Science Monthly Magazine* 5, no. 2 (Aug. 1875): 110.

31. For an account of Rudyard Kipling's post-Reconstruction surge in US popularity, see Gretchen Murphy, *Shadowing the White Man's Burden: U.S. Imperialism and the Problem of the Color Line* (New York: NYU Press, 2010), 23–57.

32. Horace Traubel, *With Walt Whitman in Camden, vol. 3*, ed. Sculley Bradley (New York: Mitchell Kennerley, 1914), 43.

33. Walt Whitman, "I Know Not How Others," in *Notebooks and Unpublished Prose Manuscripts*, vol. VI or *The Collected Writings of Walt Whitman*, ed. Edward F. Grier (New York: New York University Press, 1984), 2160. Emphasis in original.

34. Ed Folsom, "Lucifer and Ethopia: Whitman, Race, and Poetics Before the Civil War and After," in *A Historical Guide to Walt Whitman*, ed. David Reynolds (New York: Oxford University Press, 2000), 82.

35. Newell Dwight Hillis, "The Secrets of a Happy Life: Third Article: The Diffusion of Happiness through Conversation," *The Ladies' Home Journal* 26 (Aug. 1899): 22.

36. Ivy Schweitzer, *Perfecting Friendship: Politics and Affiliation in Early American Literature* (Chapel Hill: University of North Carolina Press, 2006); Caleb Crain, *American Sympathy: Men, Friendship, and Literature in the New Nation* (New Haven, CT: Yale University Press, 2001).

37. Aristotle, *Nicomachean Ethics*, trans. Terence Irwin (Indianapolis: Hackett Publishing Co., 1985), 208, 1155a 25.

38. Crain, *American Sympathy*, 4.

39. Mrs. Lyman Abbott, "Just Among Ourselves," *The Ladies' Home Journal* 10 (July 1893): 26.

40. Ruth Ashmore, "The Intense Friendships of Girls," *The Ladies' Home Journal* 15 (July 1898): 20. "Ruth Ashmore" is the penname for Isabel Allerdice Mallon.

41. Fannie L. Fancher, "Friendship," *The Ladies' Home Journal* 6 (Aug. 1889): 10.

42. Whitney, "Friendly Letter VI."

43. Alan Trachtenberg, *The Incorporation of America: Culture and Society in the Gilded Age* (New York: Macmillan, 2007).

44. On the Civil War's impact on American temporalities, see Cheryl A. Wells, *Civil War Time: Temporality and Identity in America, 1861–1865* (Athens: University of Georgia Press, 2005), especially the epilogue, which details postbellum temporality. On the Civil War in relation to postbellum federalization and the modern governmentality, see Matthew G. Hannah, *Governmentality and the Mastery of Territory in Nineteenth-Century America* (New York: Cambridge University Press, 2000).

45. T. J. Jackson Lears, *No Place of Grace: Antimodernism and the Transformation of American Culture, 1880–1920* (New York: Pantheon Books, 1981), xvii.

46. Gillian Silverman, *Books and Bodies: Reading and the Fantasy of Communion in Nineteenth-Century America* (Philadelphia: University of Pennsylvania Press, 2012), 6–7.

47. "Neighborly Confidences," *The Ladies' Home Journal and Practical Housekeeper* 5 (Sept. 1888): 10. To be sure, the *Journal* fails to tell us how individual women read literature or how they brought differing reading formations to bear on their engagements with literary texts, a failure it shares with all archives in the history of reading. Nevertheless, it succeeds in organizing a sustained and consistent program of reading that aspired toward and likely attained normative status. Specifically, the *Journal* engaged two tasks central to the discipline of "literary studies": the broad work of generic differentiation (separating the literary from the nonliterary, elaborating and specifying groups of aesthetic conventions, and assigning value) and the development of reading into a specialized skill (call it "critical reading" or "close reading") with a use value that extends beyond immediate engagement with the printed page. As a mass media genre that engaged both women's culture and literary culture, the *Journal* thus invited readers to navigate a set of parallel dialogues we might otherwise see as at odds with one another, between general reading and close reading, on the one hand, and fraternal social belonging and intimate friendship, on the other.

48. "What Should Girls Read? Mrs. Whitney to Travel with Girls in 'The World of Reading,'" *Ladies' Home Journal* 9 (Nov. 1892): 22.

49. A. D. T. Whitney, "A Friendly Letter to Girl Friends—I," *Ladies' Home Journal* 11 (Dec. 1893): 14.

50. Some *Journal* contributors take apply this value of literature to familial relationships as well, especially to the relationships between parent and child. One, for instance, writes: "It is a good thing to read excellent novels aloud in the family circle.... It affords a chance to

reach the inner life of daughter and son, and learn what they think and how they feel. Too often that life is like a sealed book to the parent" (Hester M. Poole, "Reading and Readers," *The Ladies' Home Journal* 8 (July 1891): 18).

51. A. D. T. Whitney, "A Friendly Letter to Girl Friends—II," *Ladies' Home Journal* 11 (Mar. 1894): 10.

52. Whitney, "Friendly Letter I."

53. A. D. T. Whitney, "A Friendly Letter to Girl Friends—VI," *Ladies' Home Journal* 13 (Dec. 1895): 8.

54. Whitney, "Friendly Letter VI." The Journal frequently assesses the moral worth of its subjects according to their seriousness as readers. Hence when Ralph Waldo Emerson's son, Edward W. Emerson, reminisces on his frequent childhood visits to the Alcott home in order to provide *Journal* readers with "pleasant pictures of the past that may have a lesson," he draws readers' attention to the well-used condition of the Alcott library and the daughters' skill in turning Dickens's novels into performances, both of which he presents as signs of the family's "healthy" upbringing (Edward W. Emerson, "When Louisa Alcott Was a Girl," *Ladies' Home Journal* 16 (Dec. 1898): 15). In another example, the *Journal* underscores the value of such careful attention to literature when it presents Helen Keller as a model reader: "She reads slowly, deliberately, about half as fast as we do, not so much because she feels the words less rapidly than we see them, as because it is one of her good habits of mind to do things thoroughly and well" (John Albert Macy, "Helen Keller as She Really Is: An Intimate Portrait," *The Ladies' Home Journal* 19 (Nov. 1902): 11). Well-worn books, dramatic interpretations, rereading, slow reading, deliberate attention: all describe practices for investing in the imaginative world as an essential skill for engaging the real world.

55. A. D. T. Whitney, "A Friendly Letter to Girl Friends—III," *Ladies' Home Journal* 11 (Aug. 1894): 15.

56. Hamilton W. Mabie, "Mr. Mabie Tells of the World's Greatest University," *Ladies' Home Journal* 24 (Nov.1907): 28.

57. Whitney, "Friendly Letter III," 15.

58. "Dear girl friends," Whitney writes as an opening for her second letter, "Do you know I dearly love a bit of philology—of word tracing?" (Whitney, "Friendly Letter II"). In her open letters, she encourages her readers to share in this love. She models for them the archival work of etymology, needling at multiple meanings through the consideration of one word's past and present resonance. She asks them to consider the materiality of the signifier, heeding the shape their tongues require in order to pronounce certain sounds. She tells readers to observe the text on multiple levels, considering possible allegories, symbols, metaphors, and ironies. It is up to the readers of literature, she claims, "to unroll the details 'hidden in their foundation'" (Whitney, "Friendly Letter I"). Thus, for instance, she asks her readers to "notice how certain juxtapositions of letters or sounds carry always with them the same or similar ideas" (Whitney, "Friendly Letter IV").

59. Mabie, "Mr. Mabie Tells of the World's Greatest University."

60. Helen Keller, "The Story of my Life," *Ladies' Home Journal* 19 (Aug. 1902): 28.

61. Mabie, "World's Greatest University."

62. "If You Like Short Stories Here are a Bundle Bright and Cheery," *Ladies' Home Journal* 8 (Jan. 1891): 14.

63. Ibid.

64. "Droch's Literary Talks," *Ladies' Home Journal* 14 (Dec. 1896): 23.

65. In formulating such a stringent and disciplinary program of reading, the *Journal* participated in a significant late-century trend. The 1870s and '80s witnessed a host of voices on both sides of the Atlantic who responded to what one *Journal* writer calls "an immense enlargement of the circle of reading people" by calling upon readers to refine mere literacy into systematic practice (Hamilton Mabie, "Mr. Mabie's Literary Talks," *Ladies' Home Journal* 19 (Mar. 1902): 17). Prescribing, often explicitly, an Arnoldian project of self-improvement, texts like *Books and Reading: What Books Shall I Read and How Shall I Read Them*, *The Choice of Books*, and *Hints for Home Reading* asked their audiences to cultivate an "art of reading" (Charles F. Richardson, *The Choice of Books* (New York: American Book Exchange, 1881), 5.) In language reminiscent of many an Introduction-to-the-Study-of-Literature syllabus, they advised readers to keep a sheet of paper handy for taking notes; to read a few books intensively and slowly rather than many books cursorily; to reflect and converse on what they've read; to keep a reading journal; to reread; to read from a range of genres, both fictional and not; and to persevere through difficult reading, for, their authors insist, worthwhile knowledge works in tandem with vigor and effort. Alongside these advice books, we can see how the *Journal's* prescriptions for reading may very well have merged public into private and work into leisure in order to give literature a function within the emergent middle-class "culture of professionalism" (Burton J. Bledstein, *The Culture of Professionalism: The Middle Class and the Development of Higher Education in America* (New York: Norton, 1976)). Reading, in this schema, becomes just another technocratic effect of capitalist industrialization. In particular, closer reading becomes an exhaustive program for systematizing and assigning use value to all those effects of reading (emotional investment, distraction, sentimentality, and the like) that cannot be assimilated into programs of reading as self-help.

For a useful history of "the reading habit" as a recurrent concern in the late nineteenth-century United States, see Barbara Hochman, "Highbrow/Lowbrow: Naturalist Writers and the 'Reading Habit,'" in *Twisted from the Ordinary: Essays on American Literary Naturalism*, ed. Mary E. Papke (Knoxville: The University of Tennessee Press, 2003), 217–36.

66. Kenneth Price, "Charles Chesnutt, the *Atlantic Monthly*, and the Intersection of African-American and Elite Culture," in *Periodical Literature and Nineteenth-Century America*, ed. Kenneth Price and Susan Belasco Smith (Charlottesville: University of Virginia Press, 1995), 257–76; and Heather Tirado Gilligan, "Reading, Race, and Charles Chesnutt's '"Uncle Julius" Tales,'" *ELH* 74, no. 1 (2007): 212. This is not to say that the *Journal* didn't care about the Civil War or Civil War memory. It occasionally published what it called "literature of interpretation and reconciliation which is fast making a nation out of once warring sections," including romance reunion narratives and campus novels, such as, respectively, the serialization of Julia Magruder's *Across the Chasm* in 1885 and Ralph Henry Barbour's *The Land of Joy: A Love Story of Two Harvard Students* in 1903 (Hamilton Mabie, "Mr. Mabie's Literary Talks," *Ladies' Home Journal* 19 (June 1902), 17).

67. See William Dean Howells, "Mr. Charles W. Chesnutt's Stories", *Atlantic Monthly* (May 1900): 699–701. The Atlantic *Monthly* published "The Goophered Grapevine" in August 1887, "Po' Sandy" in May 1888, "Dave's Neckliss" in October 1889, and "The Bouquet" in November 1899.

68. "Mr. Howells's Latest Novel," *Ladies' Home Journal* 7 (Mar. 1890): 13. See also a column written by the *Journal's* editor, Edward Bok, that admonishes "the most radical believers of realism in fiction" ("The Pen of a Mountaineer," *Ladies' Home Journal* 11 (July 1894), 12).

69. Annie R. Ramsey, "An Hour with New Books," *Ladies' Home Journal* 7 (Apr. 1890): 11.

70. Ibid.

71. For an excellent history of realism and the *Atlantic*-group magazines, see Nancy Glazener, *Reading for Realism*.

72. William Dean Howells, "Editor's Study," *Harper's New Monthly Magazine* 83 (June 1891): 156.

73. Annie R. Ramsey, "New Books on my Table," *Ladies' Home Journal* 7 (May 1890): 13.

74. For a more recent argument about reading's value in teaching us "to engage dialogically at a deep emotional and epistemic level" with difference, see Paula M. L. Moya, *The Social Imperative: Race, Close Reading, and Contemporary Literary Criticism* (Stanford, CA: Stanford University Press, 2016), 58.

75. In this context, we might further speculate, the *Journal's* segregation did not merely protect its white women readers from nonwhite others. It additionally protected white men and white supremacy from the disruptive potential of white women's friendships and alliances across the color line.

## Chapter 3

1. Herman Melville, *Battle-Pieces and Aspects of the War* (New York: Da Capo Press, 1995), 263.

2. Max Cavitch, *American Elegy: The Poetry of Mourning from the Puritans to Whitman* (Minneapolis: University of Minnesota Press, 2007), 5.

3. Vamik Volkan, "Large-Group Identity and Chosen Trauma," *Psychoanalysis Downunder* 6 (2005): np.

4. Stephanie Foote, *The Parvenu's Plot: Gender, Culture, and Class in the Age of Realism* (Durham, NC: University of New Hampshire Press, 2014), 6.

5. The dismissal of conventional verse additionally constitutes a refusal to acknowledge an understandable difficulty most twenty-first-century readers have with nineteenth-century American poetry more generally. We're trained in what Michael Cohen identifies as "a practice of lyric reading that values linguistic complexity, irony, and ambiguity, and that understands a poem to be the private expression of an imagined speaker whose deep subjectivity the poem makes possible" (Michael C. Cohen, "Contraband Singing: Poems and Songs in Circulation during the Civil War," *American Literature* 82, no. 2 (2010): 271). We find exceptional individuals in lyric voices because that is what we look for, what we reflect upon, and what we bring to others' attention. Yet Civil War-era poetry frequently fails to meet these preset criteria. And our limited critical lens thus misses what Cohen identifies as among the most interesting and historically influential aspects of nineteenth-century American poems: "poems and songs had wide-ranging social force *because* they were…conventional" (271). This chapter's survey of conventional elegies attempts to recuperate such social force and bring to light the playful work within the ordinary. See also Faith Barrett, *To Fight Aloud is Very Brave: American Poetry and the Civil War* (Amherst: University of Massachusetts Press, 2012).

6. Theodor Adorno, *Negative Dialectics*, trans. E. B. Ashton (New York: Continuum, 1994), 320.

7. See Mark S. Schantz, *Awaiting the Heavenly Country: The Civil War and America's Culture of Death* (Ithaca, NY: Cornell University Press, 2013), 98.

8. Ralph Waldo Emerson, "Courage," *New York Tribune*, Nov. 8, 1859. Franny Nudelman, *John Brown's Body: Slavery, Violence, and the Culture of War* (Chapel Hill: The University of North Carolina Press, 2004), 36. See also Mary H. C. Booth's elegy, "I'm Dying, Comrade," which imagines John Brown greeting soldiers at the pearly gates of heaven: "And now I'm dying, comrade, | And there is old John Brown | A standing at the Golden Gate, | And holding me a crown" (Mary H. C. Booth, *Wayside Blossoms* (Philadelphia: J. B. Lippincott, 1865), 75).

9. I draw in particular here on Drew Gilpin Faust, *This Republic of Suffering: Death and the American Civil War* (New York: Vintage, 2008); Nudelman, *John Brown's Body*; Mark S. Schantz, *Awaiting the Heavenly Country: The Civil War and America's Culture of Death* (Ithaca, NY: Cornell University Press, 2013); and Michael Warner, "What Like a Bullet Can Undeceive?" *Public Culture* 15, no. 1 (2003): 41–54.

10. Diana Fuss, *Dying Modern: A Meditation on Elegy* (Durham, NC: Duke University Press, 2013), 6.

11. Faust, *This Republic of Suffering*, 269.

12. Dana Luciano, *Arranging Grief: Sacred Time and the Body in Nineteenth-Century America* (New York: New York University Press, 2007), 4, 7.

13. Ibid., 218.

14. Adam C. Bradford, *Communities of Death: Whitman, Poe, and the American Culture of Mourning* (Columbia: University of Missouri Press, 2014), 122. Bradford and I depart on the racial politics of Whitman's gesture. Where Bradford see Whitman attempting to overcome "impediments such as geography, age, gender, race, economics, and wartime conflict" (130), I see the reconciliationist work of Whitman's poetry validating an implicitly white nation that would serve as the justification for ending Reconstruction and introducing Jim Crow. For a related argument about nationalism and Whitman's Civil War poetry, see the fourth chapter of Nudelman, *John Brown's Body*.

15. Mary Boykin Miller Chesnut, *A Diary from Dixie* (New York: D. Appleton and Company, 1905), 263.

16. Philip Shaw Faludan, *A People's Contest: The Union and Civil War, 1861–1865* (1988; reprinted Lawrence: University Press of Kansas, 1996), 367. See also Colleen McDannell and Bernhard Lang, *Heaven: A History* (New Haven: Yale University Press, 2001); and Faust, *This Republic of Suffering*.

17. Cindy Weinstein, "Heaven's Tense: Narration in The Gates Ajar," *Novel* 45, no. 1 (2012): 57.

18. Elizabeth Stuart Phelps, *The Gates Ajar*, in *Three Spiritualist Novels* (Chicago: The University of Illinois Press, 2000), 4.

19. Ibid., 135.

20. Russ Castronovo, *Necro Citizenship: Death, Eroticism, and the Public Sphere in the Nineteenth-Century United States* (Durham, NC: Duke University Press, 2001), 4.

21. Jahan Ramazani, *Poetry of Mourning: The Modern Elegy from Hardy to Heaney* (Chicago: University of Chicago Press, 1994); R. Clifton Spargo, *The Ethics of Mourning: Grief and Responsibility in Elegiac Literature* (Baltimore: Johns Hopkins University Press, 2004).

22. Ramazani, *Poetry of Mourning*, 2.

23. Michael Warner, "What Like a Bullet Can Undeceive?" *Public Culture* 15, no. 1 (2003): 43.

24. Ian Finseth, "The Civil War Dead: Realism and the Problem of Anonymity," *American Literary History* 25, no. 3 (2013): 545–6, 542.

25. Ibid., 547.

26. Edmund Wilson, *Patriotic Gore: Studies in the Literature of the American Civil War* (New York: Oxford University Press, 1966), 474, 487–8; and Daniel Aaron, *The Unwritten War: American Writers and the Civil War* (New York: Knopf, 1973), xviii.

27. Lauren Berlant, *Cruel Optimism* (Durham, NC: Duke University Press, 2011), 9.

28. Stanley Cavell, *In Quest of the Ordinary: Lines of Skepticism and Romanticism* (Chicago: University of Chicago Press, 1994), 169, 154.

29. William Cullen Bryant, "The Death of Slavery," *Atlantic Monthly* (July 1866): 121.

30. Francis Miles Finch, "The Blue and the Gray," *Atlantic Monthly* (Sept. 1867): 369–70.

31. "Protection as men, more than as voters, is what we want," *The Christian Recorder* (July 31, 1890). Cited in David Blight, *Race and Reunion*, 300.

32. Julia R. Dorr, "The Drummer-Boy's Burial," *Harper's New Monthly Magazine* (July 1864): 145–6.

33. Walt Whitman, "Reconciliation," in *Whitman: Poetry and Prose* (New York: The Library of America, 1996), 453. For a similar reading, see Natasha Trethewey, "On Whitman, Civil War Memory, and my South," *Virginia Quarterly Review* 81 (Spring 2005): 53. For an opposing reading, one speculating we see Whitman's speaker as African American, see Ed Folsom, "Erasing Race: The Lost Black Presence in Whitman's Manuscripts," in *Whitman Noir: Black America and the Good Gray Poet*, ed. Ivy G. Wilson (Iowa City: Iowa University Press, 2014), 22–3.

34. William Cullen Bryant, introduction to *The Family Library of Poetry and Song*, ed. William Cullen Bryant (New York: Fords, Howard, and Hulbert, 1878), 32.

35. *Memorial Day: Its Celebration, Spirit, and Significance as Related in Prose and Verse, with a Non-Sectional Anthology of the Civil War*, ed. Robert Haven Schauffler (New York: Dodd, Mead, & Co., 1911), xxvii.

36. "The Song of the Drum," *Harper's Weekly* (Nov. 26, 1864): 759.

37. In its emphasis on how the mechanized state produced machines out of men, the poem also echoes "The Soldier's Rest," an elegy also published by *Harper's Weekly* just six months earlier, in April 1864.

38. S. R. Elliot, "With the Tread of Marching Columns," *Century Illustrated Magazine* (May 1893): 140.

39. Thomas Bailey Aldrich, "Fredericksburg," in *Poems of Places: America – The Southern States*, ed. Henry Wadsworth Longfellow (Cambridge, MA: Houghton, Osgood & Co., 1879), 74.

40. Thomas Bailey Aldrich, "Fredericksburg," in *Our Country in Poems and Prose*, ed. Eleanor A. Persons (New York: American Book Company, 1899), 148.

41. Luciano, *Arranging Grief*, 2; David L. Eng and David Kazanjian, "Introduction: Mourning Remains," in *Loss: The Politics of Mourning*, ed. Eng and Kazanjian (Berkeley: University of California Press, 2003), 4.

42. Sianne Ngai, *Ugly Feelings* (Cambridge, MA: Harvard University Press, 2005), 3.

43. Sigmund Freud, "Mourning and Melancholia," *The Journal of Nervous and Mental Disease* 56, no. 5 (1922): 543–5.

44. Thomas Bailey Aldrich, "Accomplices," *Atlantic Monthly* (July 1865): 107.

45. "Mr. Aldrich's Poetry," *Atlantic Monthly* (Dec. 1874): 673–4; "The Poems of Thomas Bailey Aldrich," *The Century Magazine* (Sept. 1891): 660.

46. F. A. Moore, "In the Hospital," *Peterson's Magazine* (Feb. 1863): 114.

47. "Our Dead at Andersonville," *Harper's Weekly* (Aug. 19, 1865): 518.

48. For more on the horror and memory of Civil War prisons, see Benjamin G. Cloyd's *Haunted by Atrocity: Civil War Prisons in American Memory* (Baton Rouge: Louisiana State University Press, 2010).

49. Nathaniel Graham, Shepherd, "Roll-Call," *Harper's New Monthly Magazine* (Dec. 1862): 49–50.

50. Mary H. C. Booth, "While God He Leaves Me Reason, God He Will Leave Me Jim," in *Anecdotes, Poetry, and Incidents of the War: North and South, 1860–1865*, ed. Frank Moore (New York: Printed for Subscribers, 1866), 318.

51. Maud Mornington, "The Nation's Dead," *Peterson's Magazine* (May 1864): 361.

52. Russ Castronovo, *Necro Citizenship*, 17.

53. Judith Butler, *Precarious Life: The Powers of Mourning and Violence* (New York: Verso, 2004), 22–3.

54. Melville, *Battle-Pieces*, 63.

55. Warner, "What Like a Bullet Can Undeceive?," 44; Randall Fuller, *From Battlefields Rising: How the Civil War Transformed American Literature* (New York: Oxford University Press, 2011).

56. Eva Cherniavsky, *Incorporations: Race, Nation, and the Body Politics of Capital* (Minneapolis: University of Minneapolis Press, 2006), xxii.

## Chapter 4

1. Isaac S. Grant, "What I Have Heard," *The Christian Recorder*, Mar. 10, 1887.

2. Annie E. Gwynn, "Revival—Woman Preacher," *Star of Zion* (Dec. 2, 1897).

3. *God Struck Me Dead: Religious Conversion Experiences and Autobiographies of Ex-Slaves*, ed. Clifton H. Johnson (Philadelphia: Pilgrim Press, 1969), 74.

4. The original text of Jasper's sermon was recorded by William Eldridge in *John Jasper, the Unmatched Negro Philosopher and Preacher*. His version, which likely follows whites' pattern of exaggerating dialect when transcribing black speech, reads: "Our eyes goes far beyon' de smaller stars; our home is clean outer sight uv dem twinklin' orbs" ((New York: Fleming H. Revell, 1908), 148–9). The version I use, in which the dialect has been slightly modified, comes from *From my People: 400 Years of African American Folklore*, ed. Daryl Cumber Dance (New York: W. W. Norton, 2003), 277.

5. Hortense Spillers, "Fabrics of History: Essays on the Black Sermon," Ph.D. diss., Brandeis University, 1974, 4. Zora Neale Hurston makes a similar point, arguing that "the greatest poets among us are in our pulpits and the greatest poetry has come out of them. It is merely not set down. It passes from mouth to mouth as in the days of Homer" (*Zora Neale Hurston: A Life in Letters*, ed. Carla Kaplan (New York: Doubleday, 2002), 304).

6. Saidiya V. Hartman, *Scenes of Subjection: Terror, Slavery, and Self-Making in Nineteenth-Century America* (New York: Oxford University Press, 1997), 127.

7. Max Weber, *The Protestant Ethic and the Spirit of Capitalism*, trans. Talcott Parsons (Mineola, NY: Dover, 2003), 140, 143.

8. E. Franklin Frazier, *The Negro Church in America* (New York: Schocken Books, 1974), chap. 3. On the black church as a civic and political institution, see also Eugene D. Genovese, *Roll, Jordon, Roll: The World the Slaves Made* (New York: Pantheon Books, 1974); and Steven Hahn, *A Nation Under our Feet: Black Political Struggles in the Rural South from Slavery to*

*the Great Migration* (Cambridge, MA: Harvard University Press, 2003). For a wonderful survey of the historiography pertaining to African American Christianity, see Judith Weisenfeld, "On Jordan's Stormy Banks: Margins, Center, and Bridges in African American Religious History," in *New Directions in American Religious History*, ed. Harry S. Stout and D. G. Hart (New York: Oxford University Press, 1997), 417–44.

9. Evelyn Brooks Higginbotham, *Righteous Discontent: The Women's Movement in the Black Baptist Church, 1880–1920* (Cambridge, MA: Harvard University Press, 1993), 1, 9.

10. James Weldon Johnson, *God's Trombone: Seven Negro Sermons in Verse* (New York: Penguin, 1976), 10.

11. See Gerald L. Davis, *I Got the Word in Me and I Can Sing It, You Know: A Study of the Performed African-American Sermon* (Philadelphia: University of Pennsylvania Press, 1987); Charles V. Hamilton, *The Black Preacher in America* (New York: Morrow, 1972); Cleophus J. LaRue, *The Heart of Black Preaching* (Louisville, KY: Westminster John Knox Press, 2000); Henry H. Mitchell, *Black Preaching* (Philadelphia and New York: J. B. Lippincott Company, 1970); Bruce A. Rosenberg, *Can These Bones Live?: The Art of the American Folk Preacher*, Rev. edn (Urbana: University of Illinois Press, 1988); William H. Pipes, *Say Amen, Brother! Old-Time Negro Preaching: A Study in American Frustration* (New York: William-Frederick Press, 1951); and Jon Michael Spencer, *Sacred Symphony: The Chanted Sermon of the Black Preacher* (New York: Greenwood Press, 1987).

12. See Dolan Hubbard, *The Sermon and the African American Literary Imagination* (Columbia: University of Missouri Press, 1994); E. Patrick Johnson, *Performing Blackness: Performance and the Politics of Authenticity* (Durham, NC: Duke University Press, 2003); and Marcellus Blount, "The Preacherly Text: African American Poetry and Vernacular Performance," *PMLA* 107, no. 3 (1992): 582–93.

13. Blount, "The Preacherly Text," 583.

14. Kimberly W. Benston, *Performing Blackness: Enactments of African-American Modernism* (New York: Routledge, 2000), 250. See also Tyler Hoffman, *American Poetry in Performance: From Walt Whitman to Hip Hop* (Ann Arbor: University of Michigan Press, 2013).

15. I'm drawing here from performance studies' distinction between the *archive* (the translation of performance through writing into documents and texts) and the *repertoire* (interpersonal circulation of performance through orality and performance across time and place). I use *genre* instead of *scenario*, the term frequently used by historians of performance, in order to retain that emphasis that Blount, Spillers, and others place on the gospel sermon's literariness (Diana Taylor, *The Archive and the Repertoire: Performing Cultural Memory in the Americas* (Durham, NC: Duke University Press, 2003)).

16. Franco Moretti, "The Soul and the Harpy," in *Signs Taken for Wonders: On the Sociology of Literary Forms*, trans. David Forgacs (New York: Verso, 2005), 27.

17. Paul Gilroy, *The Black Atlantic: Modernity and Double Consciousness* (Cambridge, MA: Harvard University Press, 1993), 38.

18. Henry Louis Gates, *Loose Canons: Notes on the Culture Wars* (Oxford: Oxford University Press, 1992), 39; Gilroy, *Black Atlantic*, 39.

19. Gilroy, *Black Atlantic*, 30. The Ralph Ellison allusion is to the final life of *The Invisible Man*: "Who knows but that, on the lower frequencies, I speak for you?" ([New York: Vintage Books, 1995], 581).

20. Johnson, *God's Trombone*, 1.

21. Fredric Jameson, *The Political Unconscious: Narrative as a Socially Symbolic Act* (Ithaca, NY: Cornell University Press, 1981), 145–50.

22. Michel Foucault, "Nietzsche, Genealogy, History," in *The Foucault Reader*, ed. Paul Rabinow (New York: Pantheon, 1984), 82.

23. David W. Wills, *Christianity in the United States: A Historical Survey and Interpretation* (Notre Dame, IN: University of Notre Dame Press, 2002), 10.

24. Zilpha Elaw, *Memoirs of the Life, Religious Experience, Ministerial Travels, and Labors of Mrs. Zilpha Elaw*, in *Sisters of the Spirit: Three Black Women's Autobiographies of the Nineteenth Century*, ed. William L. Andrews (Bloomington: Indiana University Press, 1986), 81; cited in Ann Taves, *Fits, Trances, & Visions: Experiencing Religion and Explaining Experience from Wesley to James* (Princeton: Princeton University Press, 1999), 102. Historian John H. Wigger traces the growing influence of African American worship practices in American Methodism from the late 1700s into the early nineteenth century, arguing that "[l]ike white women, African Americans not only were attracted by the enthusiastic nature of early Methodism but did much to shape its character" (*Taking Heaven by Story: Methodism and the Rise of Popular Christianity in America* (New York: Oxford University Press, 1998), 118).

25. Freeborn Garrettson, *American Methodist Pioneer: The Life and Journals of the Rev. Freeborn Garrettson, 1752–1782*, ed. Robert Drew Simpson (Madison, NJ: Academy Books, 1984), 95.

26. John Fanning Watson, *Methodist Error: Friendly Christian Advice to Those Methodists Who Indulge in Extravagant Emotions and Bodily Exercises*, in *Antirevivalism in Antebellum America: A Collection of Religious Voices*, ed. James D. Bratt (New Brunswick, NJ: Rutgers University Press, 2006), 37–8; emphasis in original.

27. Albert J. Raboteau, *Slave Religion: The "Invisible Institution" in the Antebellum South* (New York: Oxford University Press, 1978), 137.

28. Claudia Stokes, *The Altar at Home: Sentimental Literature and Nineteenth-Century American Religion* (Philadelphia: University of Pennsylvania Press, 2014), 26. For an excellent account of such decentralization, see Nathan O. Hatch, *The Democratization of American Christianity* (New Haven: Yale University Press, 1989).

29. Orlando Patterson, *Slavery and Social Death: A Comparative Study* (Cambridge, MA: Harvard University Press, 1982), 73.

30. Elizabeth Kilham, "Sketches in Color," *Putnam's Magazine* 5, no. 27 (Mar. 1870): 306.

31. For more specific demographic data relating to overall church membership as well as denominational membership, see C. Eric Lincoln and Lawrence H. Mamiya, *The Black Church in the African American Experience* (Durham, NC: Duke University Press, 1990), 20–163.

32. I'm tracing an argument about genre here similar to the one historians make about American Methodism, which is, as John H. Wigger argues, that "it took advantage of the revolutionary religious freedoms of the early republic to release, and in a sense institutionalize, elements of popular religious enthusiasm long latent in American and European Protestantism" (*Taking Heaven by Story*, 105).

33. Kilham, "Sketches in Color," 310.

34. Leigh Eric Schmidt, *Holy Fairs: Scotland and the Making of American Revivalism*, 2nd edition (Grand Rapids, MI: William B. Eerdmans Publishing Co., 2001), 192.

35. George Roberts, *The Substance of a Sermon (but now Enlarged) Preached to, and at the Request of the Conference of the Methodist Episcopal Church, Held in Baltimore, March, 1807* (Baltimore: Henry Foxall, 1807), 29–30; quoted in Taves, *Fits, Trances, & Visions*, 78.

36. Bruno Latour, "On Actor-Network Theory: A Few Clarifications," <www.nettime.org/Lists-Archives/nettime-l-9801/msg00019.html> (accessed July 10, 2014).

37. Hortense Spillers, "Moving on Down the Line: Variations on the African-American Sermon," in *Black, White, and in Color: Essays on American Literature and Culture* (Chicago: The University of Chicago Press, 2003), 254.

38. Bruno Latour, *Reassembling the Social: An Introduction to Actor-Network-Theory* (New York: Oxford University Press, 2005), 12; emphasis original. I am influenced in this section by two articles that nicely demonstrate Latour's potential value (and limitations) for literary history: Russ Castronovo, "State Secrets: Ben Franklin and WikiLeaks," *Critical Inquiry* 39, no. 3 (2013): 425–50; and Toni Wall Jaudon, "Obeah's Sensations: Rethinking Religion at the Transnational Turn," *American Literature* 84, no. 4 (2012): 715–41.

39. John Ashbery, "A Note on 'Variation on a Noel,'" in *Selected Prose*, ed. Eugene Richie (Ann Arbor: University of Michigan Press, 2004), 200.

40. W. M. D. Johnson, "Our Work in Georgia," *The Christian Recorder*, March 12, 1874.

41. Toni Morrison, *Beloved* (New York: Plume, 1988), 87.

42. James Baldwin, *The Evidence of Things Not Seen* (New York: Holt, Rinehart and Winston, 1985), 82; emphasis in original.

43. Ashon Crawley, "Breathing Flesh and the Sound of BlackPentecostalism," *Theology & Sexuality* 19, no. 1 (2013): 51. See also Crawley's conceptualization of "otherwise possibilities" (*Blackpentecostal Breath: The Aesthetics of Possibility* (New York: Fordham University Press, 2016), 2).

44. Johnson, "Our Work in Georgia."

45. Johnson, *God's Trombone*, 13.

46. The spiritual begins with "I" and then transitions to "Jesus":

> I must walk my lonesome valley
> I got to walk it for myself,
> Nobody else can walk it for me,
> I got to walk it for myself.
>
> I must go and stand my trial,
> I got to stand it for myself,
> Nobody else can stand it for me,
> I got to stand it for myself.
>
> Jesus walked his lonesome valley,
> He had to walk it for himself,
> Nobody else could walk it for him,
> He had to walk it for himself.

James A. Cone, *The Spirituals and the Blues: An Interpretation* (New York: Seaberry Press, 1972), 31.

47. Johnson, *Gods Trombone*, 5.

48. Zora Neale Hurston, *Jonah's Gourd Vine* (New York: HarperPerennial Library, 1990), 189.

49. Michel Foucault, "What is an Author?" in *The Foucault Reader*, ed. Paul Rabinow (New York: Pantheon, 1984), 101.

50. "The Day of Prejudiced Gone," *The Christian Recorder*, July 18, 1889.

51. Higginbotham, *Righteous Discontent*, 2.

52. Spillers, "Moving on Down the Line," 265.

53. The racialized nature of this gendered history remains too frequently overlooked. For a useful corrective to this pattern, see Marli F. Weiner, with Mazie Hough, *Sex, Sickness, and Slavery: Defining Illness in the Antebellum South* (Chicago: University of Illinois Press, 2012).

54. Moreover, women frequently responded with testimony—preaching—of their own. The memoir, *The Life and Religious Experience of Jarena Lee, A Coloured Lady* (1836), describes one service where the male preacher, Reverend Richard Williams, "seemed to have lost the spirit," opening a path for Lee to take over: "I sprang, as by an altogether supernatural impulse, to my feet, when I was aided from above to give an exhortation on the very text with my brother Williams had taken" (Jarena Lee, *The Life and Religious Experience of Jarena Lee, A Coloured Lady, Giving an Account of her Call to Preach the Gospel. Revised and Corrected from the Original Manuscript, Written by Herself* (Philadelphia: published and printed for the author, 1836), in *African American Religious History: A Documentary Witness*, ed. Milton C. Sernett (Durham, NC: Duke University Press, 1999), 179).

55. Zora Neale Hurston, *The Sanctified Church* (Berkeley: Turtle Island, 1983), 83, 82–3, 104, 80, 80, 80, 91.

56. See, for example, "Still Waiting for the Good Samaritan," *The Ladies' Home Journal* (Nov. 1904).

57. Frederick Law Olmsted, *The Cotton Kingdom: A Traveller's Observations on Cotton and Slavery in the American Slave States. Based upon Three Former Volumes of Journeys and Investigations* (New York: Mason Brothers, 1861), 309–10, 314.

58. James Bissett Pratt, *The Religious Consciousness: A Psychological Study* (New York: Macmillan, 1920), 183 n. 29. As Pratt's rather strained attempt at humor indicates, many white observations rely for laughs on the distance between caricatured African American worshipers and narrators who perform themselves as enlightened, objective, empirical, and, above all, befuddled. See also the Cook's sermon to the sharks in Herman Melville's *Moby-Dick, or, The Whale* (1851; rpt New York: Penguin, 1992), 320–2; George Makepeace Towle, *American Society* (London: Chapman and Hall, 1870), 217; and G.W.S., "Negro Sermons" *Littell's Living Age* 93 (April 13, 1867): 117–20.

59. Sianne Ngai traces a long genealogy of representing African Americans through what she terms "animatedness": "the seemingly neutral state of 'being moved' becomes twisted into the image of the over emotional racialized subject" (*Ugly Feelings* (Cambridge, MA: Harvard University Press, 2005), 91).

60. Curtis J. Evans, *The Burden of Black Religion* (New York: Oxford University Press, 2008), 65.

61. Charles Stearns, *The Black Man of the South and the Rebels; or, The Characteristics of the Former and the Outrages of the Latter* (1872; reprint New York: Negro Universities Press, 1969), 365; emphasis in original. For a similar indictment, see Charles Wesley Melick, *Some Phases of the Negro Question* (Washington, DC: D. H. Deloe, 1908), 46.

62. Useful studies to begin exploring anti-Shaker and anti-Mormon persecution include Suzanne Thurman, "The Seat of Sin, the Site of Salvation: The Shaker Body and the Nineteenth-Century American Imagination," *Nineteenth Century Studies* 15 (2001): 1–18; and Patrick Mason, *The Mormon Menace: Violence and Anti-Mormonism in the Postbellum South* (New York: Oxford University Press, 2011).

63. Jeremiah E. Rankin, "The Negro as a Preacher," *The American Missionary* 53 (July 1899): 60, 61.

64. On the psychological approach to white religious enthusiasm, see Taves, *Fits, Trances & Visions*; on social science approaches to black religion as a sign of unfitness, see Evans, *Burden of Black Religion*.

65. One account compares African Americans to "cannibals." See Julian Thomas (pseudonym for Stanley James), *Cannibals & Convicts: Notes of Personal Experiences in the Western Pacific* (New York: Cassell & Co., 1887). Thomas, an England-born world traveler, treats the nonwhite world as a roughly uniform diaspora, such that "the native ministers from Fiji and Eastern Polynesia have taken Christianity in just the same way as the American negro. They are fond of long prayers, of talk, of passionate appeal to their hearers; and religious excitement and mania is common amongst them as with the blacks in the United States" (22).

66. That such disparagement was not universally the case is evident not only in Du Bois's writings, but also in the *God Struck Me Dead* project, an effort by three middle-class, educated African Americans to value and give voice to enthusiastic religious practice.

67. Frances Ellen Watkins Harper, *Minnie's Sacrifice; Sowing and Reaping; Trial and Triumph: Three Rediscovered Novels* (Boston: Beacon Press, 1994), 187.

68. William Wells Brown, *My Southern Home: or, The South and its People* (Boston: A. G. Brown, 1880), 193, 196, 197.

69. W. E. B. Du Bois, *The Souls of Black Folk*, ed. David W. Blight and Robert Gooding-Williams (Boston: Bedford Books, 1997), 179.

70. Gilroy, *Black Atlantic*, 37.

71. "Fops and Dude Preachers," *Star of Zion*, Aug. 5, 1897.

72. Bishop G. W. Clinton, "Alarm Cry No. 3," *Star of Zion*, January 21, 1897.

73. Reverend W. S. Meadows, "Positive Preaching," *Star of Zion*, Aug. 3, 1899.

74. Reverend W.T. Biddle, "Fruitless Preaching," *Star of Zion*, May 31, 1900.

75. "Old-Time Genuine Revivals," *Star of Zion*, Jan. 14, 1897.

76. "Fops and Dude Preachers," *Star of Zion*, Aug. 5, 1897.

77. Charles Taylor, *A Secular Age* (Cambridge, MA: Harvard University Press, 2007), 299. See also Talal Asad, *Formations of the Secular: Christianity, Islam, Modernity* (Stanford CA: Stanford University Press, 2003).

78. Taylor, *A Secular Age*, 38.

79. "I am Blessed but You Are Damned," *God Struck Me Dead*, 6.

80. "I Came to Myself Shouting," *God Struck Me Dead*, 31.

81. "Everything Just Fits," *God Struck Me Dead*, 61.

82. "My Jaws Became Unlocked," *God Struck Me Dead*, 12–13.

83. Leela Gandhi, *Affective Communities: Anticolonial Thought, Fin-De-Siècle Radicalism, and the Politics of Friendship* (Durham, NC: Duke University Press, 2006), 26; Lloyd Pratt, *The Strangers Book: The Human of African American Literature* (Philadelphia: University of Pennsylvania Press, 2016), 1–14. My account departs from Pratt in two respects: first, though he describes 'stranger humanism' as a form of social organization characterized by "apostolic openness," he also argues that it sits apart from 'spiritual communitarianism;" and, second, he writes that the "African American pursuit of stranger humanism arguably declined with the onset of the U.S. Civil War, Reconstruction, and Jim Crow" (Pratt, *Strangers*, 3, 8, 13). I argue instead that the spirit-filled practices of gospel sermons became the preeminent vehicles for spreading stranger humanism as a popular practice during the nineteenth century's final decades.

84. Pratt, *Strangers Book*, 10.

85. In one sense, the reason for fellowship's tentativeness is relatively mundane. Congregations were just as likely to produce intra-black struggle as they were racial identification because differential power positions between preachers and laypeople, between competing church governing bodies, and between sharp personalities turned churches into sites of sometimes-acute conflict. Postbellum black literary history repeatedly features struggles between warring factions within single congregations, representing religious practice and institutions as occasions for disunity, competition, and even occasional acrimony. See, for example, "The Fruitful Sleeping of the Reverend Elisha Edwards," "The Ordeal at Mount Hope," and "The Trial Sermons on Bull-Skin" in Paul Laurence Dunbar, *The Complete Stories of Paul Laurence Dunbar* (Athens: Ohio University Press, 2005); and Hurston, *Jonah's Gourd Vine*.

86. Hurston, *Jonah's Gourd Vine*, 158–9.

87. Du Bois, *Souls*, 148–9.

88. Johnson, *God's Trombone*, 7.

89. The tentative and experimental nature of such religious experience is, of course, hardly unique to the black gospel sermon, and it thus points to one large field of enquiry that this chapter leaves for further study: a comparative analysis between the experience enabled through the black gospel sermon and that enabled through other forms of religious experience contemporary to it. As a starting point, we might look to William James. Writing about religion and religious experience, James seeks out a state of collective religious belief incommensurable with the existing world. He claims to be "willing that there should be real losses and real losers, and no total preservation of all that is"; so doing, he values a kind of provisionality and experimentation that seems at least formally similar to that described in this chapter. Assuming the voice of "the creator," he writes: "I am going to make a world not certain to be saved, a world the perfection of which shall be conditional merely... I offer you the chance of taking part in such a world. Its safety, you see, is unwarranted. It is a real adventure, with real danger, yet it may win through. It is a social scheme of co-operative work genuinely to be done. Will you join the procession? Will you trust yourself and trust the other agents enough to face the risk" (1907; reprint William James, *Pragmatism*, in *Writings: 1902–1910* (New York: The Library of America, 1987), 617, 614). For a nice account of James's invocation of religious experience as "habituation to the hazards of alterity," see Leela Gandhi, *Affective Communities: Anticolonial Thought, Fin-de-Siècle Radicalism, and the Politics of Friendship* (Durham, NC: Duke University Press, 2006), 131–41; the quoted phrase comes from page 134.

90. "Hewn from the Mountains of Eternity," *God Struck Me Dead*, 101.

91. For more on the importance of railroads as metaphors in African American Christian discourse, see Sundquist, *Hammers of Creation: Folk Culture in Modern African American Fiction* (Athens: University of Georgia Press, 2006), 74–7.

92. "Souls Piled Up Like Timber," *God Struck Me Dead*, 44; "A Voice Like the Cooing of a Dove," *God Struck Me Dead*, 18.

93. Hannah Arendt, "What is Freedom?" in *Between Past and Future: Eight Exercises in Political Thought* (New York: Viking Press, 1968), 151.

94. Daniel Henninger, "Wonder Land: David Mamet's Revision" *Wall Street Journal*, Mar. 20, 2008, A18; Christopher Hitchens, "Obama Stands by Pastor, but will Voters Stand by Obama?," *The Australian*, Mar. 26, 2008; Matt Patterson, "That's the Obama I Knew," *PJ*

*Media*, May 8, 2009, pjmedia.com/blog/thats-the-obama-i-knew/; Dean Barnett, "The Wrong Stuff; Why the Left Defends Rev. Wright," *The Daily Standard*, Apr. 28, 2008; Steve Sailer, "Obama's Mr. Wright," *The American Conservative*, Apr. 7, 2008, <www.theamericanconservative.com/articles/obamas-mr-wright>; Mark Steyn, "Post "Post-Racial Candidate," *"National Review Online*, Mar. 22, 2008, <www.nationalreview.com/articles/224002/post-post-racial-candidate/mark-steyn>.

95. Jonah Goldberg, "Looking for Mr. Wright," *National Review Online*, Apr. 30, 2008, <www.nationalreview.com/articles/224342/looking-mr-wright/jonah-goldberg>.

96. Jeremiah Wright, "Speech at the National Press Club" (speech, Washington, DC, Apr. 28, 2008), *New York Times*, <www.nytimes.com/2008/04/28/us/politics/28text-wright.html.>

97. For a full transcript, see Lynn Sweet, "Obama on Quitting Trinity United Church of Christ," *Chicago Sun Times*, May 31, 2008, <suntimes.com/sweet/2008/05/obama_on_quitting_trinity_unit.html>. For a fuller account of the scandal surrounding Wright's sermons, including the voices of many Trinity members, see Carl A. Grant and Shelby J. Grant, *The Moment: Barack Obama, Jeremiah Wright, and the Firestorm at Trinity United Church of Christ* (New York: Rowman & Littlefield, 2013).

98. See e.g. Andrew S. Curran, *The Anatomy of Blackness: Science and Slavery in an Age of Enlightenment* (Baltimore: JHU Press, 2011); and George M. Fredrickson, *The Black Image in the White Mind: The Debate on Afro-American Character and Destiny, 1817–1914* (New York: Harper & Row, 1971).

99. Michel Foucault, *The History of Sexuality: An Introduction*, vol. 1 of *The History of Sexuality*, trans. Robert Hurley (New York: Vintage Books, 1978), 101–2.

100. J. Kameron Carter, "Paratheological Blackness," *South Atlantic Quarterly* 112, no. 4 (2013): 589.

## Epilogue

1. Claudia Rankine, "The Condition of Black Life is One of Mourning," *New York Times Magazine* (June 22, 2015).

2. Ibid.

3. Ibid.

# { WORKS CITED }

Aaron, Daniel. *The Unwritten War: American Writers and the Civil War*. New York: Knopf, 1973.

Abbott, Lyman. "Just Among Ourselves," *Ladies' Home Journal* 10 (July 1893).

Adorno, Theodor. *Negative Dialectics*. Translated by E. B. Ashton. New York: Continuum, 1994.

"After-Dinner Stories: A Budget of Bright Anecdotes Told of Famous Folk." *The Ladies' Home Journal* 15 (May 1898).

Aldrich, Thomas Bailey. "Accomplices," *Atlantic Monthly* (July 1865).

Aldrich, Thomas Bailey. "Fredericksburg." In *Our Country in Poems and Prose*. Edited by Eleanor A. Persons. New York: American Book Company, 1899.

Aldrich, Thomas Bailey. "Fredericksburg." In *Poems of Places: America—The Southern States*. Edited by Henry Wadsworth Longfellow. Cambridge, MA: Houghton, Osgood & Co., 1879.

Aldrich, Thomas Bailey. "Mr. Aldrich's Poetry." *Atlantic Monthly* (Dec. 1874).

Aldrich, Thomas Bailey. "The Poems of Thomas Bailey Aldrich." *The Century Magazine* (Sept. 1891).

Allen, Theodore. *The Invention of the White Race, Volume 1: Racial Oppression and Social Control*. London: Verso, 1994.

Anderson, Olive San Louie. *An American Girl, and her Four Years in a Boys' College*. Ann Arbor: University of Michigan Press, 2006.

Arendt, Hannah. "What is Freedom?" In *Between Past and Future: Eight Exercises in Political Thought*. New York: Viking Press, 1968.

Aristotle. *Nicomachean Ethics*. Translated by Terence Irwin. Indianapolis: Hackett Publishing Co., 1985.

Asad, Talal. *Formations of the Secular: Christianity, Islam, Modernity*. Stanford, CA: Stanford University Press, 2003.

"As a Physician Sees Women: A Frank View of Women From the Standpoint of a Successful Practitioner." *The Ladies' Home Journal (1889–1907)* (Mar. 1907).

Ashbery, John. "A Note on 'Variation on a Noel.'" In *Selected Prose*. Edited by Eugene Richie. Ann Arbor: University of Michigan Press, 2004.

Ashmore, Ruth. "The Intense Friendships of Girls," *The Ladies' Home Journal* 15 (July 1898).

Augst, Thomas. *The Clerk's Tale: Young Men and Moral Life in Nineteenth-Century America*. Chicago: University of Chicago Press, 2003.

Bagg, Lyman. *Four Years at Yale*. New Haven: Charles C. Chatfield & Co., 1871.

Baker, Bruce E. *What Reconstruction Meant: Historical Memory in the American South*. Charlottesville: University of Virginia Press, 2007.

Baldwin, James. *The Evidence of Things Not Seen*. New York: Holt, Rinehart and Winston, 1985.

Baldwin, James. *Just Above my Head*. New York: Random House, 1978.

Baptist, Edward E. *The Half Has Never Been Told: Slavery and the Making of American Capitalism*. New York: Basic Books, 2014.

Barnes, Jodi A., ed. *The Materiality of Freedom: Archaeologies of Postemancipation Life*. Columbia: University of South Carolina Press, 2011.

Barnett, Dean. "Why the Left Defends Rev. Wright." *The Daily Standard* (Apr. 28, 2008).

Barnett, Dean. "The Wrong Stuff." *The Daily Standard* (Apr. 28, 2008).

Bellis, Peter J. "Reconciliation as Sequel and Supplement: *Drum-Taps* and *Battle-Pieces*." *Leviathan: A Journal of Melville Studies* 17, no. 3 (2015): 79–93.

Benston, Kimberly W. *Performing Blackness: Enactments of African-American Modernism*. New York: Routledge, 2000.

Berlant, Lauren. *Cruel Optimism*. Durham, NC: Duke University Press, 2011.

Berlant, Lauren. *The Female Complaint: The Unfinished Business of Sentimentality in American Culture*. Durham, NC: Duke University Press, 2008.

Beveridge, Edith Carter. "Where Southern Memories Cluster." *The Ladies' Home Journal* 23 (Sept. 1906).

Biddle, Reverend W. T. "Fruitless Preaching." *Star of Zion* (May 31, 1900).

Bledstein, Burton J. *The Culture of Professionalism: The Middle Class and the Development of Higher Education in America*. New York: Norton, 1976.

Blight, David W. *Race and Reunion: The Civil War in American Memory*. Cambridge, MA: Belknap Press of Harvard University Press, 2001.

Blount, Marcellus. "The Preacherly Text: African American Poetry and Vernacular Performance." *PMLA* 107, no. 3 (1992): 582–93.

"The Blue and the Gray." Advertisement. *The Ladies' Home Journal* 9 (Jan. 1892).

Blum, Edward J. *Reforging the White Republic: Race, Religion, and American Nationalism*. Baton Rouge: Louisiana State University Press, 2005.

Bok, Edward. "The Magazine with a Million." *The Ladies' Home Journal* 20 (Feb. 1903).

Bok, Edward. "The Pen of a Mountaineer." *Ladies' Home Journal* 11 (July 1894).

Bok, Edward. "The Two Centuries and this Magazine." *The Ladies' Home Journal* 18 (Jan. 1901).

Bold, Christine, ed. *U.S. Popular Print Culture, 1860–1920*. New York: Oxford University Press, 2011.

"Books of the Month." *Atlantic Monthly* (Jan. 1886).

Booth, Mary H. C. *Wayside Blossoms*. Philadelphia: J. B. Lippincott, 1865.

Booth, Mary H. C. "While God He Leaves Me Reason, God He Will Leave Me Jim." In *Anecdotes, Poetry, and Incidents of the War: North and South, 1860–1865*. Edited by Frank Moore. New York: Printed for Subscribers, 1866.

Bourdieu, Pierre. *The Logic of Practice*. Translated by Richard Nice. Stanford, CA: Stanford University Press, 1980.

Boym, Svetlana. *The Future of Nostalgia*. New York: Basic, 2001.

Bradford, Adam C. *Communities of Death: Whitman, Poe, and the American Culture of Mourning*. Columbia: University of Missouri Press, 2014.

Brown, Bill. *The Material Unconscious: American Amusement, Stephen Crane & the Economies of Play*. Cambridge, MA: Harvard University Press, 1996.

Brown, Helen Dawes. *Two College Girls*. Boston: Ticknor, 1886.

Brown, William Wells. *My Southern Home: or, The South and its People*. Boston: A. G. Brown, 1880.

Bryant, William Cullen. "The Death of Slavery." *Atlantic Monthly* (July 1866).

Bryant, William Cullen, ed. *The Family Library of Poetry and Song*. New York: Fords, Howard, and Hulbert, 1878.

Butler, Judith. *Gender Trouble*. New York: Routledge, 1999.

Butler, Judith. *Precarious Life: The Powers of Mourning and Violence*. New York: Verso, 2004.

Calhoun, Charles W. *Conceiving a New Republic: The Republican Party and the Southern Question, 1869–1900*. Lawrence: University Press of Kansas, 2006.

Carter, J. Kameron. "Paratheological Blackness." *South Atlantic Quarterly* 112, no. 4 (2013): 589–611.

Castronovo, Russ. *Necro Citizenship: Death, Eroticism, and the Public Sphere in the Nnineteenth-Century United States*. Durham, NC: Duke University Press, 2001.

Castronovo, Russ. "State Secrets: Ben Franklin and WikiLeaks." *Critical Inquiry* 39, no. 3 (2013): 425–50.

Cavell, Stanley. *In Quest of the Ordinary: Lines of Skepticism and Romanticism*. Chicago: University of Chicago Press, 1988.

Cavitch, Max. *American Elegy: The Poetry of Mourning from the Puritans to Whitman*. Minneapolis: University of Minnesota Press, 2007.

Cherniavsky, Eva. *Incorporation: Race, Nation, and the Body Politics of Capital*. Minneapolis: University of Minnesota Press, 2006.

Chesnut, Mary Boykin Miller. *A Diary from Dixie*. New York: D. Appleton and Company, 1905.

Clarke, Ednah Proctor. "Of Santa Claus." *The Ladies' Home Journal* 18 (Dec. 1901).

Clarkson, Lida. "Letter 6." *The Ladies' Home Journal and Practical Housekeeper* 3 (May 1886).

Clinton, Bishop G. W. "Alarm Cry No. 3." *Star of Zion* (Jan. 21, 1897).

Cloyd, Benjamin G. *Haunted by Atrocity: Civil War Prisons in American Memory*. Baton Rouge: Louisiana State University Press, 2010.

Cohen, Michael C. "Contraband Singing: Poems and Songs in Circulation during the Civil War." *American Literature* 82, no. 2 (2010): 271–304.

Cone, James A. *The Spirituals and the Blues: An Interpretation*. New York: Seaberry Press, 1972.

Cook, Robert. "The Quarrel Forgotten? Toward a Clearer Understanding of Sectional Reconciliation." *The Journal of the Civil War Era* 6, no. 3 (2016): 413–36.

Cooper, Frederick, Thomas Holt, and Rebecca Scott. *Beyond Slavery: Explorations of Race, Labor, and Citizenship in Postemancipation Societies*. Chapel Hill: University of North Carolina Press, 2000.

Crane, Stephen. *The Red Badge of Courage*. New York: Norton, 1994.

Culler, Jonathan. *The Literary in Theory*. Stanford, CA: Stanford University Press, 2007.

Cummings, Emmy. "Tenth Letter." *The Ladies' Home Journal* 15 (Feb. 1898).

Curran, Andrew S. *The Anatomy of Blackness: Science and Slavery in an Age of Enlightenment*. Baltimore: JHU Press, 2011.

Damon-Moore, Helen. *Magazines for the Millions: Gender and Commerce in the Ladies' Home Journal and the Saturday Evening Post, 1880–1910*. Albany: SUNY Press, 1994.

Dance, Daryl Cumber. *From my People: 400 Years of African American Folklore*. New York: W. W. Norton, 2003.

Davis, Gerald L. *I Got the Word in Me and I Can Sing It, You Know: A Study of the Performed African-American Sermon*. Philadelphia: University of Pennsylvania Press, 1987.

"The Day of Prejudiced Gone." *The Christian Recorder* (July 18, 1889).

Dayan, Colin. *The Law is a White Dog: How Legal Rituals Make and Unmake Persons.* Princeton: Princeton University Press, 2011.

Dayan, Joan. *Haiti, History, and the Gods.* Berkeley: University of California Press, 1995.

Derrida, Jacques. "The Law of Genre." Translated by Avital Ronell. *Glyph* 7 (1980): 176–201.

Derrida, Jacques. *Politics of Friendship.* Translated by George Collins. New York: Verso, 1997.

Dimock, Wai Chee. "The Egyptian Pronoun, Lyric, Novel, the Book of the Dead." *New Literary History* 39, no. 3 (2008): 619–43.

Dimock, Wai Chee. "Introduction: Genres as Fields of Knowledge." *PMLA* 122, no. 5 (2007): 1377–88.

Dirlik, Arif. "Race Talk, Race, and Contemporary Racism." *PMLA* 123, no. 5 (2008): 1363–79.

Dorr, Julia R. "The Drummer-Boy's Burial." *Harper's New Monthly Magazine* (July 1864).

Douglass, Frederick. "The Color Question." In *The Frederick Douglass Papers, Series One: Speeches, Debates, and Interviews.* Edited by John W. Blassingame and John R. McKivigan. New Haven: Yale University Press, 1991.

"Droch's Literary Talks." *Ladies' Home Journal* 14 (Dec. 1896).

Du Bois, W. E. B. *The Autobiography of W. E. B. Du Bois: A Soliloquy on Viewing my Life from the Last Decade of Its First Century.* New York, International Publishers, 1969.

Du Bois, W. E. B. *Black Reconstruction in America, 1860–1880.* New York: The Free Press, 1992.

Du Bois, W. E. B. "The College Bred Negro." In *Proceedings of the Fifth Conferences for the Study of the Negro Problems.* Atlanta, GA: Atlanta University Press, 1900.

Du Bois, W. E. B. *Dusk of Dawn: An Essay Toward an Autobiography of a Race Concept.* 1940; New York: Oxford University Press, 2007.

Du Bois, W. E. B. *The Souls of Black Folk.* Edited by David W. Blight and Robert Gooding-Williams. Boston: Bedford Books, 1997.

Dunbar, Paul Laurence. *The Complete Stories of Paul Laurence Dunbar.* Athens: Ohio University Press, 2005.

Duquette, Elizabeth. *Loyal Subjects: Bonds of Nation, Race, and Allegiance in Nineteenth-Century America.* New Brunswick, NJ: Rutgers University Press, 2010.

Elaw, Zilpha. *Memoirs of the Life, Religious Experience, Ministerial Travels, and Labors of Mrs. Zilpha Elaw.* In *Sisters of the Spirit: Three Black Women's Autobiographies of the Nineteenth Century.* Edited by William L. Andrews. Bloomington: Indiana University Press, 1986.

Elliott, Mark. *Color-Blind Justice: Albion Tourgée and the Quest for Racial Equality from the Civil War to Plessy v. Ferguson.* New York: Oxford University Press, 2006.

Elliott, Michael A. *The Culture Concept: Writing and Difference in the Age of Realism.* Minneapolis: University of Minnesota Press, 2002.

Elliot, S. R. "With the Tread of Marching Columns." *Century Illustrated Magazine* May 1893.

Ellison, Ralph. *The Invisible Man.* New York: Vintage Books, 1995.

Emerson, Edward W. "When Louisa Alcott Was a Girl." *Ladies' Home Journal* 16 (Dec. 1898).

Emerson, Ralph Waldo. "Courage." *New York Tribune* (Nov. 8, 1859).

Eng, David L. and David Kazanjian, eds. "Introduction: Mourning Remains." In *Loss: The Politics of Mourning.* Berkeley: University of California Press, 2003.

Eudell, Demetrius L. *The Political Languages of Emancipation in the British Caribbean and U.S. South.* Chapel Hill: University of North Carolina Press, 2002.

Evans, Curtis J. *The Burden of Black Religion.* New York: Oxford University Press, 2008.

Faludan, Philip Shaw. *A People's Contest: The Union and Civil War, 1861–1865*. Lawrence: University Press of Kansas, 1996.

Fancher, Fannie L. "Friendship," *The Ladies' Home Journal* 6 (Aug. 1889).

Faulkner, William. *Absalom, Absalom!* New York: Vintage, 1990.

Faust, Drew Gilpin. *This Republic of Suffering: Death and the American Civil War*. New York: Vintage, 2008.

Finch, Francis Miles. "The Blue and the Gray." *Atlantic Monthly* (Sept. 1867).

Finseth, Ian. "The Civil War Dead: Realism and the Problem of Anonymity." *American Literary History* 25, no. 3 (2013): 535–62.

Fitzgerald, F. Scott. *This Side of Paradise*. New York: Penguin, 1990.

Folsom, Ed. "Lucifer and Ethopia: Whitman, Race, and Poetics Before the Civil War and After." In *A Historical Guide to Walt Whitman*. Edited by David Reynolds. New York: Oxford University Press, 2000.

Folsom, Ed. " 'That Towering Bulge of Pure White': Whitman, Melville, the Capitol Dome, and Black America." *Leviathan: A Journal of Melville Studies* 16, no. 1 (2014): 87–120.

Foner, Eric. *Reconstruction: America's Unfinished Revolution, 1863–1877*. New York: Harper and Row, 1988.

Foote, Stephanie. *The Parvenu's Plot: Gender, Culture, and Class in the Age of Realism*. Durham, NC: University of New Hampshire Press, 2014.

"Fops and Dude Preachers." *Star of Zion* (Aug. 5, 1897).

Foucault, Michel. "Friendship as a Way of Life." Translated by John Johnston. In *Essential Works of Foucault 1954–1984, Volume 1: Ethics: Subjectivity and Truth*. Edited by Paul Rabinow. New York: New Press, 1997.

Foucault, Michel. *The History of Sexuality: An Introduction*. Volume 1 of *The History of Sexuality*. Translated by Robert Hurley. New York: Vintage Books, 1978.

Foucault, Michel. "Nietzsche, Genealogy, History." In *The Foucault Reader*. Edited by Paul Rabinow. New York: Pantheon, 1984.

Foucault, Michel. *The Order of Things: An Archaeology of the Human Sciences*. Translated by Alan Sheridan. New York: Vintage, 1994.

Foucault, Michel. "What is an Author?" In *The Foucault Reader*. Edited by Paul Rabinow. New York: Pantheon, 1984.

Frankenberg, Ruth. *White Woman Race Matters: The Social Construction of Whiteness*. London: Routledge, 1993.

Frazier, E. Franklin. *The Negro Church in America*. New York: Schocken Books, 1974.

Fredrickson, George M. *The Black Image in the White Mind: The Debate on Afro-American Character and Destiny, 1817–1914*. New York: Harper & Row, 1971.

Freud, Sigmund. "Mourning and Melancholia." *The Journal of Nervous and Mental Disease* 56, no. 5 (1922): 543–5.

Frye, Northrop. *Anatomy of Criticism: Four Essays*. Princeton: Princeton University Press, 1957.

Fuller, Caroline. *Across the Campus: A Story of College Life*. New York: Scribner's, 1899.

Fuller, Randall. *From Battlefields Rising: How the Civil War Transformed American Literature*. New York: Oxford University Press, 2011.

"The Game the Waiter Preferred." *The Ladies' Home Journal* 22 (Jan. 1905).

Gandhi, Leela. *Affective Communities: Anticolonial Thought, Fin-De-Siècle Radicalism, and the Politics of Friendship*. Durham, NC: Duke University Press, 2006.

Gannon, Barbara A. *The Won Cause: Black and White Comradeship in the Grand Army of the Republic*. Chapel Hill: University of North Carolina Press, 2011.

Garrettson, Freeborn. *American Methodist Pioneer: The Life and Journals of the Rev. Freeborn Garrettson, 1752–1782*. Edited by Robert Drew Simpson. Madison, NJ: Academy Books, 1984.

Gates, Henry Louis. *Loose Canons: Notes on the Culture Wars*. Oxford: Oxford University Press, 1992

Genovese, Eugene D. *Roll, Jordon, Roll: The World the Slaves Made*. New York: Pantheon Books, 1974.

Gillespie, Michele K., and Randal L. Hall, eds. *Thomas Dixon Jr and the Birth of Modern America*. Baton Rouge: Louisiana State University Press, 2006.

Gilligan, Heather Tirado. "Reading, Race, and Charles Chesnutt's 'Uncle Julius' Tales." *ELH* 74, no. 1 (2007): 195–215.

Gilroy, Paul. *The Black Atlantic: Modernity and Double-Consciousness*. Cambridge, MA: Harvard University Press, 1995.

Glazener, Nancy. *Reading for Realism: The History of a U.S. Literary Institution, 1850–1910*. Durham, NC: Duke University Press, 1997.

Goldberg, Jonah. "Looking for Mr. Wright." *National Review Online* (Apr. 30, 2008). <www. nationalreview.com/articles/224342/looking-mr-wright/jonah-2goldberg>.

Grant, Carl A., and Shelby J. Grant. *The Moment: Barack Obama, Jeremiah Wright, and the Firestorm at Trinity United Church of Christ*. New York: Rowman & Littlefield, 2013.

Grant, Isaac S. "What I Have Heard." *The Christian Recorder* (Mar. 10, 1887).

Gwynn, Annie E. "Revival—Woman Preacher." *Star of Zion* (Dec. 2, 1897).

Hager, Christopher, and Cody Marrs. "Afterword: Archiving the War." In *A History of American Civil War Literature*. Edited by Coleman Hutchison. New York: Cambridge University Press, 2016.

Hahn, Steven. *A Nation under our Feet: Black Political Struggles in the Rural South from Slavery to the Great Migration*. Cambridge, MA: Harvard University Press, 2003.

Halberstam, Judith. *In a Queer Time and Place*. New York: New York University Press, 2005.

Hamilton, Charles V. *The Black Preacher in America*. New York: Morrow, 1972.

Hannah, Matthew G. *Governmentality and the Mastery of Territory in Nineteenth-Century America*. New York: Cambridge University Press, 2000.

Harper, Frances Ellen Watkins. "An Appeal to the American People." In *The Complete Poems of Frances E. W. Harper*. Edited by Maryemma Graham. New York: Oxford University Press, 1988.

Harper, Frances Ellen Watkins. *Minnie's Sacrifice; Sowing and Reaping; Trial and Triumph: Three Rediscovered Novels*. Boston: Beacon Press, 1994.

Harris, M. Keith. *Across the Bloody Chasm: The Culture of Commemoration among Civil War Veterans*. Baton Rouge: Louisiana State University Press, 2014.

Hart, William. "Never Fade Away." *The American College Novel: An Annotated Bibliography*. Lanham, MD: Scarecrow, 2004.

Hartman, Saidiya V. *Scenes of Subjection: Terror, Slavery, and Self-Making in Nineteenth-Century America*. New York: Oxford University Press, 1997.

Hatch, Nathan O. *The Democratization of American Christianity*. New Haven: Yale University Press, 1989.

Hatcher, William Eldridge. *John Jasper, the Unmatched Negro Philosopher and Preacher*. New York: Fleming H. Revell, 1908.

"He Knew his People." *The Ladies' Home Journal* 23 (Apr. 1906).

"He Put Him Off, All Right." *The Ladies' Home Journal* 21 (Oct. 1904).

Henninger, Daniel. "Wonder Land: David Mamet's Revision." *Wall Street Journal* (Mar. 20, 2008).

Higginbotham, Evelyn Brooks. *Righteous Discontent: The Women's Movement in the Black Baptist Church, 1880–1920.* Cambridge, MA: Harvard University Press, 1993.

Hillis, Newell Dwight. "The Secrets of a Happy Life: Third Article: The Diffusion of Happiness through Conversation." *The Ladies' Home Journal* 26 (Aug. 1899).

Hitchens, Christopher. "Obama Stands by Pastor, but will Voters Stand by Obama?" *The Australian* (Mar. 26, 2008).

Hochman, Barbara. "Highbrow/Lowbrow: Naturalist Writers and the 'Reading Habit.'" In *Twisted from the Ordinary: Essays on American Literary Naturalism.* Edited by Mary E. Papke. Knoxville: The University of Tennessee Press, 2003.

Hoffman, Tyler. *American Poetry in Performance: From Walt Whitman to Hip Hop.* Ann Arbor: University of Michigan Press, 2013.

Hogwarth Press Bookshop. Advertisement. *New York Times* (Nov. 12, 1932).

Hood's Sarsaparilla. Advertisement. *The Ladies' Home Journal* 8 (May 1891).

Horowitz, Helen Lefkowitz. *Campus Life: Undergraduate Cultures from the End of the Eighteenth Century to the Present.* Chicago: University of Chicago Press, 1987.

Horton, Thaddeus Mrs. "The Story of the Nancy Harts," *The Ladies' Home Journal* 21 (Nov. 1904).

Howells, William Dean. "The Bouquet." *Atlantic Monthly* (Nov. 1899).

Howells, William Dean. "Dave's Neckliss." *Atlantic Monthly* (Oct. 1889).

Howells, William Dean. "Editor's Study." *Harper's New Monthly Magazine* (June 1891).

Howells, William Dean. "The Goophered Grapevine." *Atlantic Monthly* (Aug. 1887).

Howells, William Dean. "Mr. Charles W. Chesnutt's Stories." *Atlantic Monthly* (May 1900).

Howells, William Dean. "Mr. Howells's Latest Novel." *Ladies' Home Journal* 7 (Mar. 1890).

Howells, William Dean. "Po' Sandy." *Atlantic Monthly* (May 1888).

Hubbard, Dolan. *The Sermon and the African American Literary Imagination.* Columbia: University of Missouri Press, 1994.

Hunt, Robert. *The Good Men Who Won the War: Army of the Cumberland Veterans and Emancipation Memory.* Tuscaloosa: University of Alabama Press, 2010.

Hurston, Zora Neale. *Jonah's Gourd Vine.* New York: HarperPerennial Library, 1990.

Hurston, Zora Neale. *The Sanctified Church.* Berkeley: Turtle Island, 1983.

Hurston, Zora Neale. *Zora Neale Hurston: A Life in Letters.* Edited by Carla Kaplan. New York: Doubleday, 2002.

Hutchins, Zach. "Miscegenetic Melville: Race and Reconstruction in *Clarel*." *ELH* 80, no. 4 (2013): 1173–203.

"The Ideas of a Plain Country Woman." *Ladies' Home Journal* 24 (Sept. 1907).

"If You Like Short Stories Here are a Bundle Bright and Cheery." *Ladies' Home Journal* 8 (Jan. 1891).

Ignatiev, Noel. *How the Irish Became White.* New York: Routledge, 1995.

Jackson, Virginia. "The Function of Criticism at the Present Time." *Los Angeles Review of Books* (Apr. 12, 2015).

Jacobson, M. F. *Whiteness of a Different Color: European Immigrants and the Alchemy of Race.* Cambridge, MA: Harvard University Press, 1998.

James, Henry. *The Bostonians.* New York: Vintage, 1991.

James, William. "Letter to Henry James, 5 Dec. 1869." In *William and Henry James: Selected Letters*. Edited by Ignas K. Skrupskelis and Elizabeth M. Berkeley. Charlottesville: University of Virginia Press, 1997.

James, William. *Pragmatism*. In *Writings: 1902–1910*. New York: The Library of America, 1987.

Jameson, Frederic. *The Political Unconscious: Narrative as a Socially Symbolic Act*. Ithaca, NY: Cornell University Press, 1981.

Janney, Caroline. *Remembering the Civil War: Reunion and the Limits of Reconciliation*. Chapel Hill: University of North Carolina Press, 2013.

Jaudon, Toni Wall. "Obeah's Sensations: Rethinking Religion at the Transnational Turn." *American Literature* 84, no. 4 (2012): 715–41.

Johnson, Clifton H., ed. *God Struck Me Dead: Religious Conversion Experiences and Autobiographies of Ex-Slaves*. Philadelphia: Pilgrim Press, 1969.

Johnson, D. W. M. "Our Work in Georgia." *The Christian Recorder* (Mar. 12, 1874).

Johnson, E. Patrick. *Performing Blackness: Performance and the Politics of Authenticity*. Durham, NC: Duke University Press, 2003.

Johnson, James Weldon. *God's Trombone: Seven Negro Sermons in Verse*. New York: Penguin, 1976.

Johnson, Mat. *Pym*. New York: Spiegel & Grau, 2011.

Johnson, Owen. *Stover at Yale*. New York: Frederick A. Stokes, 1912.

Jordan, Brian Matthew. *Marching Home: Union Veterans and their Unending Civil War*. New York: Livewright, 2014.

"Just Told in A Talkative Way." *Ladies' Home Journal* 21 (Dec.1904).

Keely, Karen A. "Marriage Plots and National Reunion: The Trope of Romantic Reconciliation in Postbellum Literature." *The Mississippi Quarterly* 51, no. 4 (1998): 621–48.

Keller, Helen. "The Story of my Life." *Ladies' Home Journal* 19 (Aug. 1902).

Kellor, Frances A. "The New Department: The Housewife and her Helper." *The Ladies' Home Journal* 22 (Sept. 1905).

Kikant, Thomas. "Melville's *Battle-Pieces* and the Environments of War." *ESQ* 60, no. 4 (2014): 557–90.

Kilham, Elizabeth. "Sketches in Color." *Putnam's Magazine* 5, no. 27 (Mar. 1870).

Kim, Ju Yon. *The Racial Mundane: Asian American Performance and the Embodied Everyday*. New York: New York University Press, 2015.

L., H. "Letter 4." *The Ladies' Home Journal* 4 (Oct. 1887).

"The Lady from Philadelphia's Heart-to-Heart Talks with Girls." *The Ladies' Home Journal* 23 (Oct. 1906).

LaRue, Cleophus J. *The Heart of Black Preaching*. Louisville, KY: Westminster John Knox Press, 2000

Latour, Bruno. "On Actor-Network Theory: A Few Clarifications" (10 July, 2014). <www.nettime.org/Lists-Archives/nettime-l-9801/msg00019.html>.

Latour, Bruno. *Reassembling the Social: An Introduction to Actor-Network-Theory*. New York: Oxford University Press, 2005.

Lears, T. J. Jackson. *No Place of Grace: Antimodernism and the Transformation of American Culture, 1880–1920*. New York: Pantheon Books, 1981.

Lee, Jarena. "The Life and Religious Experience of Jarena Lee, A Coloured Lady, Giving an Account of her Call to Preach the Gospel." In *African American Religious History: A Documentary Witness*. Edited by Milton C. Sernett. Durham, NC: Duke University Press, 1999.

Lefebvre, Henri. *Critique of Everyday Life. Volume 1: Introduction.* Translated by John Moore. London: Verso, 1991.

Lefebvre, Henri. *Critique of Everyday Life. Volume 2: Foundations for a Sociology of the Everyday.* Translated by John Moore. New York: Verso, 2002.

Levine, Caroline. *Forms: Whole, Rhythm, Hierarchy, Network.* Princeton: Princeton University Press, 2015.

Levine, Robert S. *Dislocating Race and Nation: Episodes in Nineteenth-Century American Literary Nationalism.* Chapel Hill: University of North Carolina Press, 2008.

Lichtenstein, Joy. *For the Blue and Gold: A Tale of Life at the University of California.* San Francisco: Robertson, 1901.

Lightfoot, Natasha. *Troubling Freedom: Antigua and the Aftermath of British Emancipation.* Durham, NC: Duke University Press, 2015.

Lilley, Jeremy D. *Common Things: Romance and the Aesthetics of Belonging in Atlantic Modernity.* New York: Fordham University Press, 2013.

Lincoln, C. Eric, and Lawrence H. Mamiya, *The Black Church in the African American Experience.* Durham, NC: Duke University Press, 1990.

Lipsitz, George. "The Possessive Investment in Whiteness: Racialized Social Democracy and the 'White' Problem in American Studies." *American Quarterly* 47, no. 3 (1995): 369–87.

Loring, Frederick. *Two College Friends.* Boston: Loring, 1871.

Lott, Eric. *Love & Theft: Blackface Minstrelsy and the American Working Class.* New York: Oxford University Press, 1993.

Love, Heather. "Critique is Ordinary." *PMLA* 132, no. 2 (2017): 364–70.

Luciano, Dana. *Arranging Grief: Sacred Time and the Body in Nineteenth-Century America.* New York: New York University Press, 2007.

Lybeer, Edward. "Whitman's War and the Status of Literature." *Arizona Quarterly* 67, no. 2 (2011): 23–40.

M., M. M. "Letter 2," *The Ladies' Home Journal* 6 (Dec. 1888).

Mabie, Hamilton W. "Mr. Mabie's Literary Talks." *Ladies' Home Journal* 19 (Mar. 1902).

Mabie, Hamilton W. "Mr. Mabie's Literary Talks." *Ladies' Home Journal* 19 (June 1902).

Mabie, Hamilton W. "Mr. Mabie Tells of the World's Greatest University." *Ladies' Home Journal* 24 (Nov. 1907).

McDannell, Colleen and Bernhard Lang. *Heaven: A History.* New Haven: Yale University Press, 2001.

MacFarlane, Isabella. "The Two Slave Mothers." 3 *The Anglo-African* (Nov. 7, 1863).

MacFarlane, Isabella. "The Two Slave Mothers." 4 *Continental Monthly* (Nov. 1863).

MacHenry, Laury. "Talks with the Doctor," *The Ladies' Home Journal* 7 (May 1890).

MacHenry, Laury. "Whooping Cough, Etc.: Talks with the Doctor No. 5," *The Ladies' Home Journal* 6 (Dec. 1888).

McPherson, Tara. *Reconstructing Dixie: Gender, Race, and Nostalgia in the Imagined South.* Durham, NC: Duke University Press, 2003.

Macy, John Albert. "Helen Keller as She Really Is: An Intimate Portrait." *The Ladies' Home Journal* 19 (Nov. 1902).

Marrs, Cody. *Nineteenth-Century American Literature and the Long Civil War.* New York: Cambridge University Press, 2015.

Martin, Theodore. *Contemporary Drift: Genre, Historicism, and the Problem of the Present.* New York: Columbia University Press, 2017.

Mason, Patrick. *The Mormon Menace: Violence and Anti-Mormonism in the Postbellum South*. New York: Oxford University Press, 2011.

Meadows, Reverend W. S. "Positive Preaching." *Star of Zion* (Aug. 3, 1899).

Melick, Charles Wesley. *Some Phases of the Negro Question*. Washington, DC: D., H. Deloe, 1908.

Melville, Herman. *Battle-Pieces and Aspects of the War*. New York: Da Capo Press, 1995.

Melville, Herman. *Moby-Dick, or, The Whale*. New York: Penguin, 1992.

Mills, Charles W. *Blackness Visible: Essays on Philosophy and Race*. Ithaca, NY: Cornell University Press, 1998.

Mills, Charles W. *The Racial Contract*. Ithaca, NY: Cornell University Press, 1997.

Mills, Charles W. "Racial Exploitation and te Wages of Whiteness." In *What White Looks Like: African American Philosophers on the Whiteness Question*. Edited by George Yancy. New York: Routledge, 2004.

Mitchell, Henry H. *Black Preaching*. Philadelphia and New York: J. B. Lippincott Company, 1970.

Moffatt, Michael. "Inventing the 'Time-Honored Traditions' of 'Old Rutgers': Rutgers Student Culture, 1858–1900." *The Journal of the Rutgers University Libraries* 47, no. 1 (1985): 1–11.

Moore, F. A. "In the Hospital." *Peterson's Magazine* (Feb. 1863).

Moreton-Robinson, Aileen. *The White Possessive: roperty, Power, and Indigenous Sovereignty*. Minneapolis: University of Minnesota Press, 2015.

Moretti, Franco. *Graphs, Maps, and Trees: Abstract Models for Literary History*. New York: Verso, 2005.

Moretti, Franco. "The Soul and the Harpy." In *Signs Taken for Wonders: On the Sociology of Literary Forms*. Translated by David Forgacs. New York: Verso, 2005.

Moretti, Franco. *The Way of the World: The Bildungsroman in European Culture*. New York: Verso, 2000.

Mornington, Maud. "The Nation's Dead," *Peterson's Magazine* (May 1864).

Morrison, Toni. *Beloved*. New York: Plume, 1988.

Morrison, Toni. *Playing in the Dark: Whiteness and the Literary Imagination*. New York: Random House, 1992.

"Mothers' Monuments." *The Ladies' Home Journal* 20 (Oct. 1903).

Moya, M. L. *The Social Imperative: Race, Close Reading, and Contemporary Literary Criticism*. Stanford, CA: Stanford University Press, 2016.

Murphy, Gretchen. *Shadowing the White Man's Burden: U.S. Imperialism and the Problem of the Color Line*. New York: NYU Press, 2010.

Neff, John. *Honoring the Civil War Dead: Commemoration and the Problem of Reconciliation*. Lawrence: University Press of Kansas, 2005.

"Neighborly Confidences." *The Ladies' Home Journal and Practical Housekeeper* (Sept. 1888).

Ngai, Sianne. *Ugly Feelings*. Cambridge, MA: Harvard University Press, 2005.

Nudelman, Franny. *John Brown's Body: Slavery, Violence, and the Culture of War*. Chapel Hill: The University of North Carolina Press, 2004.

Nurmi, Tom. "Shadows in the Shenandoah: Melville, Slavery, and the Elegiac Landscape." *Leviathan: A Journal of Melville Studies* 17, no. 3 (2015): 7–24.

O'Brien, Colleen C. *Race, Romance, and Rebellion: Literatures of the Americas in the Nineteenth Century*. Charlottesville: University of Virginia Press, 2013.

O'Brien, Jean M. *Firsting and Lasting: Writing Indians out of Existence in New England.* Minneapolis: University of Minnesota Press, 2010.

"Old-Time Genuine Revivals." *Star of Zion* (Jan. 1897).

O'Leary, Cecilia Elizabeth. *To Die For: The Paradox of American Patriotism.* Princeton: Princeton University Press, 1999.

Olmsted, Frederick Law. *The Cotton Kingdom: A Traveller's Observations on Cotton and Slavery in the American Slave States. Based upon Three Former Volumes of Journeys and Investigations.* New York: Mason Brothers, 1861.

"Our Dead at Andersonville." *Harper's Weekly* (Aug. 19, 1865).

Packard, Chris. *Queer Cowboys and Other Erotic Male Friendships in Nineteenth-Century American Literature.* New York: Palgrave, 2005.

Palmieri, Patricia A. "From Republican Motherhood to Race Suicide: Arguments on the Higher Education of Women." In *Educating Women Together: Coeducation in a Changing World.* Edited by Carol Lasser. Chicago: University of Illinois Press, 1987.

Parsons, Amy. "Desire, Forgetting, and the Future: Walt Whitman's Civil War." *Arizona Quarterly* 71, no. 3 (2015): 85–109.

Patterson, Matt. "That's the Obama I Knew." *PJ Media* (May 8, 2009). pjmedia.com/blog/thats-the-obama-i-knew/

Patterson, Orlando. *Slavery and Social Death A Comparative Study.* Cambridge, MA: Harvard University Press, 1982.

Perkins, Linda. "The African American Female Elite: The Early History of African American Women in the Seven Sister Colleges, 1880–1960." *Harvard Educational Review* 67, no. 4 (1997): 718–57.

Phelps, Elizabeth Stuart. *Donald Marcy.* Boston: Houghton Mifflin, 1893.

Phelps, Elizabeth Stuart. *The Gates Ajar.* In *Three Spiritualist Novels.* Chicago: The University of Illinois Press, 2000.

Pipes, William H. *Say Amen, Brother! Old-Time Negro Preaching: A Study in American Frustration.* New York: William-Frederick Press, 1951.

Poole, Hester M. "Reading and Readers." *The Ladies' Home Journal* 8 (July 1891).

Porter, Noah. *The American Colleges and the American Public.* New Haven: C. C. Chatfield & Co., 1870.

Portor, Laura Spencer. *Those Days in Old Virginia. The Ladies' Home Journal* 19 (Feb.–May 1902).

Pratt, James Bissett. *The Religious Consciousness: A Psychological Study.* New York: Macmillan, 1920.

Pratt, Lloyd. *The Strangers Book: The Human of African American Literature.* Philadelphia: University of Pennsylvania Press, 2016.

"The President: Mr. Roosevelt's Views on Race Suicide." *The Ladies' Home Journal* 23 (Feb. 1906).

Preston, Alice. "A Girl and her Prejudices." *The Ladies' Home Journal* 24 (Nov. 1907).

Price, Kenneth. "Charles Chesnutt, the *Atlantic Monthly*, and the Intersection of African-American and Elite Culture." In *Periodical Literature and Nineteenth-Century America.* Edited by Kenneth Price and Susan Belasco Smith. Charlottesville: University of Virginia Press, 1995.

Prince, K. Stephen. *Stories of the South: Race and the Reconstruction of Southern Identity, 1865–1915.* Chapel Hill: University of North Carolina Press, 2014.

Raboteau, Albert J. *Slave Religion: The "Invisible Institution" in the Antebellum South.* New York: Oxford University Press, 1978.

Ramazani, Jahan. *Poetry of Mourning: The Modern Elegy from Hardy to Heaney.* Chicago: University of Chicago Press, 1994.

Ramsey, Annie R. "An Hour with New Books." *Ladies' Home Journal* 7 (Apr. 1890).

Ramsey, Annie R. "New Books on my Table." *Ladies' Home Journal* 7 (May 1890).

Rankine, Claudia. "The Condition of Black Life is One of Mourning." *New York Times Magazine* (June 2015).

"The Real Miracle." *The Ladies' Home Journal* 22 (Jan. 1905).

"Record of the Democratic Speaker." *The Republic: A Political Science Monthly Magazine* (Aug. 1875).

Renker, Elizabeth. "Melville and the Worlds of Civil War Poetry." *Leviathan: A Journal of Melville Studies* 16, no. 1 (2014): 135–52.

Richardson, Charles F. *The Choice of Books.* New York: American Book Exchange, 1881.

Richardson, Heather Cox. *The Death of Reconstruction: Race, Labor, and Politics in the Post-Civil War North, 1865–1901.* Cambridge, MA: Harvard University Press, 2001.

Rifkin, Mark. *Settler Common Sense: Queerness and Everyday Colonialism in the American Renaissance.* Minneapolis: University of Minnesota Press, 2014.

Robbins, Bruce. "Afterword." *PMLA* 122, no. 5 (2007): 1644–51.

Robinson, Cedric. *Black Marxism: The Making of the Black Radical Tradition.* Chapel Hill: University of North Carolina Press, 2000.

Rosen, Hannah. *Terror in the Heart of Freedom: Citizenship, Sexual Violence, and the Meaning of Race in the Postemancipation South.* Chapel Hill: University of North Carolina Press, 2009.

Rosen, Jeremy. *Minor Characters Have their Day: Genre and the Contemporary Literary Marketplace.* New York: Columbia University Press, 2016.

Rosenberg, Bruce A. *Can These Bones Live?: The Art of the American Folk Preacher.* Rev. edition. Urbana: University of Illinois Press, 1988.

Rotundo, Anthony. *American Manhood: Transformations in Masculinity from the Revolution to the Modern Era.* New York: Basic Books, 1993.

S., G. W. "Negro Sermons." *Littell's Living Age* 93, no. 193 (Apr. 13, 1867): 117.

Sailer, Steve. "Obama's Mr. Wright." *The American Conservative* (Apr. 7, 2008). <www.theamericanconservative.com/articles/obamas-mr-wright>.

Sanipure Milk. Advertisement. *The Ladies' Home Journal* 24 (Oct. 1907).

Santayana, George. "A Glimpse of Yale." *The Harvard Monthly* (Dec. 1892).

Scanlon, Jennifer *Inarticulate Longings: The Ladies' Home Journal, Gender, and the Promises of Consumer Culture.* New York: Routledge, 1995.

Schantz, Mark S. *Awaiting the Heavenly Country: The Civil War and America's Culture of Death.* Ithaca, NY: Cornell University Press, 2013.

Schauffler, Robert Haven, ed. *Memorial Day: Its Celebration, Spirit, and Significance as Related in Prose and Verse, with a Non-Sectional Anthology of the Civil War.* New York: Dodd, Mead, & Co., 1911.

Schmidt, Leigh Eric. *Holy Fairs: Scotland and the Making of American Revivalism.* 2nd edition. Grand Rapids, MI: William B. Eerdmans Publishing Co., 2001.

Scott, Rebecca. *Degrees of Freedom: Louisiana and Cuba after Slavery.* Cambridge, MA: Harvard University Press, 2005.

Seelye, L. Clark. "The Influence of Sororities." *The Ladies' Home Journal* 24 (Sept. 1907).

Sharpe, Christina. *In the Wake: On Blackness and Being*. Durham, NC: Duke University Press, 2016.

Shepherd, Nathaniel Graham. "Roll-Call." *Harper's New Monthly Magazine* (Dec. 1862).

Silber, Nina. "Reunion and Reconciliation, Reviewed and Reconsidered." *The Journal of American History* 103, no. 1 (2016): 59–83.

Silber, Nina. *The Romance of Reunion: Northerners and the South, 1865–1900*. Chapel Hill: University of North Carolina Press, 1993.

Silverman, Gillian. *Books and Bodies: Reading and the Fantasy of Communion in Nineteenth-Century America*. Philadelphia: University of Pennsylvania Press, 2012.

Smith, F. Hopkinson. "Let Us Go Back." *The Ladies' Home Journal* 22 (Sept. 1905).

"The Soldier's Rest." *Harper's Weekly* (Apr. 1864).

"The Song of the Drum." *Harper's Weekly* (Nov. 1864).

Solomon, Barbara Miller. *In the Company of Educated Women: A History of Women and Higher Education in America*. New Haven: Yale University Press, 1985.

Spargo, R. Clifton. *The Ethics of Mourning: Grief and Responsibility in Elegiac Literature*. Baltimore: Johns Hopkins University Press, 2004.

Spencer, Jon Michael. *Sacred Symphony: The Chanted Sermon of the Black Preacher*. New York: Greenwood Press, 1987.

Spillers, Hortense. "Fabrics of History: Essays on the Black Sermon." Ph.D. diss. Brandeis University, 1974.

Spillers, Hortense. "Moving on Down the Line: Variations on the African-American Sermon." In *Black, White, and in Color: Essays on American Literature and Culture*. Chicago: The University of Chicago Press, 2003.

Stearns, Charles. *The Black Man of the South and the Rebels; or, The Characteristics of the Former and the Outrages of the Latter*. New York: Negro Universities Press, 1969.

Steyn, Mark. "Post 'Post-Racial Candidate.'" *National Review Online* (Mar. 22, 2008). <www.nationalreview.com/articles/224002/post-post-racial-candidate/mark-steyn>.

Stokes, Claudia. "Novel Commonplaces: Quotation, Epigraphs, and Literary Authority." *American Literary History* 30, no. 2 (2018): 201–221.

Stokes, Claudia. *The Altar at Home: Sentimental Literature and Nineteenth-Century American Religion*. Philadelphia: University of Pennsylvania Press, 2014.

Sundquist, Eric. *Hammers of Creation: Folk Culture in Modern African American Fiction*. Athens: University of Georgia Press, 2006.

Sweet, Lynn. "Obama on Quitting Trinity United Church of Christ." *Chicago Sun Times* (May 31, 2008). <suntimes.com/sweet/2008/05/obama_on_quitting_trinity_unit.html>.

Sweet, Timothy. "Battle-Pieces and Vernacular Poetics." *Leviathan: A Journal of Melville Studies* 17, no. 3 (2015): 25–42.

Sweet, Timothy, ed. "Introduction: Shaping the Civil War Canon." In *Literary Cultures of the Civil War*. Athens: University of Georgia Press, 2016.

"Talking about our Ailments." *The Ladies' Home Journal* 15 (Dec. 1897).

Tamarkin, Elisa. *Anglophilia: Deference, Devotion, and Antebellum America*. Chicago: University of Chicago Press, 2008.

Taves, Ann. *Fits, Trances, & Visions: Experiencing Religion and Explaining Experience from Wesley to James*. Princeton: Princeton University Press, 1999.

Taylor, Charles. *A Secular Age*. Cambridge, MA: Harvard University Press, 2007.

Taylor, Diana. *The Archive and the Repertoire: Performing Cultural Memory in the Americas.* Durham, NC: Duke University Press, 2003.

Teichgraeber, Richard F. *Building Culture: Studies in the Intellectual History of Industrializing America, 1867–1910.* Columbia: University of South Carolina Press, 2010.

Towle, George Makepeace. *American Society.* London: Chapman and Hall, 1870.

Trachtenberg, Alan. *The Incorporation of America: Culture and Society in the Gilded Age.* New York: Macmillan, 2007.

Traubel, Horace. *With Walt Whitman in Camden, Volume 3.* Edited by Sculley Bradley. New York: Mitchell Kennerley, 1914.

Veblen, Thorstein. *The Higher Learning in America: A Memorandum on the Conduct of Universities by Business Men.* New York: Sagamore Press, Inc., 1957.

Veysey, Laurence R. *The Emergence of the American University.* Chicago: The University of Chicago Press, 1965.

Warner, Michael. "Uncritical Reading." In *Polemic: Critical or Uncritical.* Edited by Jane Gallop. New York: Routledge, 2004.

Warner, Michael. "What Like a Bullet Can Undeceive?" *Public Culture* 15, no. 1 (2003): 41–54.

Washburn, William Tucker. *Fair Harvard; A Story of American College Life.* New York: Putnam, 1869.

Washington, Booker T., and W. E. B. Du Bois. *The Negro in the South: His Economic Progress in Relation to his Moral and Religious Development.* Philadelphia: George W. Jacobs and Company, 1907.

Watson, John Fanning. "Methodist Error: Friendly Christian Advice to Those Methodists Who Indulge in Extravagant Emotions and Bodily Exercises." In *Antirevivalism in Antebellum America: A Collection of Religious Voices.* Edited by James D. Bratt. New Brunswick, NJ: Rutgers University Press, 2006.

Watts, Trent. *One Homogenous People: Narratives of White Southern Identity, 1890–1920.* Knoxville: University of Tennessee Press, 2010.

Weber, Max. *The Protestant Ethic and the Spirit of Capitalism.* Translated by Talcott Parsons. Mineola, NY: Dover, 2003.

Weiner, Marli F., and Mazie Hough, *Sex, Sickness, and Slavery: Defining Illness in the Antebellum South.* Chicago: University of Illinois Press, 2012.

Weinstein, Cindy. "Heaven's Tense: Narration in The Gates Ajar." *Novel: A Forum for Fiction* 45, no. 1 (2012): 56–70.

Weisenfeld, Judith. "On Jordan's Stormy Banks: Margins, Center, and Bridges in African American Religious History." In *New Directions in American Religious History*, edited by Harry S. Stout and D. G. Hart. New York: Oxford University Press, 1997.

Wells, Cheryl A. *Civil War Time: Temporality and Identity in America, 1861–1865.* Athens: University of Georgia Press, 2005.

"What Should Girls Read? Mrs. Whitney to Travel with Girls in 'The World of Reading.'" *Ladies' Home Journal* 9 (Nov. 1892).

Whitman, Albery A. "A Bugle Note." *The Christian Recorder* (Mar. 19, 1891).

Whitman, Walt. "I Know Not How Others." In *The Collected Writings of Walt Whitman.* Edited by Edward F. Grier. New York: New York University Press, 1984.

Whitman, Walt. "Reconciliation." In *Whitman: Poetry and Prose.* New York: The Library of America, 1996.

Whitney, A. D. T. "A Friendly Letter to Girl Friends—I." *Ladies' Home Journal* 11 (Dec. 1893).

Whitney, A. D. T. "A Friendly Letter to Girl Friends—II." *Ladies' Home Journal* 11 (Mar. 1894).

Whitney, A. D. T. "A Friendly Letter to Girl Friends—III," *Ladies' Home Journal* 11 (Aug. 1894).

Whitney, A. D. T. "A Friendly Letter to Girl Friends—VI." *Ladies' Home Journal* 13 (Dec. 1895).

Whittier, John Greenleaf. '"Ein feste Burg ist unser Gott."' In *Selected Poems*. Edited by Brenda Wineapple. New York: Library of America, 2004.

Whittier, John Greenleaf. *The Letters of John Greenleaf Whittier, Volume III*. Edited by John B. Pickard. Cambridge, MA: Harvard University Press, 1975.

Wiegman, Robyn. *Object Lessons*. Durham, NC: Duke University Press, 2012.

Wiegman, Robyn. "Whiteness Studies and the Paradox of Particularity." *boundary 2* 26, no. 3 (1999): 115–50.

Wigger, John H. *Taking Heaven by Story: Methodism and the Rise of Popular Christianity in America*. New York: Oxford University Press, 1998.

Williams, Jeffrey J. "The Rise of the Academic Novel." *ALH* 24, no. 3 (2012): 561–89.

Wills, David W. *Christianity in the United States: A Historical Survey and Interpretation*. Notre Dame, IN: University of Notre Dame Press, 2002.

Wilson, Edmund. *Patriotic Gore: Studies in the Literature of the American Civil War*. New York: Oxford University Press, 1966.

Wister, Owen. *Philosophy 4: A Story of Harvard University*. New York: Macmillan, 1903.

Wolfe, Patrick. "Settler Colonialism and the Elimination of the Native." *Journal of Genocide Research* 8, no. 4 (2006): 387–409.

Wood, John Seymour. "Rev. of Yale Yarns." *Daily Inter Ocean* (June 1895).

Wood, John Seymour. *Yale Yarns: Sketches of Life at Yale University*. New York: Putnam, 1895.

Wright, Jeremiah. "Speech at the National Press Club." *New York Times* (Apr. 28, 2008). <www.nytimes.com/2008/04/28/us/politics/28text-wright.html>.

Yancy, George. *Look, a White!: Philosophical Essays on Whiteness*. Philadelphia: Temple University Press, 2012.

Yothers, Brian. "Melville's Reconstructions: 'The Swamp Angel,' 'Formerly a Slave,' and the Moorish Maid in 'Lee in the Capitol.'" *Leviathan: A Journal of Melville Studies* 17, no. 3 (2015): 63–78.

# { INDEX }